DOPE

DOPE

HOW DRUGS CHANGED SPORT

James Witts

First published in the UK in 2026 by Blink Publishing
An imprint of Bonnier Books UK
5th Floor, HYLO, 105 Bunhill Row,
London, EC1Y 8LZ

A CIP catalogue record for this book is available from the British Library.

Hardback ISBN: 978-1-78512-974-2
Trade Paperback ISBN: 978-1-78512-978-0
Paperback ISBN: 978-1-78512-977-3

Also available as an ebook and an audiobook

1 3 5 7 9 10 8 6 4 2

Design and Typeset by Envy Design Ltd
Printed and bound in Great Britain by CPI (UK) Ltd, Croydon CR0 4YY

At Bonnier Books UK, we are committed to publishing sustainably.
Find out more here: bonnierbooks.co.uk/sustainability

The authorised representative in the EEA is
Bonnier Books UK (Ireland) Limited.
Registered office address:
Block B, The Crescent Building
Northwood, Santry
Dublin 9, D09 C6X8
Ireland
compliance@bonnierbooks.ie

www.bonnierbooks.co.uk

For the sportspeople whose performances we can trust.
Victory is competing fairly.

CONTENTS

CHEATING THE CLOCK: A HISTORY OF DOPING

'I've just been handed a piece of paper here that if it's right will be the most dramatic story of these Olympics or any others. It says Ben Johnson of Canada has been caught taking drugs and is expected to be stripped of his 100m gold medal, according to International Olympic Committee sources.'

The warm, calm and effortlessly authoritative Des Lynam, Seoul Olympics, 1988. The moustachioed Lynam, armed with blazer, crisp shirt and striped purple-and-gold tie, against a banner that read 'The Olympics Today', shattered my innocence on that late September day and inadvertently set me on the path to writing this book. The 11-year-old me was at first confused and then saddened by the news that the planet's fastest man, who'd set a new world record in that South Korean final of 9.79 seconds, had tested positive for the banned anabolic steroid stanozolol.

'It's confirmed Ben Johnson is stripped of his medal, he's out of the Games, out of Korea, home in shame,' Lynam continued.

Within 24 hours, Johnson had morphed from hero to zero. Fame to infamy. Dream-maker to ruiner of dreams.

I consoled myself that Johnson was an outlier, a droplet of pollution in a sea of purity. As it transpired, I was wrong. Ten athletes tested positive at the 1988 Olympics from 1,598 drug tests. I didn't know it then but 12 athletes had also failed tests at the 1984 Los Angeles Olympics. Drug-assisted sports folk was no new phenomenon.

One by one, the protagonists from the fastest race in history failed drug tests at some point in their careers; in fact, only Calvin Smith of the original top five never tested positive. It's why the fastest race in history became known as the dirtiest race in history, captured in the late Richard Moore's magnificent book of the same name.

Into my teens and the 1990s I began a love affair with road cycling that'd later dominate my professional writing career. Channel 4's coverage of the Tour de France captured the beauty and awe of riding 3,500km around this stunning country. Legendary commentator Phil Liggett brought the pain of endurance alive . . . and the reality, when in 1998 several teams were thrown off the race due to what turned out to be rampant abuse of the drug EPO, or erythropoietin. This was one of the (many, many . . .) drugs that'd fuel Lance Armstrong to his seven Tour titles and one that you'll read a lot more about in the pages that follow.

The Festina affair coincided with my time at university where a fascination with elite sporting performance and disappearing into a book led me to the unusual degree combo of sport science and English literature. In the classroom, I learned the impact of training protocols and nutrition strategies on peak performance in many sports (plus the joys of rhyming couplets and iambic pentameter!).

Away from it, I read column inch after column inch on sport, including frequent doping scandals, that'd ultimately see me write several sporting books and thousands of magazine features before reaching where I am now.

For sport as a whole, the Festina affair led to the foundation of the World Anti-Doping Agency (WADA) in 1999 and the formation of the anti-doping framework that is the WADA Code in 2003. Until then, anti-doping rules were fragmented, inconsistently enforced, and largely controlled by individual sports federations and the International Olympic Committee (IOC). As you'll discover, how much that has changed remains to be seen.

Drug testing actually began at the 1968 Olympics, with major competitions the primary testing ground. Out-of-competition testing was rare before the 1990s, and many sports had minimal or no regular random testing. This allowed systematic doping programmes to operate undetected in several countries during the 1970s and 1980s, including one of the most toxic and pervasive, the East German doping scandal where government funds were used to subsidise research on performance-enhancing substances. Seen through an official prism, the studies aimed to simply discover whether or not certain drugs were performance-enhancing. Not surprisingly, when promising effects were discovered, these products found their own way into the sporting arena rather quickly.

In the 1976 Montreal Summer Olympics, the world took notice as East Germany, a relatively small country with few previous Olympic wins, triumphed with 40 gold medals. The women's swim team alone won 11 out of 13 swim events. US swimmer Wendy Boglioli described her opponents' performance thus: 'They were very strong women; they were very fast; we thought they were machines. Here (we) were, four of America's best athletes ever put together on a team, and every single day the East German women were winning every, every event.'

It wasn't until decades later and the reunification of Germany that the secret to the East's success came to light. Operating under the authority of the country's elite sports federation, led by Manfred Ewald and overseen by the ministry of state security – aka the Stasi – performance-enhancement was embedded within a broader political strategy. Sporting success was engineered as a vehicle for international prestige.

Girls as young as 12 were scouted and enrolled into elite programmes. Unbeknown to many of them, they were routinely administered experimental anabolic steroids and male hormones as part of their training regime. The medals came at a profound human cost. Numerous athletes later suffered severe side effects, including excessive hair growth, deepened voices, liver and heart disease, infertility, miscarriages, depression and, in some cases, premature death.

More than 3,000 Stasi informants operated within the sports system, monitoring coaches, scientists and athletes alike. This dense surveillance network ensured secrecy and compliance; questions or dissent were met with swift consequences. Behind the medals stood a tightly controlled system in which performance, politics and pharmacology were inseparably linked.

Of course, such a state-run programme couldn't operate today. Could it? The notorious Russian state-sponsored programme of recent times answers that one. That's despite the 700-plus scientific and educational anti-doping projects invested in by WADA since 1999. But, again as you'll discover, the usefulness of many of those projects is questionable. Is the money really swilling around the system to catch the cheats? Is the political will really there to catch them?

Since Des Lynam unknowingly changed my life, the moniker of 'dirtiest race' has been redirected to the women's 1,500m final at the 2012 London Olympics, in which six of the top-nine finishers would at some point test positive for performance-enhancing drugs. That's the statistic. But there's a very human cost to doping, both for the doper and the clean athlete.

British runner Lisa Dobriskey, who finished 10th that day, told the *Independent*, 'I remember after the race, I wanted to cry and I needed to get out of the stadium. It should have been a joyous moment in front of my home crowd but I felt humiliated. I just wanted the ground to swallow me up. I felt I had to apologise for my performance to my family and friends. I felt I'd let people down.

'The most upsetting thing is that, when you take 1988, I just felt our sport had moved on so much more,' Dobriskey added. 'It should be harder to cheat than back then but that doesn't seem to be the case.'

There's a belief that the increasing commercialisation of sport, the billions flowing to this most passionate of entertainments via broadcasting deals, sponsorship and ticket entry, naturally raises the stakes. And when those stakes are highest, so too is the temptation to cheat, in the case of this book, to dope.

Sport in the 2020s is wealthier than it's ever been. Does that mean the number of athletes taking illegal performance-enhancers is potentially higher than it's ever been? That's impossible to verify equivocally, though I give it a detailed stab in chapter two. There are simply too many variables for a definitive answer – rigour of tests in different countries, difficulty in convicting an athlete, ease of hiding . . . But on a theoretical level, and a scientific one, it's logical and is arguably one of the drivers behind the Enhanced Games, which we delve into in chapter 12. (As is money, money, money . . .)

That said, drug taking to improve sporting performance has existed for millennia. One of the earliest known records of athletes improving performance above their own natural ability comes from the Ancient Olympic Games with opium juice a favourite among the ancient Greek athletes. Although not illegal today, the practice of over-indulging on meat products such as animal hearts and testicles was tested for its performance-enhancing properties. Similarly, Roman gladiators used different forms of food and drink to increase energy during battles, enticed by the rewards of victory, including homes and avoiding military service.

Documented corruption cranked up at the modern Olympics, starting with the inaugural Games in Athens, 1896, where athletes reportedly resorted to injections of strychnine and tinctures of cocaine to elicit peak performance.

At the 1904 Olympics, American brass-worker Thomas Hicks ran to marathon victory fuelled by strychnine and brandy. Struggling as the race rolled on, Hicks was given approximately 1mg of strychnine sulphate, which appeared to revive him, but not for long. So, he was given a second dose of strychnine. When he crossed the finish line he collapsed and was too weak to collect his medal. Much more 'help' from his team and Hicks might have been killed. That's because strychnine, a powerful stimulant of motor neurons, which control muscle contractions, can result in body convulsions that kill by paralysing the breathing muscles. But he did recover, and lived until the age of 76, though he never competed again.

Incredibly, the marathon of 1904 also highlighted further corruption. Frederick Lorz, a bricklayer by trade, dropped out at mile nine before nipping into a car that'd drive him back to the stadium to collect things. Unfortunately, the car broke down at mile 19. Lorz, revitalised from the journey, jogged on, crossing the line first. He was stripped of the gold medal, though he claimed it was a joke.

Over 120 years later, doping, match-fixing, illegal betting and corruption are commonplace in sport. And despite WADA celebrating its 25th birthday, in 2024 Ben Johnson told Radio Jamaica that he believed nothing had changed and, if anything, doping was worse than during his career.

A French sports medicine doctor recently echoed Johnson's assessment, telling French newspaper *La Dépêche* that high-level sport is '100 per cent medicalised', so how are the dopers getting away with it? What products do they use to boost performance? What methods do the authorities use to catch the cheats? How does politics impact and influence WADA's work? How much money's ploughed into anti-doping and where's the money coming from? What's the evidence these illegal performance-enhancers actually enhance performance? Why are football's indiscretions glossed over while cycling and athletics are lambasted? What products do the dopers use to mask their illegal actions?

We start by looking at the modern athlete's medical cabinet and, as mentioned, finish with the Enhanced Games, a sporting event where illegal drugs are legal. Along the way, I'll hopefully illustrate the mixed picture of doping in sport. At the end of the day, this subject matter, while at times sad and desperate, is often bizarre, including the story of why the world's greatest footballer used a prosthetic penis to hide his drug taking. In fact, talking bizarre, sport and penises, just as I'm penning this a controversy dubbed 'Penisgate' has emerged at the 2026 Winter Olympics, where ski jumpers were accused of injecting hyaluronic acid into their genitals to inflate 3D body measurements and for aerodynamic suit sizing. WADA's Polish president, Witold Bańka, clearly as amused as the rest of us, said, 'Ski jumping is very popular in Poland, so I promise you I'm going to look at it.'

Welcome to the world of Dope…

STRONGER, DANGER . . . BANNED?

How far would you go in search of peak performance? Inject yourself with the inners of a lugworm? A Tour de France rider would. Or tried to. Haemoglobin from *Arenicola marina* lugworms is utilised for medical use because of the worm's startling oxygen-transporting abilities. Hemarina, the French company founded by Dr Franck Zal, says that lugworm haemoglobin can transport 40 times more oxygen than human haemoglobin, which is why it's so effective for organ transplants. And why it'd appeal to endurance athletes. 'A well-known cyclist whose team participates in the Tour de France contacted me because he wanted the product ahead of the 2020 race,' Zal told *L'Équipe*. Zal declined the request and passed on the information to the police, who confirmed the discussions but didn't add any further information.

WADA (World Anti-Doping Agency) said that they were aware of the risks of the lugworm haemoglobin but that they hadn't caught anyone using it yet.

'We bought the product and put it in the hands of the

anti-doping laboratories,' Professor Olivier Rabin, the scientific director of WADA, said. 'If this substance had been found in an athlete, we would have made it public. I can't guarantee that this hasn't happened somewhere in the world, but to my knowledge this is not the case.'

Lugworms fuelling an athlete towards gold? It's inexplicable and highlights the difficulty – and absurdity – of beating the cheats. It also begs the question, what separates the illegal from the legal? At the end of the day, why would a worm be banned but a proven performance enhancer like creatine be allowed?

'A substance makes it onto WADA's Prohibited List if it meets two of three criteria,' explains Dr Matthew Dunn, associate professor in the school of health and social development at Deakin University, Australia, and an internationally recognised expert in the field of sports doping. 'It enhances, or has the potential to enhance, performance; it may pose a risk to the athlete's health; or it violates the "spirit of sport". The third criteria is a bit nebulous, but the first two are factual.'

The Prohibited List is updated annually and, for 2026, its number is over 400. All this is documented in a 26-page PDF[1] with any additions or deletions coming into effect from 1 January of that year. This becomes an athlete and their support team's Bible, be it to identify the substances to avoid (the clean competitors) or to act as a shopping list (the dopers).

These substances are either prohibited at all times or in-competition only. Why the distinction? It's down to longevity and impact. There's evidence that anabolic steroids, EPO (erythropoietin) and human growth hormone (HGH) can improve

---

1 https://www.wada-ama.org/sites/default/files/2025-09/2026list_en_final_clean_september_2025.pdf

training adaptation, recovery or long-term physiology, so they're banned at all times. So are masking agents that can disguise evidence of doping, which include diuretics. Stimulants, on the other hand, deliver short-term, transitory gains so are solely banned in the competition amphitheatre – we're talking drugs such as ephedrine here.

Then there's a third category that prohibits drugs only in certain sports. Beta blockers are an example, which are commonly used to lower blood pressure. They also slow down heart rate, ease anxiety and dampen down a general shakiness. So, it's no great leap of the imagination to see how their calming properties can pay dividends in sports that require steadiness, precision and serenity. It's why beta blockers are banned – at least in competition – for archers, drivers, darts players, golfers (and mini-golfers!), shooters, and those who partake in billiards, pool or snooker.

Beta blockers have been a no-no in-competition since the IOC (International Olympic Committee) banned them in 1985. But the ban wasn't universal and didn't include the non-Olympic sport of snooker. Still, controversy reigned in 1987 when then 23-year-old snooker player Neal Foulds admitted taking them for a heart complaint. The UK's sports minister Colin Moynihan branded the Englishman a cheat and urged the sport's international governing body to ban their use, of which they did in 1988.

Foulds wasn't alone in their use; the ban would soon end the career of Canadian Bill Werbeniuk. Werbeniuk, once eighth in the world, was as prodigious at downing pints as potting balls, prepping for matches with eight pints of lager followed by a pint per frame. It was, he said, the only way to prevent an arm tremor that hampered his play, which is why he once attempted to offset his lager expenditure against tax.

Werbeniuk was ultimately prescribed the beta blocker Inderal to counter the effects of the alcohol. 'I would always maintain that Inderal was performance enabling, not performance enhancing,' he said. 'I got a letter one day saying, "Don't bother to turn up because you're not playing." I don't think I was treated fairly.'

Werbeniuk played his last professional match in 1990, commenting afterwards, 'I've had 24 pints of extra-strong lager and eight double vodkas and I'm still not drunk.' Why the Canadian didn't sidestep the pub and go straight to the chemist remains to be seen. He died in 2003 at the age of 56 due to heart failure.

WADA also allows certain substances below specific threshold levels without triggering an anti-doping violation. These thresholds exist because some drugs are essential for therapeutic reasons. Salbutamol is a good example. Nearly half a billion people are affected by asthma and chronic obstructive pulmonary disease around the world with, according to GSK,[2] around 300 million salbutamol inhalers sold each year. Many of those are prescribed for endurance athletes due to exercise-induced asthma, caused by a number of factors including training hard in cold or dry environments; the chlorine in swimming pools; and rapid rates of ventilation.

It's why the likes of Olympic swimming legends Michael Phelps and Ryan Lochte both used inhalers. As did cross-country skier Matti Heikkinen and a number of cyclists including Sir Bradley Wiggins. All legitimate. No violations there.

But it was Wiggins' teammate Chris Froome who attracted headlines for blurring the lines between enabling and enhancing back in 2017. The Brit, who'd win four Tour de France titles,

---

2 https://www.gsk.com/en-gb/media/press-releases/gsk-announces-positive-pivotal-phase-iii-data-for-next-generation-low-carbon-version-of-ventolin-salbutamol-metered-dose-inhaler/

returned a urine sample that showed elevated levels of salbutamol during the 2017 Vuelta a España, which he won. WADA's threshold is set at 1,600µg over a 24-hour period without requiring a Therapeutic Use Exemption (TUE), which allows you to use a prohibited substance for medical reasons (and which we dig into in chapter five). That's the equivalent of 16 puffs of a standard inhaler. Tip over that threshold and there's evidence of mild anabolic or endurance-boosting effects. Froome argued his elevated reading didn't stem from performance reasons but due to a combination of dehydration and the hot conditions.

His team, Team Sky, supplied pharmacokinetic data to show the result was consistent with permitted use rather than abuse. After months of legal and scientific wrangling, the Union Cycliste Internationale closed the case in July, 2018, without sanction, accepting that Froome had not intentionally exceeded permitted use.

The ruling sparked backlash, with critics accusing authorities of opacity and preferential treatment, while supporters said it exposed the scientific uncertainty around salbutamol thresholds.

The case highlighted one of the many grey areas inherent in the anti-doping framework, as did the 2025 media storm around the carbon monoxide rebreathing method – a diagnostic instrument used by practitioners to assess an athlete's haemoglobin mass.

Haemoglobin mass is essentially how much oxygen the muscles have to work with. As oxygen is like nectar to an athlete, especially endurance athletes, in general the higher your mass the better.

When an athlete heads to altitude in an effort to increase their oxygen-boosting red blood cells – vis-à-vis their haemoglobin mass – the support team measure whether training and living above 1,500m is having the desired impact via a device that entails the athlete inhaling a small bolus of carbon monoxide. After a few minutes of rebreathing this mix, a small blood sample is taken and analysed for carbon monoxide content. The expert can then calculate the mass figure. It's legal, doesn't impact performance and, contrary to its name, not suffocating.

A 2024 study,[3] however, concluded that carbon monoxide rebreathing twice a day for three weeks mimicked the blood-boosting effects of altitude. Previous research[4] saw the haemoglobin mass levels of 11 subjects increase by an average of 5% after they inhaled carbon monoxide five times a day for three weeks. A similar improvement was seen in endurance performance. The reports of carbon monoxide resulting in an athletic boost saw WADA add the 'non-diagnostic use of carbon monoxide' to the Prohibited List from 2026.

'To a degree we were forced to make changes due to inaccurate reporting,' says Professor Yorck Olaf Schumacher, chair of the WADA Prohibited List Working Group. 'Determining haemoglobin mass that way has been used for years, but the press made this big thing out of it that people are using it to increase performance. We had stakeholder pressure from different federations and authorities that it should be on the list. Now it is, although there was little evidence of its abuse for performance purposes.'

Maybe not in the laboratories. A professional cyclist who wished to remain anonymous told me, 'I haven't done it personally, but I know teammates that have. Basically, it gives your red blood cells a higher affinity to oxygen. Strangely, this is similar to smokers heading to altitude. They're often less affected

---

3   https://pubmed.ncbi.nlm.nih.gov/39236115/

4   https://pubmed.ncbi.nlm.nih.gov/32118696/

by altitude sickness than seemingly healthier folk because they already have reasonably high levels of carbon monoxide coursing through their system.'

If all of this presents an amphitheatre of ambiguity, then it should. Because keeping sport 'clean' is far from a clean-cut business. Cue the Monitoring Program that, like the Prohibited List, is updated annually. This is a list of substances that aren't banned but are making the WADA experts twitchy, which might be down to their potential to improve performance, affect health or their growing use in sport. Often a drug will sit on the Monitoring List while the relevant parties go through statistical analysis, research and testing whether it should be promoted to the banned list or drop off and remain legal.

One of the most recent graduates was tramadol. Tramadol is a potent painkiller. That's clearly beneficial in a therapeutic environment. But if you can kill the pain in a sporting setting you can sustain a higher level of performance. It's why tramadol ran roughshod through many elite sports, especially rugby and cycling, where it was often dished out with water bottles.

And it's why WADA funded a study by Professor Lex Mauger of the University of Kent, England, who specialises in pain. Mauger and his team recruited 27 highly trained cyclists who pedalled for 30 minutes at a fixed intensity followed by a competitive self-paced 25-mile time trial. They followed this template twice after taking either a placebo or 100mg of soluble tramadol, resulting in an average 1.3% performance improvement on the tramadol.

'That was after a relatively low dose of 100mg, meaning the effect could have been even greater in races or matches,' says Mauger. That raised the alarm as, according to Mauger's paper, 'three of the participants expressed and displayed adverse effects in the tramadol condition after the time-trial completion. For one participant these effects were mild (nausea, mild dizziness), whereas for two these were more pronounced (drowsiness or vomiting).'

Mauger's study showed irrefutable evidence that tramadol enhanced performance and was potentially dangerous, and was duly banned.

Just to highlight the never-ending finish line, Mauger's currently undertaking another WADA-funded study into tapentadol. 'It's much more powerful than tramadol. It's an opioid, has analgesic effects similar to morphine and can therefore raise the pain threshold.'

Tapentadol is on the Monitoring List for 2026 while Mauger completes his research. It's saddled up with another relative newcomer to the sporting scene – weight-management drugs or GLP-1 agonist semaglutides – that have witnessed unprecedented growth, due to not only the fact that they seemingly work, but also driven by endorsements from celebrities and influencers, including actress Rebel Wilson, TV personality and businesswoman Sharon Osbourne and billionaire owner of X, Elon Musk.

According to market research company Grand View Research, the global semaglutide market size was estimated at $28.43 billion in 2024 and is projected to reach $93.59 billion by 2035. The global semaglutide industry is driven by the increasing prevalence of Type-2 diabetes and obesity, plus the growing adoption of weight-management treatments. Ozempic, Wegovy and Mounjaro are well-known examples.

Obesity and elite sport aren't synonymous with each other. Creep towards the former and it'll inevitably mean curtailment of the latter. So why have WADA recently funded Morten Hostrup, associate professor of physiology at the University of Copenhagen, Denmark, to the tune of £216,000 to undertake research into the long-term effects of semaglutide use on body composition and performance in running?

'Anti-doping agencies have observed via survey and from hearsay that an increasing amount of athletes are using a drug like Ozempic,' he says. 'There were plenty who used it in the build-up to the 2024 Games in Paris. If you compete in a sport where weight (or lack of it) really matters, like swimming, boxing and long-distance running, the appeal of these weight-loss drugs is strong.'

One strand of Hostrup's research is to observe these drugs' impact on performance. It's too simplistic to think that calorie restriction equals weight loss and faster running. 'Their performance might actually suffer because these starvation drugs are so effective. The athlete might lose muscle mass and muscle function. Those are significant negatives when it comes to sport.

'The other aspect is how do these drugs affect hormonal balance, what we call the endocrine system? When you put the body into massive calorie restriction, you negatively affect its metabolism. That can be severe in all athletes but especially females, who are more prone to eating disorders than the male athlete. If you're an athlete who's already predisposed to this condition, these drugs could push you into a dangerous situation.'

The potential danger is why semaglutides are on the Monitoring List, though the chair of WADA's health, medical and research committee, Lars Engebretsen, has already made his feelings known, publicly stating that they should be placed immediately onto the Prohibited List, citing ethical issues around elite athletes taking obesity drugs.

Prohibiting these drugs would arguably be the simplest part.

Detecting them would be a much bigger issue, especially as pharmaceutical companies, buoyed by the success of the market leaders, will research and identify hitherto unknown compounds that would present a headache for WADA and its testing limitations.

Hostrup says that athletic users would take the likes of Ozempic in cycles – unless they are prone to body dysmorphia, where they might take it all of the time – perhaps in the off-season if they've added weight. 'There's also evidence that these drugs work very well for around 16 weeks but then you plateau. Then again, look at cyclists who excel in the mountains. They're already stick-thin. What would stop them persisting with these weight-loss drugs if they felt it'd speed them up?'

That'd return us to the muscle-mass-loss scenario, though another question: What would stop athletes countering this with steroids? 'That could definitely happen,' says Hostrup, 'but obviously steroids are on the Prohibited List already. That, of course, might not prevent some athletes and their support teams from trying this combination.'

Leaner, stronger. That's the foundations for elite sport. That's known. What's less clear are the empirical benefits of prohibited drugs in a sporting setting. Remember, the drug in question has generally been adopted from a clinical backdrop. Take EPO (erythropoietin), a hormone that stimulates red blood cell production, and was approved as a treatment for anaemia in 1989. Understandably, the clinical trials focused on treating patients, not performers.

Surprisingly, perhaps, there have been a few studies investigating the performance bump from EPO, mostly in endurance sports like rowing, cycling and distance running. In 2017,[5] a

---

5 https://pubmed.ncbi.nlm.nih.gov/28669689/

research group injected a group of well-trained cyclists with EPO or a placebo for eight weeks. The EPO group showed a statistically significant increase in power output, aerobic capacity and efficiency, all conducive to improved endurance performance. Across the literature, the norm is around a 5% boost, and these are at relatively low doses. Too high and the proposal wouldn't have passed the ethics committee.

That's the data. The anecdotal is even greater, says American Joe Papp. Papp is a law enforcement officer who's also an anti-doping advocate. This goodness wasn't always so. Former professional cyclist Papp served a two-year suspension in 2006 after his urine sample tested positive for metabolites of testosterone following the Tour of Turkey. That was extended to eight years after being found guilty of dealing performance-enhancing drugs (PEDs). Papp also testified against Floyd Landis, who was stripped of his 2006 Tour de France win because of doping. In short, few appreciate the effects of PEDs more than Papp.

'I took many drugs but EPO was truly the one that gave you wings,' he tells me from his American home. 'I reckon I enjoyed a 10-to-12% improvement in aerobic capacity, which is huge. That compares to around 2% from micro-dosing [which is more common now since the athlete biological passport was introduced. This is the focus of chapter three]. Honestly, the effect was tangible.'

Papp says his physician would prescribe him a four-week cycle of EPO based on his base blood parameters and body weight. Three times each week he'd inject himself with a syringe before they'd reevaluate both his physiological and performance status.

'I could just train that bit harder and recover quicker,' he says. 'I remember racing with a clean rider shortly after I started my doping programme in 2001. We broke off the front and I must have pulled us for nearly two hours. He just sat beside me clinging on. It was incredible – my lungs were consuming all of the air in the world that I needed. I beat him.'

Papp admitted to using over 100 different drugs during his professional career but pinpointed five as the most effective for an endurance athlete: 'You had EPO and testosterone, plus human growth hormone, the occasional amphetamine and steroids.'

Papp's experience matches the data, with steroids the most widely used, or abused, substance by athletes according to the Anti-Doping Database. As of September, 2023, the steroid stanozolol had been implicated in over 3,000 cases in track-and-field alone. Notable cases include Ben Johnson, who won, then quickly lost, the 1988 Olympic 100m title, while the steroid became popular among baseball players, with 2015 seeing four pitchers test positive: Jenrry Mejia (Mets), Ervin Santana (Minnesota), Arodys Vizcaíno (Atlanta) and David Rollins (Seattle).

As such, there's a much greater body of evidence than EPO showing that anabolic steroids crank up strength, power, muscle and sprinting speed. Take a landmark human study featured in an edition of the *New England Journal of Medicine* all the way back in 1996.[6] Forty-three healthy men were split into four groups for ten weeks and either took a placebo with no training; the steroid testosterone with no training; placebo plus strength training; or testosterone plus strength training.

Those in the testosterone and strength group increased their bench-press maximum by up to 38% compared to the no-training group, with squat strength a seismic 60% higher. Remarkably, the group taking testosterone without training still gained more muscle than the placebo group that trained.

---

6 https://pubmed.ncbi.nlm.nih.gov/8637535/

These are startling improvements, albeit you'd expect the boost for elites to be lower as they have less room to grow. Still, myriad studies into the impact of steroids on athletes have shown that 10–30m sprint times improved by 1–3%, and vertical jump height (useful for basketball, soccer, rugby, etc) by 5–10%, plus a significant improvement in repeated sprints, again useful for many sports. Even a 1% improvement in any of these can mean the difference between success and failure. Which the likes of Victor Conte knew better than anyone . . .

Conte drew infamy for founding the infamous Bay Area Laboratory Co-operative (BALCO) that supplied anabolic steroids to a wide range of athletes in the early 2000s. The list reads like a Who's Who of track-and-field, whose achievements were celebrated . . . and then scrubbed: Marion Jones won three gold medals and two bronze at the 2000 Olympics in Sydney, which were all stripped after admitting to using steroids supplied by BALCO; Tim Montgomery, doped, and had his 100m world record annulled; and Dwain Chambers, who tested positive for THG (tetrahydrogestrinone), a designer steroid developed out of BALCO.

In 2005 Conte pleaded guilty in a US court to conspiracy to distribute steroids, and in the process revealed the impact of his PEDs. 'Steroids can help a female sprinter to lower her 100m time by about four-tenths of a second or four metres faster,' he said. 'The effects of steroids upon male 100m sprinters are about two-tenths of a second or two metres faster.'

I looked to contact Conte to dig deeper into this assessment but the American, who served four months in federal prison for dealing steroids, was suffering from pancreatic cancer and died at his Californian home in November, 2025.

Arguably, Conte's stats stack up, with several female Olympic and world records set prior to a greater focus on anti-doping and the creation of WADA in 1999. Florence Griffith Joyner's 100m and 200m world records of 10.49 and 21.34 seconds, respectively, have stood since 1988, the year she won Olympic gold in both, plus the 4x100m relay. Though the American never tested positive, rumours circulated due to her sharp progression – her best 100m prior to 1988 was 10.96 seconds the year previous – plus a significant change in physique between 1987 and 1988. FloJo died unexpectedly in her sleep in 1998 at 38 years old.

There are further studies into a range of performance enhancers, but arguably drawing conclusions on how much higher, faster or stronger an athlete can go is futile. Not only do elites rarely partake in research – they're strangely none too enamoured with common sport-science lab practices like muscle biopsies (where you slice off muscle for analysis) – but as Papp's medical cabinet revealed, a doping athlete is a doping athlete many times over, as they're seeking to optimise training gains, accelerate recovery and stave off injury.

Take a look at boxer Larry Olubamiwo's litany list. The Brit was banned for four years after 12 substances were detected in his body. They comprised boldenone, fluoxymesterone, methandienone, methyltrienolone, oxymetholone, trenbolone, EPO, human growth hormone, anastrozole, letrozole, exemestane and tamoxifen. His ban was reduced to 13 months and 20 days after he offered information to UKAD (United Kingdom Anti-Doping). Countryman and rugby league player Terry Bridge went two better than Olubamiwo with 14. Bodybuilders Maciej Pietrewicz and Dawid Cnota rattled to 15. Tallying up the combined physiological and performance benefit is an impossible task.

And then there are the unknowns, like whether the drug actually works. 'There were guys on Lance Armstrong's US Postal team who said they weren't really responders to the drugs that they were taking,' says professional cyclist Rory Townsend. They clearly worked for Lance, although there's a school of thought that the American maximised the effect of EPO, blood bags and steroids not solely from the physiological impact, but because he believed they worked more than anyone else. His doping dogma dug deeper than anyone else's.

'I'm a clean rider and anti-doping advocate, but this responder/non-responder theme applies to me, too,' adds Townsend. 'I just don't respond well to altitude. The idea is for your blood oxygen saturation levels to drop, so you create more EPO [legally] to create more red blood cells. But mine just won't drop below 97%. You really want to dip lower than that to optimise adaptations.'

So, PEDs don't always enhance. But as we've seen, there's sufficient evidence that for many, they do. That flags them up to WADA. But what about part two of the Code: that a drug hits the Prohibited List if it's dangerous? On the face of it, taking any drug at higher doses than recommended is far from ideal. But swallowing, rubbing or injecting it for performance reasons when your base level's presumably 'normal' is surely fraught with danger, leading to damaging side effects, illness and even death?

(Whether that's an issue for some/elite athletes remains to be seen. A well-known sports survey in the 1980s, known as the Goldman Dilemma, presented the world's best with a Faustian bargain: would you take a drug that guaranteed gold but would also kill you within five years? Over 50 per cent of athletes said yes. Goldman repeated the survey biannually for the next decade and the results were always the same. That said, a WADA-funded

Goldman-styled study in 2011[7] refuted this idea, suggesting that only two out of 212 athletes would make this gold-winning deal with the devil. Like much in doping and anti-doping in sport, who can you trust?)

There are a number of scientific reviews that examine the link between doping and increased mortality, including a 2024 study[8] out of Denmark that showed the chances of dying in regular anabolic steroid users was three times higher than that of the 'normal' population. Among those deaths, a notable proportion of natural deaths were due to cardiovascular disease and cancer, with suicide and accidents the primary causes of unnatural death. The steroid users also endured more frequent hospital admissions. Earlier research[9] revealed that pathological heart changes were behind 33 cases of deaths in predominantly male steroid users.

They're just a snapshot of the damage this particular PED can do. But much of the research stems from bodybuilders and strength athletes, not from elite athletes who are likely monitored by an expert. So, it's difficult to extrapolate those results to all doping cases.

A 2007 study[10] in the journal *Sports Medicine* focused on the dangers of another PED, revealing that 'EPO use is a suspect in nearly 20 deaths in four years in European cyclists'. One of those riders was Johannes Draaijer. He was 26, Dutch and had finished 20th in the 1989 Tour de France. In February the following year, just days after racing in Italy, he died in his sleep from a heart blockage. An autopsy failed to establish a definitive cause of death.

---

7   https://www.wada-ama.org/sites/default/files/2023-11/connor_2011_-_wada_report_final_gold.pdf

8   https://pmc.ncbi.nlm.nih.gov/articles/PMC10941020/

9   https://pubmed.ncbi.nlm.nih.gov/33158202/

10 https://pubmed.ncbi.nlm.nih.gov/17465616/

He had been declared fit to ride. Later, in a television interview, his widow said she hoped what happened to him might serve as a warning to others who were taking the drug.

Between 2003 and 2004 alone EPO use reportedly accounted for eight deaths, including 21-year-old Belgian amateur Johan Sermon, who died of a heart attack; French rider Fabrice Salanson, 23, who died of a heart attack in his sleep and was found by his roommate just before the Tour of Germany; and 16-year-old Italian Marco Ceriani, who experienced a heart attack during a race, fell into a coma and never recovered consciousness. Between 1989 and 1992, seven young Swedish orienteering enthusiasts died mysteriously.

More recently in 2024, Kenyan middle-distance runner Kipyegon Bett, who won the 800m bronze at the 2017 World Championships held in London, died from kidney and liver failure. He'd previously tested positive for EPO in 2018 and received a four-year ban. Then there's the passing of Mexican boxer Moisés Calleros, who tested positive for cocaine after his stoppage defeat by Olympic champion Galal Yafai in April, 2023. He died in March, 2024, of a suspected cardiac arrest.

In all of these cases doping was suspected or cited as a possibility behind the deaths but remained unproven. The uncertainty is down to myriad reasons. Often, deaths happen years after doping; some athletes may have a genetic risk that's simply not known; post-mortem toxicology often doesn't take place or is inconclusive; and dose, duration, cocktails of drugs and other extreme behaviours, like a heavy training load or weight-loss regime, make it nigh-on impossible to isolate a single drug's impact.

One anti-doping expert, who wished to remain anonymous, isn't convinced that EPO abuse leads to deaths. 'I hate to say this but I think all the horror stories about EPO thickening the blood and leading to heart issues are wrong. There really is very little evidence that backs this up,' he explains. 'There are also plenty of examples of people living at altitude, like mine workers who work in Peru at over 3,000 metres – their haematocrit is commonly over 55, if not 60, and they're absolutely fine.'

Haematocrit is the percentage of blood volume made up of red blood cells and is in the 40–50% range. As we've seen with Townsend's unrewarding efforts, athletes head to altitude to raise this figure, the rarefied air forcing the body to generate more red blood cells in a desperate attempt to cling on to oxygen. With haematocrit raised, a return to sea level and the greater access to oxygen should mean more fuel to fan the flames of working muscles, especially for endurance athletes.

Historically, if a male athlete's haematocrit tipped over 50% and a female 47%, WADA would investigate. But the introduction of the biological passport in 2008 for cycling, and all sport in 2009, means there's no longer a blanket figure; instead, it's an individualised, longitudinal approach to detect potential doping. This is deemed more effective as haematocrit values can deviate significantly due to factors like hydration status, training intensity and illness. Critics suggested this limit was arbitrary and potentially penalised clean athletes.[11]

'Genetic mutations can cause naturally high haematocrit readings, which are again safe to the individual,' adds our expert. 'Take the Finnish cross-country skier Eero Mäntyranta. He won multiple Olympic medals [seven between 1960 and 1968, three of which were gold] and [it was later proved by genetic sequencing that] he had a naturally high haematocrit of over 60%. All of the

---

11 https://www.researchgate.net/publication/288979238_Hematocrit_levels_in_elite_athletes

Mäntyranta men did. As far as I'm aware, Eero lived a healthy and happy life in Northern Finland working as a reindeer farmer until his death at 76.'

The Eero supra-physiological story isn't an entirely innocent one. In 1972 he tested positive for amphetamines at a competition, becoming the first Finn known to have been caught doping. He also later admitted to taking hormones, which weren't then prohibited.

'Arguably you should be more concerned that EPO stimulates cancer cells,' our expert continues. 'That's the potential danger rather than thickening the blood. EPO is a growth factor that works on the [blood-boosting] erythropoietic cells in the bone marrow. But does it also work on mutated cells that float around the body and that cause cancer? That's a possibility. Ultimately, though, no athlete should take EPO.'

That didn't deter Papp, who saw himself as a fairly enthusiastic doper. 'Still, there were substances and methods on the Prohibited List that even I wouldn't try: insulin, because of the risk of severe hypoglycaemia leading to brain dysfunction, coma and death; synthetic oxygen carriers that could lead to potentially lethal renal toxicity; and blood transfusions, which would result in acute septic reaction from a contaminated component. If I was racing now, I'd definitely steer away from GW1516.' We'll come back to GW1516 shortly.

'That's got me thinking about Mauro Gianetti being hospitalised after alleged PFC use,' Papp adds. Gianetti was a journeyman professional who fell ill at the 1998 Tour de Romandie. Two doctors believed he's been given perfluorocarbon emulsions, an artificial blood substitute. They've never been approved for human use but at the time it was rumoured they were being abused by cyclists. The case didn't go anywhere because Gianetti refused to share his medical records. He's now the team principal of Tadej Pogačar's UAE Team Emirates. 'I'm also thinking about Riccardo Riccò being hospitalised after a botched autologous transfusion, and Frank Vandenbroucke attempting suicide with an overdose of insulin and Château Pétrus!'

Papp also suffered the side effects of drug abuse. In 2005 he was hospitalised after an episode of tachycardia. The same year, adrenal suppression resulting from 'excessive, season-long glucocorticoid use' left him wrestling with heavy fatigue. 'But the worst incident happened in 2006. I crashed while taking anticoagulants to decrease blood viscosity after having used EPO to raise my haematocrit levels. I suffered severe internal bleeding and again spent time in hospital.'

Assessing a substance's danger is made harder as there are so many around, be it on the regulated or unregulated markets. The 2026 WADA Prohibited List identifies 68 steroids that are banned under the 'S1.1 Anabolic Androgenic Steroids (AAS)' classification. It also mentions 'and other substances with a similar chemical structure or similar biological effect(s) including their esters', meaning their number could swell into the hundreds.

Dr Matthew Dunn's research includes the harms associated with PEDs.

'Those who use steroids do largely indicate that trenbolone has an increased risk profile,' he says. Trenbolone, or 'tren', has really strong anabolic properties and is implicated for causing psychological harm, including bringing out violent or aggressive tendencies. Arguably, this is exacerbated by the higher doses used in sport compared to the clinical patient.

'But there are common side effects for a healthy individual taking most steroids, the impact and severity of which is varied,' says Dunn. 'Some are seen as more nuisance effects, like increased acne on the body, as well as soreness at the injecting site and increased sweating during the night. Some effects might even be seen as desirable, such as an increased libido.

'There are, however, more serious effects that include headaches, increased blood pressure, lymph-node swelling, liver problems, kidney problems and possible infections. Some of the mental-health issues reported include aggression, anxiety, mood swings and insomnia.

'Some steroids might also pose more of a risk because they are taken orally, which can impact the liver,' Dunn continues. 'The steroids that are injected intramuscularly pose other risks, such as abscesses, tissue or muscle damage, and risks that come from sharing injecting equipment or not using sterile-injecting equipment.'

Much of Dunn's work has centred on taking steroids for image-enhancing reasons rather than performance, and he suggests that if (or when) steroids are being used in professional sport, they're probably under medical supervision so should be safely managed. 'Whether they're used to administering the doses athletes take in search of improved performance is an unknown. I do believe that the higher doses contribute to an increased risk.'

As does the increased commercialisation of sport that, Dunn believes, has led to more PED use. He also feels that we're naturally reaching the limits of what humans can do without enhancement. 'We need to think about how the sporting world may set someone up to consider using substances like steroids.' We take a deep-dive into that topic in chapter 12.

So, there are PEDs where clear evidence points to danger. But not enough according to a 2023 paper by Jo Morrison, professor of kinesiology at Longwood University, USA, whose research in *Performance Enhancement & Health*[12] pulled no punches: 'Lack of evidence that doping is harmful to the health of elite athletes.'

Morrison's snapshot summary is even more brutal. Yes, elite athletes use banned substances. No, their morbidity and mortality aren't higher than the rest of the population. In fact, former elites tend to live longer, healthier lives than age-matched controls. Her point: we keep insisting PEDs are uniquely dangerous despite the awkward truth that many of these drugs are routinely prescribed to people far less robust than Olympic finalists.

The anti-doping claim of 'harm' leans heavily on anecdotes, she says: black-market gear, outrageous dosing, no medical oversight and the occasional underground chemist knocking together compounds never intended for humans. Morrison argues that none of this translates into meaningful evidence that PEDs, when used by tested elite athletes, cause measurable harm.

Or an improvement in performance. Morrison cites a 2019 review[13] examining 23 categories of substances on WADA's Prohibited List. The authors found no evidence of enhancement in most categories. Either the studies didn't exist or they showed no effect. For the five classes that *did* show benefits, the sum total of the evidence rested on just 11 studies and 266 athletes.

One of those authors, Jules Heuberger of the Centre for Human Drug Research in Leiden, Netherlands, set about testing the PEDs with the same rigour as he would when approving medicines for patients. 'Treat it,' he says, 'as if we were studying a disease called "cycling slowly".'

On the health-risk side, the review found nothing that justified

---

12 https://www.sciencedirect.com/science/article/abs/pii/S2211266923000026?via%3Dihub
13 https://pubmed.ncbi.nlm.nih.gov/30411235/

the blanket assumption that banned substances pose unique dangers to athletes. Without evidence of specific harm, the logic underpinning WADA's criteria looks arbitrary, says Heuberger.

Heuberger's not saying PEDs are harmless – high doses of anything carry risk – and some drugs, like growth hormone or immune-modulators, demand caution. But with over 400 substances on WADA's Prohibited List, Heuberger suggests the evidence isn't strong enough for far too many of them. A spokesman for WADA stresses that protecting athlete health is central to its mission, even if not every listed substance is dangerous.

Heuberger argues for a simpler, more scientific model, one that identifies the drugs that genuinely boost performance, study them properly and build sensitive detection methods. And ditch the 'spirit of sport' clause – a catch-all so nebulous that it's simply vague.

Professor Olivier Rabin, Senior Director, Science and Medicine at WADA, wishes it were that simple. Instead, the goalposts of doping in sport are always moving. 'I believe one of the reasons WADA employed me in 2002 is that when you work in the pharmaceutical industry you see substances 10, 12, 15 years before they become medicines,' he says. Rabin was previously with biopharmaceutical company Ipsen. 'I said we need to forge strong ties with pharma; we need to identify the drugs that are the doping substances of tomorrow. Let's work together and develop the detection method, so that we can control the drug before it becomes an issue in sport.'

Most pharmaceutical companies must satisfy shareholders, meaning they must communicate what's in the pipeline. Their portfolio of 'drugs in development' will be categorised by therapeutic needs.

'That comes in many forms, starting from clinical trials,' says

Rabin. 'If you see a pharmaceutical company is recruiting subjects with anaemia, that means they want to boost their production of red blood cells. This would be of interest to WADA because it could become the new EPO.'

On joining WADA, Rabin ensured they started using a database called 'Pharmaprojects' that's become the go-to hub for monitoring and analysing global pharmaceutical R&D.

'This is how we spotted heat stabilisers,' he adds. Heat stabilisers in medicine are added chemicals that shield an ingredient – commonly peptides, proteins or hormones – from degrading when exposed to heat. They ensure a drug remains active during transport, storage or use.

'They're perfectly legitimate and not harmful. But seen through a doping lens, they make prohibited substances easier to transport illegally and harder to detect. Many illegal substances, especially peptide hormones [which boost stamina and accelerate recovery], break down quickly unless refrigerated. Heat-stable versions allow athletes to store them for longer in hotel rooms, gyms or race vehicles without fear of becoming inactive.' They are also associated with shorter detection windows.

'We were able to test those substances before they were marketed and made available to athletes,' says Rabin. 'Generally, the pharmaceutical industry is collaborative because they don't want their drugs abused by healthy people and for doping purposes. Sometimes they even share the drug itself, so that we can put it in the hands of our anti-doping laboratories and undertake ADME. That's the absorption, distribution, metabolism and excretion of a drug through the human body.'

Rabin's understandably guarded when asked about future substances that are on WADA's radar. 'But there are tons of new substances we're following. Of course, some are discontinued during the early development phase, so aren't a threat. In fact, the rule in pharma is you need 10,000 new chemical entities to make one medicine, so the attrition rate is huge. Some, however, are discontinued later in that cycle and can become an issue. Take Cardarine, which was developed by GlaxoSmithKline [and Ligand Pharmaceuticals]. The molecule was discontinued because animal testing showed it caused cancer to develop rapidly in several organs. But the drug made it to the internet and we found several athletes using it.'

Cardarine reportedly improved metabolism and cranked up physical endurance, appealing to most athletes. WADA were so concerned about Cardarine, also known as GW1516, that beyond banning it in 2009, they took the rare steps of warning 'cheats' of the dangers of the developmental drug.

That hasn't deterred many. According to the Anti-Doping Database, between 2015 and 2024, 90 athletes tested positive for Cardarine, the most (21) emanating from those working in track-and-field. That includes coach Gerald Phiri, who was provisionally suspended by the Athletics Integrity Unit (AIU) earlier in 2025 for possession of GW1516.

Phiri's most famous protégé was Issam Asinga, the teenage phenomenon who rewrote the sprint record books in 2023 after breaking the under-20 world 100m record in 9.89 seconds. Soon after, Asinga underwent an out-of-competition test that detected the presence of GW1516 metabolites. Asinga blamed the positive result on contaminated gummies (see chapter eight for more on contamination), taking Gatorade to court. The American sports-nutrition manufacturer won the lawsuit, resulting in a four-year ban for the company's national player of the year.

Another area of concern, says Rabin, are novel psychoactive substances, which aren't regulated and are frequently sold as alternatives to classic street drugs such as ecstasy or LSD. According to the European Union Drugs Agency (EUDA), between 2009 and 2022, 139 countries and territories reported the emergence of 1,182 new psychoactive substances. These included PMMA, a dangerous synthetic stimulant similar to MDMA but much more toxic and responsible for a number of fatalities, particularly in the UK, Ireland, Netherlands and Canada.

'There's seemingly one released each week by rogue scientists working in illegal laboratories,' says Rabin. 'They can be anything – opioids, cannabinoids, stimulants – and they can be used in sports. SARMs are a particular concern. It stands for Selective Androgen Receptor Modulators and they're not approved anywhere in the world.'

SARMs are essentially designer steroids. They increase lean muscle mass, slash fat and may reduce injury recovery time. Because these drugs are unregulated, users believe that SARMs are undetectable. A number of cases – 39 between 2014 and 2017 involving ostarine, says USADA (United States Anti-Doping Agency) – suggests otherwise. 'They're found in some regions of the world in dietary supplements,' says Rabin. 'Many athletes invoked the contamination supplement defence, but that still leads to a suspension.'

We'll soon discover that this contamination supplement defence is 'the' defence for positive athletes.

From lugworm haemoglobin to designer steroids, performance-enhancing drugs are pervasive – if you know where to look and are open to cheating. WADA's framework rests on three pillars – performance enhancement, health risk and the spirit of sport – yet each proves porous when examined closely. Some drugs clearly work. Some are clearly dangerous. Many sit in a messy space where evidence is thin, ethics are contested and enforcement lags behind innovation.

What complicates matters further is that most substances originate in legitimate medicine. Designed to heal the sick, they're repurposed by the healthy in pursuit of marginal gains. The science often arrives late, the testing later still. As Professor Rabin makes clear, anti-doping is a race not solely against today's cheats but tomorrow's chemistry. It's clear that doping is neither uniformly deadly nor uniformly transformative. It's inconsistent, individual and often hidden behind belief as much as biology.

HOW MANY . . . AND WHY?

According to a report by WADA, assessing the effectiveness of the anti-doping programme they ran at the 2024 Olympics, a total of 6,130 samples were collected via urine, blood and dried-blood spot testing (which we will look at in the next chapter), from 4,150 athletes. That was roughly 39% of all Paris competitors. Of those, 12 recorded adverse analytical findings – a positive test – with seven having no case to answer due to valid factors like a TUE (therapeutic usage exemption) certificate.

Iraqi judo star Sajjad Sehen had the dubious honour of registering the first positive doping test in Paris for the steroids boldenone and methandienone. The Court of Arbitration for Sport banned him for four years. Boxer Cynthia Ogunsemilore of Nigeria followed two days later, testing positive for the masking agent furosemide. The other three positives were again in judo, plus aquatics and track-and-field.

So, five athletes caught out of 4,150, which nestles at around 0.001%. That compares to WADA's most recent data testing report

(2024) that showed 0.78% of samples collected returned an adverse analytical finding. The World Athletics' anti-doping agency's positive drug tests surprisingly dropped from 0.7% in 2012 to 0.5% in 2023. Which doesn't necessarily mean the number of athletes doping dropped.

We're talking tenths of percentage differences between the different bodies, but physical evidence of the number of athletes potentially abusing PEDs in elite sport is less than 1%. Well, if those figures hint that elite sport is cleaner than ever, things have certainly nudged along nicely since the 1988 Seoul Olympics. After Canadian sprinter Ben Johnson was stripped of his 100m title, a US Senate hearing was convened in 1989, chaired by future president Joe Biden, to address what was seen as rampant anabolic-steroid use in elite sport.

At that hearing, US Olympic track-and-field coach Pat Connolly claimed that 15 of the 50 American women on the 1984 Olympic team had used anabolic steroids similar to those found in Johnson's system. By the time of the Seoul Games in 1988, she believed that figure had climbed to around 40%.

In 2015, Britain's Paula Radcliffe, who held the women's marathon record of 2:15:25 for 16 years between 2003 and Kenya's Brigid Kosgei breaking it in 2019 with 2:14:04, asked by the *Guardian*'s Donald McRae if she thought most of the top Kenyan athletes were clean, commented, 'Um… I don't know at the moment. I think the majority are but I also think there is a [doping] problem there. They are realising this and starting to look at it and do something about it. But it's not just a problem in Kenya. It's a problem everywhere.'

Of course, that's hearsay and possibly hyperbole. Data and surveys don't make headlines, but they're essential in painting a picture of the problem. Is professional sport vibrant, colourful and based on Corinthian values? Or murky, monochrome and tainted by the needle? Can we trust the superhuman efforts of the minority?

Well, a 2024 study[14] by USADA suggests yes, we can, at least the majority of the time. Using anonymous self-reporting data, the survey found that 6.5–9.2% of the 1,398 respondents reported using one or more prohibited substances or methods in the 12 months prior to the survey.

Of the athletes who reported doping, the majority (84.4%) reported using only one substance or method. The most common form of doping was perhaps a surprise – cannabinoids – albeit they're not prohibited for out-of-competition use. Performance-enhancing doesn't spring to mind when you think of hashish, cannabis and marijuana, the results suggesting athlete use is more down to greater social acceptance than leaping further. The least prevalent categories of doping were diuretics or masking agents (0.1%), stem cell or gene editing (0.1%), narcotics (0.2%), and hormone and metabolic modulators (0.2%).

But a metaphorical shot in the arm for clean sport. Not perfect but far removed from one of the most controversial – and revealing – papers in the history of sport. The Tübingen study, led by Professor Rolf Ulrich of the University of Tübingen, was funded by WADA and involved surveying athletes at the 2011 Athletics World Championships in Daegu, South Korea, and the 12th Pan-Arab Games in Doha, Qatar, to assess the prevalence of doping. Ulrich and his team asked 2,167 athletes: 'Have you knowingly violated anti-doping regulations by using a prohibited substance or method in the last 12 months?'

---

14 https://link.springer.com/article/10.1186/s40798-024-00721-9

The replies were eye-opening, with 43.6% of athletes at the Worlds and 57.1% at the Pan-Arab Games saying yes, they had knowingly violated the rules in the past year. It caused uproar. Or it would have, as the IAAF (International Association of Athletics Federations, now World Athletics) were accused of deliberately suppressing the results for six years, despite the results being leaked to the *New York Times* in 2013 and later released in the UK under parliamentary privilege by the Digital, Culture, Media and Sport Committee in their report on blood doping in athletics. All the researchers were required by WADA to sign retrospective confidentiality clauses, preventing them from discussing their findings.

The IAAF, led by Lord Sebastian Coe, argued that the delay was down to issues surrounding the researchers' methodologies. The UK committee disagreed, 'There was no good reason why the Tübingen paper should not have been formally published several years ago. The IAAF's claim that it needed to check the methodology is entirely spurious, since one explicit aim of the study's authors was to test the validity of the methodology they were using, which was, in their view, one of the key areas for peer review . . . We find the IAAF's stated reasons for blocking publication of the study to be unconvincing, and we are concerned that their behaviour indicates a lack of transparency and, worse, an apparent desire to suppress revelations about doping in sport.'

Ulrich pushed back, accusing the IAAF of blocking the release of the study because they didn't like the results, and arguing that Coe's comments were damaging to the authors' reputations, efforts to combat doping and scientific freedom.

Professor Ulrich still works at the University of Tübingen and is remarkably phlegmatic about the whole saga. 'Yes, it was not easy to publish the study,' he replies when I ask him about the emotional toll of dominating the headlines. 'After 15 years, I still consider the study and its conclusions to be scientifically sound and relevant. The fundamental insight – that randomised response techniques can reveal a very different picture of doping prevalence than routine testing – remains valid today.

'It's also essential that such studies should be conducted face-to-face, as we did. This ensures that athletes understand the procedure and thus are open to eliciting an honest answer. By contrast, online studies are not suitable for this type of research and may not produce reliable data.' That raises question marks over the accuracy of the USADA study, although that applies to any estimate.

For those of you whose work doesn't comprise surveys, meta-analysis and creating a framework to elicit the truth, it's relevant to both the credibility of Ulrich's results and the potential scale of the PED problem to understand how the randomised response technique works. Over to Ulrich...

'Imagine we want to estimate the prevalence of doping – "Have you ever used prohibited doping substances?" – by surveying 1,000 athletes gathered in a large hall. Simply asking them to raise their hands if they did so wouldn't work because it's such a sensitive issue.

'Now, imagine that each athlete flips a coin and raises their hand if they've either used prohibited substances or if the coin shows heads. If someone raises their hand, we can't tell whether this is because they've used banned substances or because their coin landed on heads, which provides anonymity due to the "random masking principle".

'If nobody had ever used prohibited substances, we'd expect around 500 athletes to raise their hands. That's because probability theory tells us that about 95% of the time the coin would land on its head, which equates to between 469 and 531.

'Let's then assume that the number of raised hands is 610. This excess of 110 over the expected 500 indicates that some athletes raised their hands because they had used prohibited substances.

'Applying elementary probability theory to these data, the estimated number of such athletes would be 220 or 22% (and not 110 or 11%, as one might intuitively think). Of course, due to the random nature of the coin tosses, the excess may be smaller or larger. Therefore, the estimate may be smaller or larger as well.

'This figure can also be understood backwards: if 220 athletes had used prohibited substances, all of them would, according to this example, raise their hands. Among the remaining 780 athletes, about half would raise their hands on average because of the coin flip (approximately 390). Together, this would lead to an expected total of 220 + 390 = 610 hand raisers, which matches the observed number.'

You might need to reread that. A couple of times. Or thrice in this author's case. But essentially participants use a randomising device (like a coin flip or coded question) that determines whether they answer the sensitive question or an unrelated one, so researchers can estimate true prevalence at a population level without knowing any individual's response. Ulrich's since adapted this technique to include a 'cheater detection' that requires a strong background in 'in mathematical psychology of cognitive processes'. We'll leave it at that.

Edmund Willison is a UK journalist dedicated to investigating doping and the medicalisation of elite sport, and the man behind the Substack 'Honest Sport'. In October 2025, his work featured in the British broadsheet the *Telegraph* with the stark headline, 'One in five athletes doped at Commonwealth Games'.

At the 2022 Commonwealth Games in Birmingham, 21% of more than 900 athletes answered 'yes' to the question, 'I have intentionally used a prohibited substance or method without a therapeutic use exemption (TUE) in the last 12 months.' That same year, around 100 of 800 British athletes replied to an email doping questionnaire from UKAD saying they'd taken a PED. There's more. In 2022, the Spanish Anti-Doping Agency conducted an in-person survey of 325 athletes at the Spanish Athletics Championships, of whom 36% reported doping. A year before, it was 13% Spanish athletes of 354 surveyed.

Willison's investigate work exposed doping estimates between 13% and 36% across different countries and competitions. Sprinkle in Ulrich's results and it's a bleak picture. But what of WADA? As the international body charged with defending clean sport, what do their surveys reveal?

WADA has its own Prevalence Working Group led by senior manager James Sclater. 'We've been working on a survey for around eight years. In that time, there are many papers the team have worked on, including one that disagrees with the Tübingen findings [applying a different statistical model, doping prevalence drops to 28.2% from 43.6% at the 2011 Worlds and plummets from 57.1% to 10.6% at the Pan-Arab Games]. But the group are still working on the survey itself.'

That's eight years in the making. Or two Olympic cycles. And still no end product. That's glacial progress weighed down by methodologies and politics. Surveys are hard to standardise across countries and sports and are sensitive to small design flaws that skew results. Politically, high-prevalence estimates significantly above the positive-test rates undermines confidence in the testing system, forging headlines that the system is 'failing'. The working group must also balance scientific transparency with diplomatic consensus among numerous high-level stakeholders including governments, sports bodies and the IOC.

'Of course, eight years is a long time but we've got to get it right,' adds Tony Cunnigham, head of research and policy at WADA. 'One paper we commissioned looked at prevalence figures over a 35-year period. I think there were over 100 studies and it ranged from zero to 75% of athletes doping. Of those 100 studies, around 75% were deemed low-quality and unreliable.

'What comes through is that there are numerous variables that change the results. What is the sporting population you're assessing? What was the method used? When did you survey the group? A survey of cyclists in the 2000s is very different from a chess player. That's the rabbit hole that we've gone down.'

Sclater says that anti-doping organisations are under pressure from governments to show that their work is effective. To that end, they've begun analysing testing data using similar analytical tools to criminologists. 'Hopefully we'll reach a stage where we can identify countries and sports that might require greater resources to educate about clean sport,' he says. 'But I still think we're quite far off that . . .'

Unlike the team behind the UTMB World Series of ultra-running. Intent on gaining physical data, they collected urine samples from experimental male urinals positioned near the start line of UMTB races. These urinals were connected to a custom-made tubing system positioned on the urinal drainpipe. The participant's presence in the urinal cubicle was detected by a sensor, which triggered an antenna that read the runner's radio frequency identification tag attached to his bib. Resulting signals were computed to generate a presence-detection file associated with an encrypted tag code, thus preserving the participant's anonymity.

They discovered that among the 412 individual urine samples, 205 (49.8%) contained at least one substance and 16.3% of the samples contained one or more prohibited substances. Substances detected in urine included non-steroid anti-inflammatory drugs (NSAIDs) (22.1%), acetaminophen (15.5%), opioids (6.6%), diuretics (4.9%), hypnotics (4.4%), glucocorticoids (2.7%), beta-2 agonists (2.2%), cannabinoids (1.9%) and stimulants (1.2%). As a snapshot, 12.9% of respondents to a separate questionnaire reported using NSAIDs, nearly 10% lower than physiologically proven.

The number of footballers, swimmers, boxers, men, women, Paralympians who are using PEDs clearly varies. At times, wildly so. So do the reasons behind why an athlete dopes. Amanda Hudson is director of education at WADA. 'Athletes start in sport clean,' she says. 'No athlete ever awakes and says that they want to participate in sport because they want to inject themselves with steroids. This is a very powerful, straightforward fact.' So, what happens? 'For many reasons, they become vulnerable,' Hudson adds. 'But we know that given the choice they simply wouldn't dope.'

At a point in an athlete's career, they undertake a risk assessment of which they're both the assessor and assessed. Shall I or shan't I? Stick or twist? Sleep soundly or fear the doping officer?

'We know strong values help,' says Hudson. 'So do sound morals, beliefs and conviction that you can achieve your performance in sport the right way. As is having athlete-support people around you who are well educated. All protective factors that make athletes much less vulnerable to doping. Having a supportive family is important. In fact, I remember a campaign run by our colleagues at UKAD called "Tell Mum". It was designed to make young athletes think twice.

'Research tells us that there are many reasons behind an athlete doping: they have poor resilience; they enjoy big risk taking; they are in a win-at-all-costs coaching environment; they are under intense selection pressure and they believe that everybody's doping. Even the nature of sport where athletes are having to perform at night for the TV audience. All are risk factors to shift the doping dial for vulnerable athletes.'

This is an area of expertise of Dr Rocco Porreca, co-author of a research paper entitled, 'Explaining Elite Athletes' Corruption Behaviours: A Case Study of Doping and Match Fixing'. I meet the good doctor in a cycling café just outside the centre of Oxford, where he's senior lecturer in marketing at Oxford Brookes Business School.

We both settle down with an Americano and, before a word is uttered, have a taste of the political scepticism that permeates sport and the anti-doping movement. Caffeine is arguably the most studied ergogenic in the world. It boosts power, improves decision-making and makes exercise feel easier. Up to 2004, it was on the Prohibited List above a moderate threshold. Then it was allowed. WADA argued the decision was down to science, enforceability and fairness. But sceptics alleged long-time Olympic sponsor Coca-Cola of lobbying, something through my research I could not corroborate.

Porreca ignores my speculation. Instead, he quantifies how they set about discovering why some elite athletes will go to the extreme vampiric lengths of withdrawing blood, storing it in the fridge before reinfusing it so their levels are supraphysiological. Or taking steroids. Or peptides. Or, or, or . . .

'I knew we'd struggle to sit down with the likes of Lance Armstrong and ask about why he got involved in doping. So, we pondered how we could dig a little deeper and extract specific information from athletes without knowing them. After much deliberating, we waded through WADA and national anti-doping organisations' websites to see if they had a sanction list. After that, we searched social media, press releases . . . anything we could find around the respective athlete's doping case. As you can imagine that led us down a pretty seismic rabbit hole. In the end, we pinpointed 33 elite athletes from ten countries.'

Porreca and co-author Stacie Gray then used the 'theory of planned behaviour' as a framework to analyse real athlete statements and admissions. This theory suggests that a person's behaviour is influenced by three key factors: attitudes to the behaviour – whether they see it as positive or negative; subjective norms – perceived social pressure to perform or not perform the behaviour; and perceived behavioural control – beliefs about how easy or hard it is to perform that behaviour. 'It's often applied to consumer behaviour to try and understand why someone will buy a certain product,' says Porreca.

As an example, a positive attitude is that electric cars are eco-friendly and cheaper to run; the subjective norm might be that your friends are talking about going electric; and the perceived control is that you can afford the car and there are charging stations near you. If either of the three components weakens – for instance, the charging station's actually towns away so you'll inevitably end up stranded – then the chance of purchase lessens.

'Interestingly, and against other research in this area, the reasons to dope were more about performance-continuing than performance-enhancing. Many were athletes in the twilight stage of their career and didn't want it to end. They weren't necessarily looking for a leg up. It was more about staying relevant.'

This echoes 2007 work by Alexander Dilger, Bernd Frick and Frank Tolsdorf, who analysed 100m doping cases between 1997 and 2002 and revealed that, on average, they were around three years older than their clean-tested competition.

A 2015 paper[15] examined the economics of sporting corruption, specifically 'the special case of doping', and concluded that age-related doping likely exhibits a U-shape. A competitive athlete in their younger years has both the physical conditioning and immaturity to progress that could be the difference between mediocrity and superstardom. Against this backdrop, their expected monetary, sporting and adulatory benefits outweigh the risk of taking a PED. As the years roll by and the U flattens out, the 'endgame effect' begins to take over. 'Here, existing punishment mechanisms, such as being exempted from participating in tournament, have no credible sanctioning effect on an old athlete who is close to his retirement.'

High-profile athletes who were caught doping late in their careers – which, again, doesn't necessarily mean they were clean earlier in their careers – include sprinters Tyson Gay and Asafa Powell, who were both 30 when they recorded positives for steroids and stimulants, respectively; and baseball pitcher Bartolo Colón, who was 39 when suspended for 50 games in 2012 after testing positive for testosterone, albeit the durable Colón continued pitching at MLB (Major League Baseball) level into his 40s.

---

15 https://www.researchgate.net/publication/317823523_The_Economics_of_Corruption_in_Sports_The_Special_Case_of_Doping

This crossing the ethical line in search of career extension boiled down to myriad reasons including financial and improving health; in fact, reducing a spell on the sidelines due to injury is a vulnerable moment for any athlete with such a significant fiscal element saddled to it.

Injury has a real and quantifiable impact on an athlete's transfer or contract value. The *European Sport Management Quarterly*, *Journal of Sports Economics* and *Applied Economics* have all featured research that shows recent injury can impact market valuation by 10–20%, with that rising to over 30% for a serious or recurrent injury. This can approach 50% for players that are the wrong side of 28 years old. Naturally, this drop in market value limits an athlete's salary and earning potential.

'Andy Pettitte was a famous pitcher for the New York Yankees,' says Porreca. 'He failed a doping test twice in 2002. He was one of a number of players [86] named in the Mitchell Report that exposed the depth of the drug problem in baseball. Many denied they'd taken anything, but he admitted to taking human growth hormone in an effort to recover faster from an elbow injury. Again, that's more about performance-enabling than seeking a big jump in performance.'

Of course, you could contest the truth of these athlete statements that Porreca worked with. That they've blatantly shown their untrustworthiness and so hampers the reliability of his research. 'To be fair, they had no real reason to come out and say they'd taken the drugs,' he says. 'I guess it's like any interview. How can you trust anybody?'

Seen through the theory of planned behaviour model used by Porreca, he concluded that injury shifts an athlete's attitude towards doping. Like Pettitte, they believe it'll accelerate recovery, protect their contract and restore a sense of identity – athletes soon become lost and even depressed when injured. Doping's no longer framed as cheating but a necessary tool to survive.

In Porreca's dataset, athletes frequently reported that coaches, doctors and even teammates implied or encouraged recovery-aid doping. Injury heightens the social pressure because being unavailable threatens the team dynamic.

And injury raises perceived behavioural control – the belief that an athlete can dope with impunity. When injured athletes believe that *I can do this safely and avoid detection*, presuming testing is less likely when injured, their intention to dope increases sharply, even if they'd previously been an anti-doping advocate.

Away from injury, there's also the sheep mentality. In the previous chapter, we met anti-doping advocate, former doper and drug dealer Joe Papp, who rode professionally in the PED-fuelled 2000s. 'I managed to justify and structure the doping in my mind that, for the most part, I felt guilt-free; I made a conscious effort not to think about it and could rely on the fact that so many guys are doing it, this is what I need to continue.'

Crime can be contagious. Just reflect on your school days and the occasional spluttering of a roll-up behind the bike sheds. The use of doping might inflame a straw fire. It's called the 'spillover effect'.

'The culture of the sport is so important,' says Porreca. 'In certain periods, whether it was boxing or cycling, the dopers believed everyone was doing it and so it'd be silly for me not to take anything. It's unfair to have such a disadvantage. At least this will allow me to level the playing field. There's also pressure from teammates.'

At the Lance Armstrong trial, his US Postal teammates

testified that doping expectations were communicated through team hierarchy, and participation was framed as necessary to stay competitive and retain selection. More recently, the former CEO and sports director of the W52-FC Porto cycling team were given suspended prison sentences for running a systematic doping programme. Adriano Quintanilha financed the operation while Nuno Ribeiro bought the banned drugs and instructed the athletes on how to administer them. When the team was first suspended, the director of the Portuguese anti-doping agency faced death threats and his family was placed under police surveillance.

Athletes are placed in a prisoner's dilemma-type situation. Take two athletes. Simply put, for many reasons they'd be better off not engaging in doping in the first place. But as nobody can trust the other, both end up taking drugs in order to enhance their chances of winning.

But what happens when one of you breaks free from our metaphorical prison and doesn't need to tread the road to PED redemption? Where does that leave the doped athlete? Wrestling with guilt, says Papp. 'There was one kid in particular, a guy named Mike Friedman who was from here in Pittsburgh. He was so disappointed in me that I cheated because I was a role model for him when he was a junior. Not only that, I beat him over and over again while doping and he was clean. That, I felt pretty shitty about. When you have a concrete experience like that with someone you know isn't doping, it's hard to ignore what you've done.'

Arguably, cycling's business model doesn't forge a foundation of athlete security. Teams rely on up to 95 per cent of their income from sponsors, creating an uncertain environment for those whose mortgage, family's quality of life and survival depends on it. Sometimes, the fragility of the sporting business leads to temptation. Sometimes it's less subtle. Sometimes it's engineered by the state.

The last half a century is scarred by numerous state-sponsored doping scandals, including the East German systematic national doping programme from the 1960s to late 1980s, where many athletes were given substances without informed consent. More recently, the full extent of Russia's nationwide doping scheme was exposed by Dr Grigory Rodchenkov, former head of Russia's national doping laboratory (something we look at in more detail in chapter six). For an insider account, read *The Rodchenkov Affair: How I Brought Down Russia's Secret Doping Empire*. Both are extreme and life-altering examples that politics and sport should never meet.

Neither, according to WADA's director of education Amanda Hudson, should budding young elites and legal supplements. 'The cognitive gateway theory is a determinant of doping vulnerability in athletes,' she explains. This is a research model that describes how athletes move from *I would never break the rules* to *Maybe I could* to *I probably should* to *I most definitely will* and their actual behaviour.

'If an athlete is used to taking a pill or supplement powder, or even an injection to manage pain, it's a smaller hurdle to leap over in terms of doping,' adds Hudson. 'They've already normalised taking substances. Of course, that doesn't mean it's a green light to dope but does add to the vulnerability.'

There's also the issue of unknowing doping via contaminated supplements, which we look at in chapter eight. And then there's the unknowing athlete, doped on what they thought to be legal supplements. One of the most infamous cases is the Essendon Bombers saga of the early- to mid-2010s.

Multiple players of the Australian rules football team took prohibited substances because they trusted the club's sports-science programme, believing it was legal and safe. The programme comprised subcutaneous injections of supplements to accelerate tissue recovery time, enabling players to work harder in training and so enjoy greater physiological adaptation. After four years of investigations and legal proceedings, 34 players at the club were found guilty of having used the banned peptide Thymosin beta-4 and incurred suspensions. Players would later say they felt 'naïve', describing a culture of total trust in support staff – a recurring theme in team sports.

As Hudson mentioned earlier in the chapter, further 'pressures' on athletes come from their personality type. If they're risk takers and sensation seekers, the warning signs could flash bright. This is amplified if they fear failure, have easy access to drugs and even if they're overly tired.

That last one sounds a little absurd but it ties in with self-control. Ignoring temptation is a cognitive drain because, according to researcher Anja Achtziger, it's treated 'as the capacity of one's "more rational" self to override the decisions of a more impulsive one'. This uses up resources that, Achtziger continues, induce a state of ego depletion. Not a great state of mind for an ego-driven elite. Coupled with the constant physical and psychological pressure of training, competition and expectation, the chances of making irrational – or less rational – decisions cranks up.

The 2008 Olympic 400m champion LaShawn Merritt sought forgiveness for the 'foolish, immature and egotistical mistake' he made in taking banned substances that led to three positive tests between 2009 and 2010. In press coverage after his suspension, the American talked about 'not thinking clearly', 'not exercising self-control' and feeling 'mentally depleted'. Floyd Landis described his eventual decision to dope as psychological surrender, stating that he was 'too tired to keep doing things the hard way' and had 'no willpower left to resist what everyone else was doing'. From the same era, Tyler Hamilton echoed the fatigue sentiment: 'I was too exhausted to say no anymore.' Or is that simply a lack of accountability? That'd certainly be the argument of clean athletes.

'There's also a crossover with gym culture,' says Josh Torrance. Torrance is a researcher at the University of Bristol, England, and is writing a PhD on schemes that divert people in possession of drugs away from the criminal justice system. 'I used to work at the Bristol Drugs Project,' he says. 'We'd run a free and confidential needle exchange service for heroin and crack users. It's a great initiative and has saved innumerable lives, preventing the spread of HIV and hepatitis C.

'Well, gym goers cottoned on to the service and we had a wave of young lads coming through the door to exchange old needles for new to inject steroids. We didn't really know anything about IPEDs [image and performance-enhancing drugs], but that was a real eye-opener.'

Estimates of steroid use in the UK range from half a million to a million. A key reason why they're so prevalent, says Torrance, is body dysmorphia, which is common in teenagers and is on the rise,[16] partly due to increasing social media influence and increasing screen time. 'Sure, you get some bodybuilders who want to lift 100kg and that's their goal,' says Torrance. 'But for a lot of guys lifting weights, the underlying motivation is to be

---

16 https://pmc.ncbi.nlm.nih.gov/articles/PMC7114025/

attractive. It's the same with many women. And it's true in elite sport, too.'

Elite athletes are perceived as superhuman and focused on peak performance but, like you and I, they have their fragilities, of which appearance is one. Brazilian footballer Ronaldo tested positive for the banned stimulant sibutramine in 2011. By this time, one of the world's greatest footballers had retired from the national team, stating that he took sibutramine to manage weight after a number of injuries and a thyroid-related metabolic condition. He told Brazilian newspaper *O Globo* that jokes and mockery about his body dug deep. 'People think it's funny but it tormented me,' he said. 'I was fighting my own body.'

Arguably the finest cricketer of all time, Shane Warne, also took a banned substance for image rather than performance reasons. In 2003, the Australian leg-spinner took a pill that his mother insisted would make him look better. 'I admitted to the [anti-doping committee] hearing that I had taken a tablet in early December,' Warne said at the time. 'I was doing a lot of wine promotions. I'd had a couple too many bottles of wine and had a few late nights. It was to get rid of a double chin.' The Australian Cricket Board anti-doping panel accepted his explanation, but because athletes are responsible for anything they ingest, he was still given a 12-month ban.

Similar to society as a whole, the factors that flow into arguably one of the biggest decisions of an athlete's life are many and multifactorial. So pervasive is sport and its history of doping that researcher Wolfgang Maennig devised a formula that predicts the chances of an athlete cheating. It's lengthy, dense and complex, so the preserve of academics only. Naturally, it cuts through the emotion and focuses on probability.

Unlike Jose Canseco's *New York Times* bestseller *Juiced*, which chronicles the Cuban-American's gilded baseball career where he scored 462 home runs. Published in 2006, it 'was the book that started the steroid scandal' and, at odds with the vulnerabilities cited above, Canseco was searingly honest that steroids made his career. He had no regrets. As a snapshot from *Juiced* . . .

'So off to the big leagues I went. Lucky bat, lucky syringe – luck had nothing to do with it.

'I was educating myself on all aspects of steroids – from why they were invented, to their chemical make-up, how to use them properly, what dosages, how to cycle off, how to cycle on, which steroids did what for the body, which one was good for strength … I wanted to keep getting better and better every year, and I was seeing that steroids could help me do that.

'We were in Boston for the play-offs, and something funny happened: all around me, I heard the fans chanting: "Steroids! Steroids!" When I heard that, I paused a moment to think about how to respond. Then I just turned sideways, flexed for them, turned the other way and flexed again. The crowd went nuts.'

Canseco embraced performance-enhancing drugs and questioned why everyone wouldn't use them. For the majority – in interviews and studies, at least – their actions and belated explanations result in myriad questions: are an elite athlete's doping actions unforgivable? Should they be damned? Or is there understanding? Put yourself in their shoes. You've dreamed of this career since childhood; you've devoted your life to that dream; responsibilities like a mortgage and parenthood fast-track innocence into experience; injury damages income projections; you know nothing but this sport, this life. This is you, your identity. Cue knocking on the doctor's door. Potential financial security and ego protected.

But what about the doctor? What's in it for them? Why would they go against the Hippocratic Oath and use medicines designed for therapeutic reasons as potent performance enhancers?

Sporting history is littered with empty vials – and often empty dreams – administered by 'doping doctors'. Dr Michele Ferrari was arguably the most prominent, supercharging the likes of Lance Armstrong. He was convicted in Italy in 2004 for sporting fraud related to doping practices but didn't serve jail time because of appeals and statute limitations.

Spain's Dr Eufemiano Fuentes received a one-year suspended sentence in 2013 for endangering public health in connection with the Operación Puerto blood-doping network that saw a number of top athletes sanctioned, including 1997 Tour de France winner Jan Ullrich and Spanish distance runner Alberto García. Several Spanish football clubs and tennis players were mentioned in leaked documents but no footballer or tennis player was ever charged.

And then there's Germany's Dr Mark Schmidt, who was the brains behind Operation Aderlass, a doping ring involving numerous athletes from across many sports. Because doping is a federal offence in Germany, in 2021 he was sentenced to four years and ten months in prison.

Reputations tarnished, suspensions, even prison, so why? Why would a doctor dope? John Hoberman is the chair of Germanic studies at the University of Texas, USA, but has dedicated four decades of his life to studying doping in sport. He's written several books on the subject, including 1992's *Mortal Engines: The Science of Performance and the Dehumanisation of Sport*, and, more recently, *Testosterone Dreams: Rejuvenation, Aphrodisia, Doping*. He's also written several papers looking specifically at physicians and doping.

'There are many reasons, one of which is obviously money. But another is to be closer to their heroes. This was certainly the case when I studied American sport and American football, in particular. These are ordinary guys who just happen to study medicine. There are tales of physicians paying up to $30,000 to have a medical spot on an NFL team. It's hero worship. I'm unsure if that still happens but it certainly did in the past.'

In the world of mixed martial arts (MMA), these practitioners are known as 'mark doctors', writes Hoberman in his 2014 paper examining the physician and sports doping epidemic. 'These are fan-boy doctors who are willing to write up prescriptions for drugs to fighters in exchange for a celebrity rub.'

This professional status and influence is something that was established in German court proceedings against Dr Schmidt following Operation Aderlass. He sought power by being 'the doctor who could deliver results'. He also charged athletes thousands of euros per blood-doping cycle, with the prosecutors describing it as a sophisticated business model rather than rogue experimentation.

'This type of emotional dependence works in both directions,' Hoberman continues. 'Just as doctors can succumb to the charismatic appeal of athletes, athletes can revere doctors as if they were infallible gurus. In his memoir *The Secret Race*, the doped former professional cyclist Tyler Hamilton writes that the notorious Italian doping doctor Michele Ferrari "was our trainer, our doctor, our god".'

This god-like status was certainly true of post-war Germany, and later unified Germany, where the American observed that sports physicians were treated as intellectuals, media authorities and 'performance experts'.

'There were plenty from other countries, too, including Robert Kerr,' says Hoberman. Kerr was a polarising character in the 1980s. From his California practice, he claimed to have provided banned hormones to more than 4,000 athletes from 19 different nations, including 20 medal winners at the 1984 Los Angeles Olympic Games. Anointed by his contemporaries, athlete–patients and the media as 'the steroid guru', Kerr was a popular figure in the doping discourse of the 1980s.

'I had lunch with him a few years ago now, as he died in 2001. He was notorious in the eighties for dispensing steroids to athletes, cops, firefighters and God knows who else. He was completely promiscuous and he wasn't the only one. There are tons of them even to this day who believe in libertarian pharmacology.' (We delve into this idea in chapter 12 and the Enhanced Games.)

Another key driver of the doping doctor is medical rationalisation. The idea is that extreme athletic stress is equivalent to what early sports physicians termed 'pathological physiology' and the doctor has a duty of care to provide pharmacological treatment to athletes. Schmidt framed blood transfusions as 'controlled, safe, medical procedures' and justified his actions through a strong belief in his technical competency. In essence, the athlete is a patient, not a performer.

In a 1988 interview, controversial West German sports physician Heinz Liesen suggested that, 'Elite sport is now at the limit of human performance where extreme pathological events occur. The body of a high-performance athlete is no longer comparable to that of a normal person.' Liesen argued that injections to fortify the body 'have nothing to do with doping' and are about legitimately replacing whatever the body has lost during exercise.

Ultimately, says Hoberman, sport is a snapshot of life. Drug-taking is rife in certain parts of society, so why wouldn't that be the case in sport? And that doesn't mean the desperate populations who are, to echo George Orwell's book, down and out in Paris and London.

'I wrote a book called *Dopers in Uniform: The Hidden World of Police on Steroids*,' says Hoberman. 'There's also a chapter in there on the military, and I have additional books in my office that look at drug use during World War II. The Americans, the British, the Germans, the Soviets, they were all on amphetamines; hundreds of millions of amphetamine pills helped to drive that war. It's pervasive. Drugs are pervasive.'

They are. But to what degree, seemingly it's anyone's guess. Paris 2024 produced 6,130 samples from 4,150 athletes, yet only five sanctioned positives. Is that a sign of a failproof anti-doping system or one that's leaking? Set that against the Tübingen study's 50% confession rate – its credibility heightened, not hindered (as the IOC argued at the time), by the randomised-response method – you'd pitch for the latter.

Subsequent national surveys (Commonwealth Games, Spain) add further variance, implying prevalence swings by sport, setting and design choices. The message is not that any single figure is 'true', but that the gap between positives and prevalence is structural: athletes weigh risk, identity, injury, contracts and social norms, while institutions balance transparency with politics. The result is uncertainty and, critics argue, a credibility problem.

What is the truth? Who can you trust? The replies to both

are ambivalent. What's clearer is that, on the face of it, the anti-doping framework and its myriad national organisations and accredited labs is far more structured in 2026 than times gone by. Whether that means sport's cleaner is clearly a matter of debate, but if it is, credit must go to the physiological tracker introduced over 15 years ago. It's time to get your passport out and travel back in time . . .

STOP TARGETING DRUGS. TRACK THEM

In chapter one, Professor Olivier Rabin explained how WADA collaborates with pharmaceutical companies in an effort to identify medicines of the future that could be used and abused by athletes and doctors. It's a vital relationship, as the medicines of today are the performance-enhancing drugs of tomorrow.

And it's why 1989 proved such a pivotal year in the war on drugs, for that is when the blood-boosting drug erythropoietin (EPO) – more specifically, epoetin alfa – was approved by the Food and Drug Administration (FDA) to treat anaemia. The world must thank Chinese hamsters, for both epoetin alfa and epoetin beta were synthesised in their ovary cells. That's reportedly down to being simple to cultivate in large-scale cultures, plus they effortlessly tolerate changes in pH levels and temperature. Millions of patients have benefitted from the increase in red blood cells ever since. It's proved a lifesaver. For thousands of athletes, it soon proved a game-changer.

While amphetamines were historically the endurance athlete's drug of choice, EPO was next level. Athletes whose haematocrit levels – the percentage of red cells in your blood – came in at 44%, could now raise it to more than 55%, even 60%. The IOC were quick out of the blocks in noting its performance potential and banned it in 1990.

But the endurance-enhancing genie was out of the bottle. And into the vial. Take swashbuckling Italian cyclist Marco Pantani, nicknamed 'The Pirate' for his perma-bandana (before the days helmets became mandatory) and aggressive style of racing, who won the Giro d'Italia and Tour de France in 1998. He ascended mountains like they were dimples. In 1999, he crashed at the one-day race Milan–Torino, where reportedly the blood-thickening effects of EPO elevated his haematocrit levels to a sloppy 60.1%.

So prevalent was EPO's use that in his book, *The Death of Marco Pantani*, author Matt Rendell describes how cyclists in the 1990s monitored heart-rate frequency overnight. If their beats per minute dipped too low, an alarm would go off, awakening the athlete, who'd then hop on bike rollers for ten minutes to get their heart racing. Too low, it's said, and it'd pool, clot and potentially lead to death. 'During the day we live to ride and at night we ride to live,' an anonymous rider revealed in Rendell's fine book. The infamous Festina affair of 1998, where vials and vials of EPO and needles plus other doping accoutrements were discovered in soigneur Willy Voet's car, made public the extent of the EPO problem.

The sporting authorities were well aware that doping was endemic, but due to difficulties finding a method of differentiating between natural EPO and synthetic EPO, it took until 2000 before a reliable test hit the sporting arena.

'We have to thank Dr Françoise Lasne of the French anti-doping laboratory for that,' says Raphael Faiss, research manager at the Centre of Research and Expertise in Anti-Doping sciences at the University of Lausanne. 'She led the research for the urine test that was rolled out for the first time at the Sydney Olympics. The test is actually still valid, albeit has been refined with newer technologies.'

No athletes tested positive for EPO at the 2000 Games; in fact, the first confirmed positive cases were recorded in cross-country skiing and cycling in 2001. But the defences had been bolstered. Still, cracks remained – one of the most gaping stemming from patent expiration. Soon, as sport scientist Ross Tucker would comment, rumours of 80 different types of EPO coming out of China with molecule modifications to avoid detection flooded the market. 'That would require 80 different tests for EPO with the cost–benefit off-the-charts negative,' said Tucker.

Beyond the financial implications, this creates a significant lag, ensuring the dopers keep well ahead of the testers. The solution? What if instead of looking directly for exogenous EPO you looked indirectly, measuring the physiological impact of the drug rather than looking for the drug itself by charting over time any nefarious trends in an athlete's blood?

'That was the heart of the athlete biological passport [ABP] and is still the key weapon against doping used today,' says Faiss. The scientific concept and practical framework of the ABP are most closely associated to Professor Michael Ashenden (an Australian who we hear more from in chapter 12), but it was standardised by WADA and embedded in the WADA Code in 2009, albeit cycling implemented it a year previous.

'Here's how it works,' explains Faiss. 'EPO stimulates the

production of reticulocytes, or young red blood cells, which can push values above an athlete's normal range. But there's also a clear "off-phase". When EPO use stops, the body reacts to the earlier supra-physiological dose by suppressing its own red blood cell production in an attempt to restore balance. That leads to abnormally low reticulocyte levels. It's this rise-and-fall pattern that the ABP detects. When the passport was first introduced, many athletes suddenly presented with low reticulocyte counts because they had all stopped using EPO during competition.'

By this point, out-of-competition testing had also intensified. Together, these anti-doping advances had an immediate and measurable effect on riders' blood profiles, as highlighted in a 2010 paper by Mario Zorzoli and Francesca Rossi, 'Implementation of the Biological Passport: The Experience of the International Cycling Union'.[17] The authors reported that between 2001 and 2007, around 10% of samples showed reticulocyte values at the extremes – either below 0.4% (the so-called off-phase) or above 2% (on-phase). Following the introduction of the biological passport, that figure fell to under 3%, while the most extreme category – below 0.2% off-phase or above 2.4% on-phase – disappeared altogether.

Dr Olaf Schumacher is an anti-doping authority and is currently the sports medicine physician at the impressive Aspetar elite sports hospital in Qatar, a job he balances with his role as chair of the WADA Prohibited List group. Schumacher trained at the University Medical Centre, Freiburg University, Germany, which erupted in scandal after being implicated in doping cycling team T-Mobile. That was 2007, but it became clear that the centre began supplying and administering banned PEDs from the 1970s.

---

17 https://pubmed.ncbi.nlm.nih.gov/21204287/

An independent commission later uncovered proof of systematic drug use in German football, particularly VfB Stuttgart and SC Freiburg. Schumacher attended 'a million commissions and was exonerated at a legal level . . . I honestly didn't know that they were actively doing stuff'.

Schumacher was involved in the development and roll out of the ABP and suggests it recalibrated performance, too. 'There's a good publication from my PhD student, Sergei Iljukov. He showed how the ABP impacted the times of female middle-distance runners in Russia. The results were stark.'[18]

Iljukov and his team analysed the top eight annual performances at the Russian National Championships over a ten-year span (2008 to 2017) in five events: 800m, 1,500m, 3,000m steeplechase, 5,000m and 10,000m. After the ABP was introduced, four of the five events (excluding steeplechase) showed a significant decline in performance, the authors arguing this is consistent with stronger anti-doping controls reducing performance artificially boosted by doping. Whether it's consistent with satisfying stakeholders concerned that sub-record performances equates to dwindling audiences is another matter.

History, of course, undermines the idea that a clean test record automatically equates to a clean athlete. 'I've been tested 500 times and never failed a drug test,' Lance Armstrong liked to say. Repeatedly. The ABP was created to address that blind spot, but dopers – well, the best-resourced – aren't fools. For years, the ABP focused solely on the haematological (blood) ramifications of doping. That was a positive step, but limiting.

'Not that long after the ABP was rolled out, athletes adapted their doping regimes and we saw an increase in the use of growth

18 https://pubmed.ncbi.nlm.nih.gov/32084627/

hormones. It needed to evolve,' says Faiss. Which it did, albeit an endocrine module, which profiles markers associated with growth hormone or Insulin-like growth factor 1 (IGF-1), wasn't added to the ABP until 2023, using serum blood samples. Before then, in 2014, WADA integrated a steroidal module that, as the name implies, targets anabolic steroid use. All operate on the same principle: tracking trends over time rather than relying on single tests. The principle goes: the more data you have, the clearer the trend, the more vivid the picture of whether an athlete is doping or clean.

'The aim of the ABP is an average three tests per year, with some riders tested once, some more than ten,' says Reid Aikin, associate director of the ABP at WADA. 'This tends to vary depending on success. For instance, in cycling, the leading riders would be tested at least three times during a grand tour like the Tour de France. Complete two grand tours in a season and that's already six without taking into account other in-competition and out-of-competition tests. If you've raced for many years at the top level, your passport will have ballooned to over 130 samples that are then kept in storage, albeit a bugbear of many in anti-doping is that GDPR (General Data Protection Regulation) stipulates the data can only be stored for ten years.

'The ABP sits within a centralised clearinghouse called ADAMS,' Aiken continues. 'It stands for Anti-Doping Management System, and each athlete has their own ADAMS.' Launched in 2005, ADAMS is the backbone of WADA's global anti-doping operations. As well as storing ABP detail, it's also the home to athletes' whereabouts information – where athletes must specify a 60-minute time and location where they'll be each day – and an athlete's TUEs (Therapeutic Use Exemptions). This allows athletes to take substances on WADA's Prohibited List to treat medical conditions. We look at both in chapter five.

ADAMS has proved an effective tool, but not without its flaws. Its reliance on self-reporting, administrative complexity, privacy concerns and uneven implementation means that clean athletes often bear a heavy compliance burden in a system designed to catch cheats. There are cybersecurity and data-protection concerns, too.

The most high-profile security breach happened in 2016 when, between August and September, WADA's systems were repeatedly compromised by the Russian-linked hacking group Fancy Bears, allegedly in retaliation for WADA's actions in exposing the state-sponsored doping ring. The group accessed and leaked confidential data of hundreds of athletes, including medical and TUE information.

It read like a Who's Who of elite sport and led to much innuendo. US Olympic gymnast Simone Biles sought TUEs for methylphenidate for ADHD; 23-time grand slam champion Serena Williams' data included exemptions for various medications such as prednisone, prednisolone, methylprednisolone, oxycodone and hydromorphone; and Sir Bradley Wiggins had multiple TUEs for asthma and corticosteroid, igniting a debate over their timing in relation to major races. A report by the Digital, Culture, Media and Sport Committee accused Wiggins, Team Sky and Sir Dave Brailsford of 'crossing an ethical line', though no evidence of wrongdoing was found.

The Fancy Bears hackers also disclosed documents attributed to the International Association of Athletics Federations (IAAF), which indicated anomalies in four-time Olympic gold medallist Mo Farah's biological blood passport during the period when he trained with the Alberto Salazar-led Nike Oregon Project.

(In 2015, Salazar was named in a joint BBC *Panorama* and *ProPublica* investigation into doping allegations. In 2019, the American was banned from athletics for four years for doping offences involving athletes he coached, though Farah wasn't one of them. The Nike Oregon Project – a group of high-performance athletes sponsored by the American corporation and based at Nike's HQ campus located just outside the Portland suburb of Beaverton, Oregon – was shut down in the wake of the controversy.)

A leaked email from then IAAF medical manager Pierre-Yves Garnier stated that he and an ABP expert panel had classified Farah's profile as 'likely doping; passport suspicious' on the 23rd November, 2015. Four months later, his biological values were reported to have returned to within normal ranges. A spokesperson for Farah commented, 'Any suggestion of misconduct is entirely false and seriously misleading. Mo Farah has been subject to many blood tests during his career and has never failed a single one. We have never been informed of any of Mo's test results being outside of the legal parameters set by the relevant authorities, nor has Mo ever been contacted by the IAAF about any individual result. It is totally incorrect and defamatory to suggest otherwise, and we will pursue any claims to the contrary through all necessary legal routes.'

Fancy Bears also claimed there were a number of adverse analytical findings – potentially positive tests – with 160 alone in 2015 in football. Four were in the UK – three for cocaine and one for ecstasy.

For Farah and the quartet of footballers, no charges were ever pressed, but it does bring into sharp focus the process that follows passport anomalies. The legal side of an adverse finding forms the core of chapter eight, but it's relevant to touch upon this lightly here, too.

'If the values exceed limits, the profile is flagged as suspicious, which will be confirmed or not with another test sample,' says Reid Aiken. 'An independent ABP panel then reviews the profile.' This panel typically comprises three experts, who'll then decide whether the abnormalities could be explained by other factors. These include things like a medical condition, exposure to altitude and training effects (which we elaborate on shortly).

'Key to proceedings are those experts. So if, say, haemoglobin levels are high, we'll bring in an expert on the haematological module and altitude. The panel don't know who the athlete is, they just have a code.'

If doping can't be ruled out, the relevant anti-doping organisation will carry out targeted testing, request medical documentation and seek an explanation from the athlete. If the expert panel conclude doping is likely, it's treated as an adverse analytical finding. The wheels are then set in motion, where the burden of proof is on the athlete to prove their innocence. 'We see around 3,000 of these each year,' says WADA General Counsel Ross Wenzel.

As the anti-doping authorities become more aware of doping strategies, similar to doping itself, ADAMS has evolved. 'A couple of years ago, the ExCo [WADA's Executive Committee] removed athletes' real-time access to their ABP and haematological data,' says Aiken. 'It came off the back of Operation Aderlass, which revealed that athletes and their support teams could monitor this data in order to fine-tune their doping programme.'

Investigators found that doctors looked for directional changes, avoiding sharp skews that might attract scrutiny. They'd time 'interventions' relative to testing windows, overlaying competition calendars with likely testing periods. They'd pinpoint periods to micro-dose or adjust when to withdraw and infuse blood, all with the aim of staying just beneath the adaptive limits. They were successful . . . until they weren't.

Proponents see ADAMS as a game-changer. Critics point to statistics like that seen in chapter two. That the system is catching a mere droplet in the doping ocean of athletes. Faiss is pragmatic.

'I'd say the ABP's working because it's forcing athletes to change their attitude towards doping, which is certainly less dangerous,' says Faiss. 'Imagine you're in a car travelling from A to B. You know there are never police on that road so you can drive really fast. But what happens when you know there's a road with a speed camera on? You know you must reduce your speed. Okay, you may drive slightly over the limit but not fast enough to be flashed. It's safer and ultimately the health of an athlete is the number one concern.' Faiss's concession that ADAMS has made sport safer if not necessarily cleaner is due to many ABP challenges.

In 2015, a documentary broadcast on TV station France 2 revealed that micro-dosing athletes not only delivered meaningful performance benefits but stayed off the radar of the ABP. Physiologist Pierre Sallet led the programme.

The premise was simple. Eight amateur athletes underwent a battery of baseline tests before embarking on a 29-day protocol involving micro-doses of EPO and other substances. Performance was assessed using a VO_2max test (to measure aerobic capacity – the higher the better for most athletes), a 14km cycling time trial on a stationary bike and a 3km run. After the intervention, the athletes repeated the same tests. The results were striking. Average

VO$_2$max rose by 6.1%, cycling performance improved by 2.1% and those 3km run times cranked up by 2.8%.

The documentary concluded that these improvements were achieved without triggering the ABP, a claim that drew a swift response from WADA, who confirmed it had provided access to ABP software for the programme, but stressed it hadn't endorsed the study. In a statement, WADA noted that the findings hadn't been peer-reviewed or published.

Unlike a 2011 study, which involved Professor Michael Ashenden in the *European Journal of Applied Physiology* reporting a 10% increase in haemoglobin mass following a 12-week micro-dosing regimen of bi-weekly injections of EPO.[19] That's the equivalent of receiving two bags of reinfused blood (more in chapter five). Despite the increase, none of the ten subjects' blood profiles were flagged as suspicious.

Today, the ABP and testing tools are more sensitive. But remain fallible. A more recent study highlighted the performance as well as physiological improvements, involving 48 male and female athletes undertaking a cycling time trial after thrice-weekly injections of EPO or a placebo for four weeks.[20] The blood-boosted group increased their haemoglobin mass by around 5% compared to the baseline, with performance gains touching 4%. Again, the changes were subtle enough to fall within normal biological variability.

'Yes, there are studies that show that micro-dosing won't be picked up by the passport, but it depends on the timing of the test,' says Schumacher. 'I'm pretty certain that if you urine-test an

---

19 https://link.springer.com/article/10.1007/s00421-011-1867-6

20 https://researchprofiles.ku.dk/en/publications/microdoses-of-recombinant-human-erythropoietin-enhance-time-trial/?utm_

athlete who's taking EPO micro-doses at the right time – even just 50 units intravenously, which is a really low dose – it'll be detected and flagged up on the ABP.'

Method of test is key, says Schumacher. EPO, especially at micro levels, is fleeting in the blood. Once it's circulated and done its work, it's rapidly cleared and becomes almost indistinguishable from the body's own hormone. Recombinant EPO has a short plasma half-life of hours.

Urine is different. As EPO is filtered by the kidneys it's excreted rather than erased. In that process, subtle structural differences between natural and synthetic EPO are preserved, allowing them to be identified after the hormone has disappeared from circulation. Put simply, blood tells you what is happening now; urine tells you what has just happened. It's why, for many drugs, urine has traditionally offered a longer detection window.

That doesn't assuage the concerns of David Howman, chair of the Athletics Integrity Unit (AIU). 'In cycling, you could take something at the start of the stage and by the time you've finished five hours later, that substance wouldn't be detectable in your body, certainly not your blood. But it'd have given you a sufficient boost to make a difference. Micro-dosing is a real issue.'

What amounts are we talking? Historically, EPO use relied on large bolus injections, often 4,000–10,000IU per dose, taken two or three times a week to rapidly elevate haemoglobin and haematocrit. The physiological effect was powerful – and obvious. Micro-dosing reversed that approach. Instead of big spikes, athletes use much smaller doses, typically 300–1,000IU per injection, administered daily or near-daily. This quietly maintains red blood cell production rather than aggressively increases it. Over time, however, the total weekly volume injected could be similar to before, but spread thinly enough to produce flatter, less conspicuous blood profiles.

The difficulty of detection is confounded by a popular training intervention. From 2022, Kenya's 2008 Olympic 1,500m champion Asbel Kiprop served a four-year ban after failing a targeted and direct EPO test, following anomalies in his biological passport. It was with a certain irony that Kiprop's gold came after being promoted from silver after the Bahrani who narrowly beat him, Rashid Ramzi, tested positive for CERA, a newer version of EPO. At his defence, the AIU called Kiprop's explanation an 'à la carte menu of reasons why the charges should be dismissed'.

Among these, the AIU said, were that the 'EPO was naturally produced due to intense exercise at altitude'. The three-man panel concluded that high altitude couldn't explain the presence of EPO in the test.

But Kiprop and his team weren't alone in arguing that biological irregularities were due to rarefied air rather than injection.

'There have certainly been reports of athletes using EPO at altitude to mask its effects,' says Dr Laura Lewis, science director at USADA and expert on the haematological module and altitude. 'At altitude, your body's natural response to the low levels of oxygen is to produce its own EPO, which accelerates the production of red blood cells. Depending on the individual's response to altitude, it can deliver similar effects on the markers as blood doping – EPO and blood transfusions – but not to the same magnitude. So, it can cause the passport to flag above those upper or lower limits. It's led to some athletes using recombinant EPO at altitude as they feel they can explain the anomaly on their passport.'

A 2022 paper by Jonas Saugy highlighted the problem, the

researcher revealing that an athlete's blood profile when micro-dosing was 'hardly distinguishable from those identified after hypoxic exposure' without doping.[21]

This labyrinth is exacerbated by the increasingly frequent and extreme use of altitude training. Andorra has become a playground for endurance athletes, while athletes who've racked up years training above 1,500m often sleep in altitude tents at altitude to crank up the hypoxic strain. This altitude duet is a nightmare for anti-doping authorities to unpick.

'It's certainly a hurdle to overcome,' says Schumacher. 'We've undertaken one of the most expensive studies WADA has ever funded, where we tried to differentiate between EPO abuse and altitude. And the short conclusion is, it's really hard. Those signatures in the blood are just too similar.'

'On the positive,' adds Schumacher, 'when an athlete trains at altitude, they must flag this up on their whereabouts system. If you throw in all the main doping tests, at the right time, plus you have that information, there's a likelihood that you will catch the cheat.'

The problem is elite sport is big business. When the fiscal stakes are highest, the doping spectre looms largest. As does clinical creativity. Take the Aderlass case, which exposed athletes who headed to altitude and extracted blood while they were there to accelerate the regeneration of new red blood cells. They'd then return to a 'normal' state faster than if they were taking out blood at sea level. Or they'd go to altitude, generate a whole lot more red blood cells and then extract blood at the end of the camp that they might reinfuse back at sea level.

This resourcefulness would be impressive if it wasn't so

---

21   https://pmc.ncbi.nlm.nih.gov/articles/PMC9282833/

blatantly against the rules. Thankfully, says Lewis, the anti-doping authorities aren't averse to imagining – and then working on – solutions. This is a little technical but stay with me. Lewis regales a study when working at the Australian Institute of Sport, where they monitored riders at the 2013 Tour of Qinghai Lake in China. 'It's the highest race in the world and features one climb that peaks at over 4,100m.' In short, it's suffocatingly intense.

'The main reason we chose that race was down to two extreme and conflicting stimuli. The first is that when you're at altitude you should realise a significant increase in haemoglobin. The second is down to the number of stages [back then, China's leading multi-stage race numbered 13 but has since shrunk to eight].' Previous studies revealed that consecutive days of exercise actually diluted haemoglobin levels, which is down to the fluid component of blood, known as plasma, expanding. It's your kidneys' natural response to the stress applied day after day.

'The question that was relevant to the passport was, at altitude which one will "win" – the increase in haemoglobin or the increase in plasma volume? I thought that the altitude would win because oxygen is pretty important! But I was wrong – every rider's haemoglobin levels dropped because of the amount plasma volume that had expanded. We also tested a Chinese team who were natives at that altitude and the results were the same – haemoglobin levels drop, plasma volume rises.

'That was really important information because it showed us that plasma volume, particularly exercising over many long days, could actually be more of a confounder to the passport than altitude itself. I think we have a good handle on altitude, albeit because micro-dosing does raise the chances of false positives, it's important for anti-doping organisations to continue with EPO tests hand in hand with the ABP. But then the way that plasma volume can change with tapering or increased training loads, that's a little bit harder to quantify.'

With that in mind, WADA has channelled funding into further research on plasma volume. 'I'm part of a working group trying to measure plasma volume in real-world settings – reliably and repeatedly – rather than only under laboratory conditions,' says Lewis. 'That's difficult, but it's not beyond reach.

'A study out of Qatar by Louisa Lobigs showed you could estimate plasma volume using straightforward blood chemistry markers. We trialled that approach at an Australian cycle race in 2020, just before Covid, and it tracked changes in plasma volume remarkably well. It would mean taking an additional blood sample alongside the ABP, but it could add confidence when interpreting results, helping distinguish whether shifts are driven by plasma volume changes.' Put simply, it would better account for altitude exposure and the plasma-expanding effects of racing hard over consecutive days.

Raphael Faiss is currently utilising machine learning to estimate what a rider's plasma volume should be at any given time – artificial intelligence is used to define normal patterns and patterns that correspond with doping. This isn't solely beneficial training up a mountain. High-intensity exercise is another confounder of the ABP as it can shift plasma volume by as much as 20% within an hour. Again, unpicking anomalies from simply hammering it in the heat is a real issue.

In fact, WADA has several AI projects on the go that focus on different facets of the ABP, including the ability to flag up 'urine exchange'. That means cracking down on athletes looking to pass off somebody else as themselves during a drug test. From 2012 to

2019, WADA looked into more than 60,000 cases and discovered a doppelganger pattern in 130 of them.

The ABP has flaws. Like the athletes and support teams who dope. But it has merits. Which is why it's somewhat of a surprise that the only British athlete ever sanctioned purely on passport is Team Sky's Jonathan Tiernan-Locke, a case that remains a landmark in UK anti-doping history.

In 2014, cycling's international governing body concluded that irregular fluctuations in Tiernan-Locke's blood values could not be credibly explained by training load, illness, altitude exposure or natural variation. There was no positive drugs test, no seized substance and no admission. Instead, the case rested entirely on longitudinal data from his biological passport, assessed independently by expert panels who judged the probability of doping to be overwhelming.

Tiernan-Locke initially received a four-year ban, later reduced to two years after cooperation. The British rider was stripped of results from 2012 and 2013 – seasons in which he'd enjoyed rapid success, including overall victory at the Tour of Britain. The sanction effectively ended his professional career.

That outlier stems from the ABP monitoring suspicion. As mentioned at the start of this chapter, any empirical misgivings and the athlete is targeted for more direct testing. See a trend. Act on it. Then let the legal cogs whirl. But what if you're a young athlete who's just started on their professional journey and their ABP entries are nil? Is that another reason they're more vulnerable? That if they've doped from a young age, the ABP won't spot anomalies as those anomalies are 'normal'?

'No,' says Reid Aikin, associate director of the ABP at WADA. 'An athlete's [ABP] will still flag outliers because while their passport is individual, we still have lots of data comparing blood values relative to that population. It would show as highly abnormal.

'In fact, relatively often an athlete's first ABP test is followed by a direct test, as they'd be unaware that they're under scrutiny. We presented data recently that showed around 80 per cent of EPO positives were on athletes who'd never been direct-tested before. They didn't think they were on the radar. That said, for spotting trends, the ABP is more sensitive to doping over time.'

Does this arrow in on a greater flaw in the anti-doping framework – that of the ABP's omnipresence only applying to the pinnacle of sport? That when you're young and graduating through the respective performance pathway, you do so unchecked? Jacek Kapela thinks so.

The Pole is a keen cyclist, proud father of Marek Kapela and an anti-doping advocate, who believes flaws in the current system are impairing – if not curtailing – the chances of his son and many like him of realising their lifelong dream and contesting at the highest level.

'An ABP is mandatory for WorldTour and Pro-level riders,' says Kapela. This is divisions one and two. 'But if you're competing at Continental level [division three], it's not mandatory. That is a big problem.' Why the lack of implementation is down to cost and, as we discover in chapter nine, politics. There's simply insufficient money to regularly test athletes who, in this case, compete on the third rung of the ladder. For the ABP to be effective, that means regular testing, which not only requires all the necessary needles, vials and bottles, but also cool-storage equipment and doping control officers. This adds up financially, but comes at the cost of integrity.

'I've spoken to someone at the International Testing Agency,' says Kapela. The ITA is an independent organisation that carries out the anti-doping testing programmes, including management of the ABP, for over 60 sporting federations, including boxing, gymnastics and even esports. 'They told me that without a biological passport, tied in with rarely being tested out of competition, if an athlete has a reasonable doctor they will never get caught.'

It's why Kapela turned civilian detective when he had suspicions about a competitor of Marek's at junior level; in fact, he had suspicions about a peloton's worth of riders. 'For a long time, I suspected many on the Polish junior team, so I contacted the Belgian anti-doping agency, who then tested the entire squad before their race [the junior version of Gent–Wevelgem] at their hotel. They didn't find anything, but I was certain.'

That set off a chain of events that led Kapela down a tunnel of data. Thanks to public platforms like Strava – a popular fitness-tracking and social-networking app primarily used by cyclists and runners – if an athlete uploads their session, you can dissect their results to uncover the physical effort behind the performance. In cycling, one of the key metrics is wattage. 'I also ran some of these performances through artificial intelligence via DeepSeek and ChatGPT. It told me that this performance was impossible for that level of competition.'

The performance in question came from three-time Polish under-23 time-trial champion Kacper Gieryk. 'He's a big guy [in cycling terms] – around 1.85m tall and around 73kg – and then all of a sudden, he's in this Czech race and climbing like a goat on this 10km-long effort that averages around 8%. It's brutal and steep, and he's beating the best climbers [at that level] from around the world. It was unbelievable. Too unbelievable.

'I tipped off the Polish anti-doping agency once, twice, three times from an anonymous account. They checked him out and nothing came up. He must have had a good doctor who was advising him when to take certain drugs and when to stop using them.'

Kapela remained unconvinced of Gieryk's innocence, so contacted the ITA. 'They believed what I was saying and caught him off guard. During the 2024 world championships, he finished 40th in the time trial [Gieryk was focused on the road race four days later, albeit he didn't finish]. You don't expect to be tested that far down the field, but the ITA tested him. This time he tested positive for EPO.'

More precisely, he tested positive for dEPO or darbepoetin, which is closely related to EPO and sits beneath the same umbrella on WADA's Prohibited List. Both stimulate the production of red blood cells, albeit dEPO is a re-engineered form of EPO and is potentially more effective, as it stays in the body longer. That longevity, however, proved Gieryk's downfall. The Pole's three-year suspension ends on 26th November, 2027.

Catching the likes of Gieryk shouldn't be down to the likes of himself, Kapela says, insisting the ABP must be mandatory further down the ladder, in an effort not only to protect the reputation of sport, but also to protect the dreams of athletes like his son. 'How can you compete with such people? It's superhuman, but not in a natural way. WorldTour teams are scouting ever-younger riders in search of the next [Tadej] Pogačar.'

If a young rider finishes top three in a high-profile race, they could be signed by one of the world's best. But unless their genetics is world-class, they often seek a shortcut and dope. 'Situations like this have really demotivated my son,' says Kapela. 'He feels his chances of reaching the top level are over.'

Cycling's no outlier here. In athletics, where the AIU has won plaudits for its testing success, there's no universal ABP rollout for all elite athletes; instead, it focuses on international-level athletes and endurance disciplines, like middle- and long-distance running. Triathlon, again there's no automatic enrolment for the elites – it's primarily used for athletes in international testing pools.

This disparity is because sports aren't legally required to use the ABP. Each international federation decides whether to implement it. The respective national anti-doping organisations then run much of the testing while WADA oversees compliance. Opting out of the ABP or rolling out nominal testing isn't a good look.

As Matt Lawton wrote in *The Times*, 'If the ABP represents the most effective means of testing, compare football to athletics in terms of the number of ABP samples that are analysed each year. In football in 2023, it accounted for 3 per cent of the total. In athletics, the analysis of ABP samples amounted to 34 per cent. In England, UKAD has a national registered testing pool that uses the ABP system to monitor athletes. The size of the pool, and the names of the athletes on it, is not public knowledge, but *The Times* understands there are few, if any, footballers on it.' Chapter nine takes a broader look at sport-specific testing variation.

The athlete biological passport was designed to make cheating harder, riskier and, crucially, less extreme. By shifting the focus from detecting substances to monitoring the body's response over time, the ABP changed behaviour. Blood profiles flattened. Performances fell. Some athletes adapted; others were caught.

Yet the passport is neither infallible nor universally applied. Micro-dosing, altitude exposure, plasma volume shifts and uneven rollout across sports continue to blur the line between natural adaptation and artificial manipulation. You could argue that the ABP has made elite sport safer, perhaps fairer, but not unequivocally clean. Ultimately, it's narrowed the margins rather than eliminated the problem.

SCIENCE, SUSPICION AND CERTAINTY COLLIDE

Stroll through King's College London and you step into the shadows of giants. Author Virginia Woolf, poet John Keats, theologian Desmond Tutu and nurse Florence Nightingale all studied at the bastion of education that turns 200 years old in 2031. On this mid-June afternoon in 2025, the suffocating humidity of inner-city London is relieved through automatic doors that greet you with air-con. Many of the university students have headed home for the summer, meaning it's a lonesome ascent up several flights of stairs before arriving at the fourth floor. Heading down corridor D, I arrive at the Drug Control Centre. It has Orwellian dystopia stamped all over it.

It's an integral part of King's Forensics and its internationally recognised expertise in analytical science, one that stretches back to the 1960s, where its pioneers contributed to the scientific foundation of modern doping control with work on steroid metabolism and hormone detection. It's been WADA-accredited since WADA founded in 1999. That means many things, but fundamentally it is a green light for testing urine and blood samples for substances on the banned list.

As of December, 2025, there were 30 WADA-accredited laboratories around the world. But this number is far from fixed, says Christiaan Bartlett, the laboratory's operations manager. 'I know Brazil lost accreditation status at one point,' he says. 'And obviously Russia. Recently South Africa lost theirs, too, due to its inability to reach the standards required. WADA regularly sends teams down to assess the quality of your work and practices. It's on a points scheme. If you don't rack up enough, you could have your accreditation revoked.'

On the positive, other countries are investing in their anti-doping structure. In early 2026, the Nigerian Ministry of Sport announced that they'd set aside a budget to build the country's first anti-doping laboratory. 'Nigeria's National Sports Commission (NSC) has declared its unwavering commitment to upholding the integrity of Nigerian sports, with a renewed focus on eradicating age falsification and doping violations,' said a spokesman.

Bartlett adds that there are also WADA-affiliated labs around the world that aren't full-scale accredited but will test for the athlete biological passport (ABP), which we covered in the last chapter. For now, I'm not concerned about that. Instead, I'm here for a tour to uncover the other tools of the anti-doping trade. Bartlett is my guide. He's been at King's for over 25 years and played a key role in the running of London's 2012 Olympic anti-doping programme. He's lifted the physiological lid on tens of thousands of elite athletes to see if their performances were natural or enhanced.

'Firstly, no photos,' he explains as our anti-doping outing begins.

'Each sample has a code that's specific to the athlete. If that's made public, someone might be able to trace it back to them. That could impact things legally.'

Bartlett flashes his security pass at the sensor, the automatic doors open and we're in. Well, nearly. Before we've entered the world of ampules and mass spectrometry, a hatch opens to reveal a courier concealed by a motorbike helmet and carrying a large box. One of Bartlett's younger colleagues – most are younger, as many are PhD students – opens said box. 'That's a delivery of blood samples,' Bartlett explains. 'They're in ice packs. You know they're blood because you don't need that for urine samples.'

Bartlett shows me a couple bottles labelled with 'A' and 'B'. A is tested first; B is the sealed back-up in case A is positive. 'You probably recognise them from the Russian doping crisis.'

I do. They are Berlinger bottles. Actually, they are adapted Berlinger bottles. One of the key discoveries of the state-sponsored scandal was that early generation Berlinger bottles, which were WADA-approved and widely trusted, weren't actually impregnable. Russia's secret service found a way of opening and resealing the bottles without any perceptible damage, meaning they were easily tampered with. That discovery led to changes, including a redesigned locking mechanism, more visible markers of tampering, improved manufacturing consistency, and enhanced serialisation and traceability.

Samples that return an adverse analytical finding (positives) must be kept for a minimum of six months. 'WADA rules stipulate that the accredited labs hold on to negative test samples for at least three months,' adds Bartlett. 'The customer, be it an international federation or national anti-doping agency, can then decide to keep negative samples for up to ten years in long-term storage (at their cost) for possible re-analysis in the future. All samples collected at Olympic Games are kept for ten years in Lausanne, Switzerland, and often retested.' This, says WADA, is a key deterrent in the fight against doping. As detection methods are updated and refined, retaining samples for a decade 'means that those who have cheated cannot rest easy after they have been tested'.

Further analysis of samples collected during Beijing 2008 and London 2012 resulted in more than 130 anti-doping rule violations, with around 90 athletes sanctioned. Belarusian shot-putter Nadzeya Ostapchuk won bronze in Beijing, which was annulled in 2017 when reanalysis identified traces of the steroid turinabol and the estrogen receptor modulator tamoxifen, a drug used to treat cancer but also adopted by female dopers to counteract the side effects of steroid abuse like menstrual disruption. (Ostapchuk won gold at London 2012 but once again tested positive, this time just days later, so was disqualified before the Games was over.)

Russia's Ekaterina Poistogova had her 800m London bronze revoked, just one of many athletes who were later sanctioned after retests from the Russian doping scandal. (There's more on this in chapter six.) And Kazakhstan's Ilya Ilyin was stripped of his weight-lifting gold medals from both Beijing and London after retests showed traces of the steroids stanozolol and turinabol, which were previously undetectable. The list goes on.

'After the Paris Olympics and Paralympics, a huge truck, or maybe even trucks, collected the samples and transported them to an enormous storage facility in Switzerland,' says Bartlett.

Bartlett says his lab tests around 10,000 samples each year, with each of the urine samples following the same first analytical step. 'That's the specific gravity test,' says Bartlett. For the laboratory to analyse an athlete's sample it must fall within a normal physiological range of around 4.5 to 9. If it doesn't, the sample may be unreliable or intentionally manipulated with the use of chemicals in an attempt to degrade or destroy the drugs. This is double-checking, as the doping-control personnel would have already tested the pH at source. It's also why said urine collector will advise the athlete not to overhydrate – too dilute a sample and, again, the sample is invalid.

Deeper into the lab are two of the most powerful tools anti-doping authorities possess – mass spectrometry machines. There's the gas chromatography version and the liquid chromatography version. Like the PEDs that dopers inject, rub or swallow, these machines were researched, designed and developed for the medical arena before their anti-doping benefits became clear.

Bartlett explains how these mechanical sniffer dogs sniff out the dopers. 'There is some degree of crossover but, broadly speaking, the substances detected by each technique come into the following categories. The gas machine focuses on anabolic steroids, some narcotics and carboxy THC [cannabis metabolite], while the liquid machine looks to detect stimulants, diuretics, narcotics, beta-2 agonists, beta blockers, glucocorticoids and some anabolic steroids.'

The gas detector is for urine. A small amount of the athlete's urine sample – just 2ml – is injected into the machine, where it's heated to around 280°C, vaporising the sample into gas. The gas then flows through a long, coiled capillary forged from copper.

This separates the urine into individual compounds based on molecular size, shape and chemical interactions with the coil coating. These then enter the mass spectrometry, where molecules are broken down further into fragments with each drug creating a unique 'fingerprint'. The result of this forensic work is displayed on a computer screen.

The liquid machine – again, a staple of WADA labs – tests both urine and blood, which are both cleaned and filtered before the separation process. Via high pressure and ionisation, the liquid is broken down into its rawest form in search of 300-plus substances.

'Again, all of this creates a fingerprint,' says Bartlett. 'Take testosterone, which the gas machine measures. You can see it on the screen. Now, the old-school way would be to solely focus on the ratio between testosterone and epitestosterone. Yes, this machine does that, too, but it can also directly detect synthetic testosterone.'

WADA compared the ratio as, when synthetic testosterone is used, while testosterone rises, epitestosterone (a naturally occurring steroid hormone but with no significant muscle-building effect) doesn't. If your ratio of testosterone to epitestosterone measured 6:1 or over, historically, that would arouse suspicion. WADA then reduced that to 4:1, which doesn't automatically mean guilt but will lead to further investigation. 'That's required,' says Bartlett, 'as testosterone is one substance that is particularly complex.'

Though its sporting vessel often isn't. In 2014, Major League Baseball suspended shortstop and third baseman Alex Rodriguez for 162 games for his role in the Biogenesis doping scandal. Biogenesis was a Miami clinic accused of supplying PEDs to professional athletes including Rodriguez, who then tried to obstruct the investigation by intimidating witnesses and attempting to discredit evidence.

Key testimony came in the form of clinic founder Anthony Bosch, who claimed Rodriguez used a sophisticated doping programme designed to avoid detection. Speaking to the American

TV programme *60 Minutes*, Bosch claimed Rodriguez took PED-laced lozenges that he called 'gummies' 15 minutes before taking to the field. The gummies resembled candy or chewing gum, and traces of the chemicals would wear off by the time he was drug-tested after the game.

In a meticulous operation, Bosch claimed he even injected Rodriguez in the bathroom of a Miami nightclub. To ensure he never tested positive for PEDs, he was taught to submit only urine from the middle part of his stream, because drug-laced metabolites gather in the beginning and end of the stream.

Swede Jenny Schulze is another expert on testosterone, though comes at the PED from a slightly more academic angle. Schulze studied biomedical engineering at university. Her Masters took her to Umeå University, one of Sweden's largest educational institutes, with over 34,000 students. There, she developed an interest in pharmaceuticals, resulting in her writing her thesis at AstraZeneca.

'After that, I wondered what to do next,' she says. 'Everyone at AstraZeneca with really fun jobs seemed to have a PhD. So, I looked around and ended up at the Karolinska Institute.'

The Karolinska Institute is world-famous for medical research – so much so that its Nobel Assembly of 50 senior professors selects the Nobel Prize in Physiology or Medicine each year. Key discoveries and the award-winning scientists who made them include Frederick Banting and Charles Best's finding of insulin in 1923; Alexander Fleming, Howard Florey and Ernst Boris Chain, penicillin, 1945; James Watson, Francis Crick and Maurice Wilkins, DNA structure, 1962; and, more recently in 2023, Katalin Karikó and Drew Weissman, whose mRNA vaccine technology enabled rapid development of Covid-19 vaccines.

'Karolinska had just received a grant from WADA to study why East Asians had such a naturally low ratio of testosterone to epitestosterone. In Europe and in America, most people have a ratio of 1, but the further east you go, the lower the ratio, and many Asians basically don't have any testosterone in their urine at all. It intrigued me, so that's what my PhD focused on.'

Her research led her to 'gene deletion'. A single dose of 360mg of testosterone was given to 55 healthy men, of whom 17 featured gene deletion. 'We measured their levels in urine for two weeks and we noted that all of the subjects with this mutation would not fail the doping test.' Their urine seemed fine, with no excess testosterone, even though the men clearly had taken the drug.

It was an anti-doping eye-opener, as those 17 men could forge strength with testosterone – they responded normally to the hormone – but because they were missing both copies of the gene used to convert the testosterone into a form that dissolves in urine, they could technically inject it with impunity. 'The study was published just before the Olympics in Beijing in 2008 and led to my 15 minutes of fame. I was in *The New York Times* and *The Economist!*'

Schulze discovered that around 10 per cent of Swedes also have this mutation, as well as about 80 per cent of the Japanese. 'Basically, the further east you go, the more common it is. It seems like it's a very old mutation that started in the east and spread to the west.'

Schulze's interest in population variance was aroused. 'It turned out that all of the testosterone research on athletes had been undertaken on men. Why, I can't say for sure, but it's doubtless down to the majority of sport-science research taking place on men, plus it's hard to secure ethical approval to start injecting women with testosterone. But I presumed that things like the menstrual cycle and contraception could skew things.'

Schulze proved correct. Her results were an eye-opener for WADA. 'In women, epitestosterone in particular is highly sensitive to hormonal fluctuations. So, if you take contraceptives, you sort of switch off your hormone production, meaning your epitestosterone will be very low, resulting in a high ratio. It means that if you hadn't taken testosterone but you were taking contraceptives, you could have tested positive.'

The findings threatened the credibility of the anti-doping system, but WADA took note. The introduction of the steroidal module in 2014 has helped to close the loophole. 'All in all, female athletes are simply more complex,' says Schulze. And nuanced. And surprising.

'I recall the case of Norwegian footballers who returned samples containing DMBA,' she explains. DMBA, or 1,3-dimethyl-butylamine, is a synthetic substance that stimulates the central nervous system and is sometimes used in dietary supplements, although it is banned in Norway, the European Union and by WADA if it exceeds the threshold of 50ng/ml. 'This was after playing on artificial turf.

'The laboratory thought there's something strange going on here, so they began measuring everything – the water, fruit, anything that could have contaminated the players,' Schulze adds. 'They then began analysing the rubber crumb infill that cushions the impact when players hit the ground, the theory being that the shredded tyre granulate on the pitch had contained DMBA. Sprinkle in air moisture and the players would have inhaled the substance.'

While the urine of four players from each women's side –

Vålerenga versus LSK Kvinner at LSK-Hall in Lillestrøm – revealed the presence of DMBA, only one player tipped over that 50ng/ml threshold.

After the seven-month investigation by Anti-Doping Norway, the player was proven faultless. Harriet Rudd, the Vålerenga CEO, told the *Guardian*: 'Environmental factors really need to be high on the radar moving forwards. It's about having a holistic overview of what in the environment you risk finding in a doping test. Anti-doping work has to develop and issues like this have to become a much larger part of the things you take into consideration.'

'A large study is currently underway into the potential issue,' counters Schulze. 'The air theory remains a hypothesis.'

Back in London, Barrett is detailing the minutiae of machines that detect growth-hormone releasing factors and immunoassay techniques for protein hormones, like EPO and HGH. 'And this one is for dried blood spot testing. This has been a development of the past few years.'

Dried blood spot testing involves placing a small amount of blood onto special filter paper. It's then dried and later analysed in the laboratory. The idea of dried blood spot analysis goes back to the early 20th century, but it became popular in the 1960s in detecting illicit drugs in forensic cases. It's commonly used in paediatrics for extracting blood from newborns and children.

Dr Jakob Mørkeberg is senior science manager at Anti-Doping Denmark (ADD). He's a man whose life's work has centred on fighting the dopers, starting from his Masters and PhD that focused on blood doping to his current expertise in dried blood spot testing.

'During my PhD, one study looked at gene expression and

involved withdrawing three bags of blood from the subjects and then reinfusing them,' he says. 'That's a relatively large amount of blood as we're talking around 450ml a bag. We saw around 70 genes that were either up- or down-regulated that could be a certain signature of doping.'

In other words, intimated doping. But hints dissipated into nothing when micro-dosing, silencing further funding channels. (It's something Professor Yannis Pitsiladis builds on in chapter nine.) Mørkeberg and his team also investigated whether they could find 'signs of bad' on the surface of the reinfused blood, as storage changes the cell's surface. 'We didn't.'

Promising research hit the buffers – an anti-doping theme – and the potential game-changer died a death. But ever the resilient scientist, Mørkeberg moved on. From his base at Denmark's House of Sport, which sits next door to Brøndby IF's football stadium, around 20km west of Copenhagen, he's pioneered WADA's newest test. 'Basically, every anti-doping organisation can use the dried blood spot test,' he says. 'They tend to use one of two models.'

One involves a doping officer finger-pricking the athlete. The blood spots are collected on a cellulose material. This dries out and is boxed up into a tamper-proof container akin to a credit-card holder before sending out to the lab. 'There's also the Tasso device. It looks like a Kinder Surprise egg – well, half of it – and you place it onto your upper arm. You push a red button that sends an array of tiny needles through your skin. It's virtually painless [see below]. The blood then flows into four pellets, which store the blood. You discard the egg and send the pellets off to the lab. It takes two to three minutes.'

Though WADA only formally accepted the test in 2023, the

Tasso kits were sent to athletes during Covid. The athlete would then have to show the sampling online while the doping control officer looked on.

'The Oslo lab are leaders in the field of dried blood spot testing, which is why in Denmark, WADA approved its use in our testing programmes in 2021. We do around two- to three-hundred collections each year, but that number is growing.' Of those, Mørkeberg says they've seen five or six adverse analytical findings from dried blood spot testing.

That nominal number, Mørkeberg says, is down to the nominal number of substances tested, the Danes predominantly focusing on steroids. That's why much of his early work's taken place in gyms. 'The rules in Denmark regarding steroid use are similar to narcotics in that it's not a crime to have it in your body but, if you're in possession, it's a criminal offence. If the samples come out positive in the gyms, you're excluded from that gym and all other gyms that we collaborate with for four years. The politicians want clean fitness centres for the youngsters to train in.'

Though its substance list is currently limited, the benefits over urine and venous blood collection are many. With each test taking ten minutes, you can test significantly more athletes than the other tests at major championships, like the Olympic Games. Sample volume's another win.

'For urine, you need around 90ml of urine to analyse, which isn't always possible, especially after a hot event or games,' says Mørkeberg. 'Athletes don't particularly love having a venous blood sample, especially if they're tested a lot. Some athletes are tested up to ten times a month for the ABP. Understandably, they're not overly happy that sporting success turns them into a pin cushion.'

Not only do you require far less blood, but the method of extraction is painless. 'We've run studies where we dried blood spot-tested around 110 elite athletes via both the finger and the upper arm, and they didn't feel a thing. They preferred it over conventional sample collections.'

Transportation and storage is another boon. 'It's much more stable at room temperature than urine or normal blood. Yes, you still want to get it to the lab within a week or two. They will then refrigerate it or freeze it down if they want to store it for a longer period.'

Sample collection and sending is cheaper than both urine and blood testing. Practicality is a huge benefit. As its analytical list grows, it begs the question: is this the anti-doping panacea? Not according to Professor Yannis Pitsiladis of the University of Hong Kong.

'WADA has directed a lot of their money to dried blood spot testing and said it's "game-changing",' says Pitsiladis. 'But it's only game-changing if you want to justify that you're testing more people than you were testing before.

'But if you're testing more people with a test that's worse than what you had before, what's the point? Most of the budget or a major part of the budget of every federation goes to pay for anti-doping that doesn't work. I mean, it's just so bad. That money could be used on grassroots to support the athletes when they retire, when they're ill . . . but it's used to do more and more weaker tests.' The Greek disruptor takes centre stage in chapter nine, detailing his genetic test that's tinged with vexation.

Mario Thevis is more pragmatic about the current limitations of dried blood spot testing. The German is professor of preventative doping research at the German Sport University Cologne. Like

Mørkeberg, he's a dried-blood-spot expert. He's recently received $150,000 from WADA for further work in this area.

'When it comes to dried blood spot testing, you're looking at maybe 100 microlitres [µl] compared to a venous blood sample where you take around 3ml, or a urine sample that's 90ml,' he says. 'As 1ml is equivalent to 1,000 microlitres, you don't have an enormous volume to work with. That means it's currently only suitable for a relatively small amount of substances.'

Thevis says it's currently best at detecting peptide hormones and protein-based drugs because these substances circulate in the blood. Though the Danes have focused on the gyms, he says it's not perfect for testosterone and steroid detection because their metabolites stick around longer in urine than blood. The reduced volume also closes the detection window. As micro-dosing EPO is often undetectable after half a day, that's clearly a major hurdle.

DBS is also limited with 'threshold drugs'. As we explained in chapter one, these are substances that are permitted up to a limit. 'It's public knowledge that dried blood spots can't be applied to substances that have a decision or reporting limit,' says Thevis. 'A simple example: if you have a cold, you have to be careful because it [cold drugs] could contain pseudoephedrine. Pseudoephedrine is prohibited if you exceed a certain concentration in a urine sample.'

More specifically, it's banned in-competition if urine concentration exceeds 150µg/mL. It's banned because it's chemically related to amphetamines, meaning at high or repeated doses it can improve endurance and power output while reducing perception of fatigue, all favourable for the high-performing athlete.

'The problem with dried blood spot testing in this case is that the concentration has, unlike urine, yet to be established. So, we won't test for it because if we do find something, we don't know whether we should call it a positive, an adverse finding or not. Unless the information is there, how does a urinary concentration correspond to a dried blood spot concentration?' It's the same for threshold drugs like salbutamol and formoterol.

Unlike Pitsiladis, Thevis is confident in the test and of its future. 'We're expanding our knowledge of this all the time. The thing is, there's such a broad spectrum of substances for athletes to abuse – and understandably such tight legal regulations – that it'll take time to refine and expand the dried blood spot testing.'

WADA is aiming for every accredited lab to be capable of dried blood spot analysis by the end of 2027, while Mørkeberg and USADA are undertaking a joint study into whether it could ultimately be comparable with venous supply, with an eye on replacing venous samples.

As for Thevis, 'I must go now,' he says. 'I've got a call imminently with the UK police force. We're undertaking forensic work with them . . .' The global battle to keep sport clean is never-ending.

Christiaan Bartlett says cost – efficiency – is a great driver of implementing any new test. At the one-day WADA Conference in London during October, 2025, Professor Olivier Rabin, senior director of science and medicine at WADA, announced that WADA had invested over $100 million. That's a healthy amount, but rapidly shrinks when set against the context of the 20-year-plus period Rabin was talking about. Balancing the books and investment into groundbreaking science is also a balancing act – at times, political – and one we delve into in chapter nine. But if you can create a test that's both statistically significant and fiscally prudent, there's a good chance WADA will listen.

★

Around 60 miles east of King's College London is the University of Kent in Canterbury, most famous for its cathedral and Geoffrey Chaucer's 14th-century book, *The Canterbury Tales*, which was widely banned due to its sexual innuendo and perceived criticism of the Church. Forwards to the 2020s and the university's become its own centre of censure, as the academic institution has become an anti-doping research hotspot. Professor Lex Mauger took top billing in chapter one for his research into tramadol, but he's not the only anti-doping epoch maker.

For nearly a decade, James Hopker, the university's professor of sport science, has worked with a number of anti-doping organisations in keeping sport clean. His interest stemmed from his research into how athletes respond to exercise and training.

'We really wanted to pin down why some people respond better to certain training prescriptions than others,' Hopker explains. Why do some react better to short high-intensity sessions than others, for example, or why some athletes will recover faster than their contemporaries between sessions?

'From there, it wasn't a million miles to then identifying the "normal" performance evolution of an athlete compared to the "abnormal". That's when we started to head down the anti-doping route whereby we used performance as a tool to identify athletes who might be committing doping offences.'

After receiving funding from the Partnership for Clean Competition – an American organisation separate from WADA that funds anti-doping research and projects – Hopker started performance modelling. By charting an athlete's results over time you can identify if it's biologically plausible without doping.

'We're interested in how one athlete performs over their career in relation to other athletes who are age-matched, and how quickly someone's performance changes in relation to other athletes.

'We started by analysing the performances of athletes who were sanctioned against athletes who hadn't been sanctioned. We did this with weight-lifting and track sprinting before moving on to pool-based swimming. We've also looked at track cycling. Performance modelling works best in controlled environments and for individual sports. Team sports and road running have far more confounding factors, so there's much more variability in performance. It makes this type of modelling trickier.'

Hopker says his performance modelling can identify anti-doping violations in 'simple' sports like weight-lifting as good as, if not better than, the athlete biological passport. 'It's interesting that something as crude as performance outperforms the physiological gold standard.' But unlike the passport, you can't sanction an athlete from the modelling tool, though it does explain performance jumps that might normally be regarded as 'having a good day'.

Hopker's performance modelling tools have been used by the ITA (International Testing Agency) for the past two Olympic cycles, primarily for pool-based swimming and weight-lifting. 'They use it to assist risk-assessing athletes within their registered testing pools. They also use it to target athletes for out-of-competition testing.

'This targeting is also used in real time. At the last Olympics [Paris 2024] and the recent World Aquatic Championships [Singapore 2025], the system was used as follows. An anti-doping officer sits beside the pool. Once the respective race finishes, the results are fed through our performance-modelling system and to the ITA. If the performance of the swimmer looks an outlier compared to their career trajectory, this is flagged up to the officer, who will then take the swimmer to doping control. This is all rather rapid with the revised risk score for that individual updated within 30 seconds.'

Hopker says that data is king, with the modelling software proving statistically significant when an athlete has racked up at least a handful of competition results. 'If someone appears from nowhere and delivers a world-class performance, the model won't pick that up. But after five sets of results it can begin working on its predictive calculations.'

Despite its controlled-setting raison d'être, Hopker says they are spreading their net to other disciplines where the environment might be variable but you can still collect standardised data.

'We've just started working with the UCI to recruit WorldTour road-cycling teams, so that we can analyse riders' power data.' Power meters are a popular training tool used by nearly every professional cyclist because they measure the force generated by a rider independent of terrain, weather, tactics or emotion, making them particularly powerful for data analysis. 'Only yesterday I was chatting about this to Jeroen Swart, one of the guys at UAE Team Emirates [Tadej Pogačar's team]. I mention it because one of Swart's students is working on a new method of eye-tracking technology to detect doping. It's similar to a lie detector. It'll be worth sounding him out.' Good idea . . .

'A lie detector test, I'm a proponent of that, frankly. I wouldn't challenge a lie detector test, with good equipment, properly administered.' The words of Lance Armstrong's lawyer, Tim Herman, back in 2012 when interviewed on BBC Radio 5 Live. Herman, defending the Texan, added that he'd be keen for the 26 witnesses who testified against the then seven-time Tour de France winner to take lie detector tests, too. As it transpired, three months later, Oprah Winfrey dispensed with the need for a peloton's worth of polygraph examination as Armstrong confessed his nefarious actions, which would lead to the erasing of that septet of Tour titles from the history books.

A spokesman for WADA says polygraph tests have been used but they rarely carry much weight and have even been found to be inadmissible on occasion.

'Our position is typically to argue that they carry no more weight than mere party assertion. Also, there have been occasions where polygraphs have been successfully cheated, as was the case with Marion Jones. So WADA does not use them proactively and would argue against their relevance when they are used against it.'

That's definitive. But agreeing to their use at least holds weight with an athlete's supporters. During the investigation into Alberto Contador's clenbuterol case in 2010 (more on this in chapter eight), the Spaniard voluntarily underwent a test, which he passed, to support his claim of 'no intent to dope'. The Court of Arbitration for Sport (CAS) acknowledged the existence of the test, allowed it to be submitted as part of the defence narrative but didn't treat it as scientific evidence. Contador ended up with a two-year ban and being stripped of his Giro d'Italia and Tour de France titles.

In 2001, the Singapore Football Association introduced random polygraph spot-testing as a deterrent tool against match-fixing and corruption. The Singapore FA's approach received support from Asia's FIFA vice-president Prince Ali Bin Al-Hussein of Jordan, who described polygraph testing as one method that appeared to be effective and suggested it could become more widely adopted over time.

In September of the same year, Bulgarian club Lokomotiv Plovdiv required players and coaching staff to undergo polygraph tests following allegations of match fixing. This move was strongly criticised by Wil van Megen, a lawyer for global footballing union FIFPRO, who highlighted that many scientists question the accuracy of lie-detector tests and remain unconvinced that they 'reliably distinguish between truth and deception'.

At the heart of the debate lies the fundamental unreliability of polygraph testing. Lie detectors are prone to error, which significantly undermines their credibility as tools for detecting deception. A purported accuracy rate of 95 per cent still implies a 5 per cent false-positive rate, meaning that one in 20 individuals could be wrongly implicated.

But what about the optical version? It certainly piqued Swart's interest. 'Jeroen was keen for someone to study this area,' says researcher Belinda Adigun. 'My background is in the pharmaceutical industry, a manufacturing site for ethical drugs, but a couple years back, I thought it'd be nice to undertake a doctorate. I then came across Jeroen. It's ironic. On one hand I make drugs; on the other I'm looking to find them.'

Similar to the ABP, the idea behind ocular deception testing is an indirect one in that your guilty eye movements would expose that you'd taken an illegal performance enhancer. 'You wouldn't use it as incriminating evidence but as aggravating evidence,' says Adigun. 'So, if you already have a case against an athlete that they're taking substances, then this would add to the prosecution.'

Similar to the dried blood spot test and performance modelling, its potential appeal lies in its economics and simplicity.

'You use a computer with an eye-tracking device attached to the base of the screen. It tracks the movement of your eyes while you're busy reading and answering questions. It takes about 20 minutes to calibrate after you're told to answer truthfully and falsefully.

'The technology is based around the fact that lying creates a measure of cognitive load, so you actually have to think about being deceptive; it requires greater brain power than telling the truth. This is reflected and picked up by your eyes. Factors like how fast your eyes respond, pupil diameter . . . there are various parameters that are analysed to determine whether you're lying or not.'

Adigun and Swart devised a study to investigate whether ocular motion testing would catch athletes concealing their PED abuse. Twenty subjects were randomly split into a control or doping group and provided with a 12-week cycle training programme. Subjects in the doping group received placebo capsules under the guise of a performance-enhancing substance for the duration of the training programme.

'We didn't tell them what the substance was; we just let them believe that it is an existing drug on the market and that it hadn't been added to the list of prohibited substances but is showing promise to be used as a performance-enhancing drug.

'So, we kind of led them down the road without delivering specific information. And then we simply popped some glucose into a capsule and gave them that instead. It created the psychological anticipation of taking a performance-enhancing drug.

'The subjects then undertook oculomotor deception testing at certain intervals to see if we could pick up on it. We could.' Adigun says for some right at the beginning, even before they'd taken their first placebo. 'We're still processing the data but the results are strong.'

Adigun says it would certainly reduce costings as a front-line filtering tool of who to target, but recognises there are hurdles to overcome, the first being recruiting professionals for further research.

'It's proving difficult,' she says. 'The amateur study took two years for human ethics approval. To recruit professional sports people you need the approval of their respective sporting federation and then the individual. And the team . . . Consent from event organisers and the local anti-doping organisation. Many stakeholders.'

Adigun knows these are early days, with a number of questions that need answering from that first study. One is the longevity of guilt and how that manifests itself in the brain. 'We did include this in that original study, but it needs more work. We tested them straight after the intervention and then seven weeks later to see if they'd forgotten about it. Of course, this wouldn't be a direct correlation with an athlete who knows they've doped, potentially for years, but there was an impact. Presently, it's not as effective if the athlete's not currently on a PED, possibly because, technically speaking, they're not lying about presently using it.'

Adigun's sporting research is built off credibility elsewhere. In the United States, police use ocular motion testing, specifically the Horizontal Gaze Nystagmus (HGN) test, as a standard part of their sobriety tests. It's also used in Canada, Australia and New Zealand, to name but a few. 'Certainly in my country of South Africa, they use it as pre-employment screening,' she says.

Back at the WADA-accredited lab at King's College London, Bartlett's rounding off our tour by returning to the liquid chromatography machine. 'At the moment, one of the most commonly found substances with this machine is ostarine. It's proving "popular".'

All around the world. According to the Anti-Doping Database, there have been 164 sanctions for ostarine since 2016. That includes the relatively fallow Covid years of 2020 and 2021 when testing dropped significantly.

Ostarine is a SARM (Selective Androgen Receptor Modulator, which we talk about in chapter one) that promotes muscle protein synthesis and preserves lean mass without the water retention associated with anabolic steroids, making it an attractive PED for weight-category sports.

A number of high-profile athletes have tested positive for ostarine, including boxer Ryan Garcia. In 2024, the American beat Devin Haney in a super-lightweight contest, albeit was ineligible to win the world title due to weighing 3.2lbs over the championship limit; instead, he forfeited up to $600,000 of his purse to Haney.

Soon after, the Voluntary Anti-Doping Association notified all parties that Garcia's A and B samples showed traces of the performance-enhancing drug. Garcia took to social media and denied having knowingly taken ostarine, citing his willingness to take the drug test. His team pointed to contaminated supplements. The bout was changed to a 'no contest', Garcia was suspended for a year and was fined $1.1 million after accepting the plea deal over taking it to trial.

Again highlighting the labyrinth that is anti-doping and doping in sport, prior to the 2024 Olympics, the French fencer Ysaora Thibus was temporarily suspended after testing positive for ostarine. She was cleared to fence in Paris after proving the result was down to having sex with her partner, fellow fencer Race Imboden. 'He took a product that contained ostarine and infected Ysaora. The transmission that caused the infection occurred through bodily fluids,' her lawyer Joëlle Monlouis said at the time.

What emerges from King's College London is the eternal equation of dopers adapt equals scientists respond. Then rerun the fun. The gap narrows, widens, then narrows again. Some of these developments are cutting-edge and based on hundreds of peer reviews. Others feel more rudimentary and in their infancy. Will they become an anti-doping tool or consigned to the literature?

Experts like Bartlett have devoted their professional careers to chasing certainty. By looking for patterns rather than proof, likelihood rather than confession. The battle is unglamorous, imperfect and never-ending. Oh, so never-ending. But inside these labs, amid the fingerprints of chemistry and data, sport's credibility is still being quietly defended.

HOW ATHLETES EXPLOIT THE MARGINS BETWEEN RULES AND REALITY

Go to YouTube, type in 'Max Hauke' and you'll face one of the saddest images in sport. There, the lean and fresh-faced cross-country skier looks through the camera as Austrian police raid the apartment block where he based himself for the 2019 Nordic World Ski Championships in Seefeld.

Hauke's right hand nervously rubs his left calf muscle, while his left arm nestles on a yellow sofa cushion. Out of his inner elbow and an oversized plaster flows a tube containing his blood. In 2014, Hauke had competed for Austria at the Winter Olympics. Now, in 2019, he'd been caught in the middle of a blood transfusion. Hauke understandably confessed his guilt, was handed a four-year ban, a suspended prison sentence, retired from the sport and would later admit he felt an unburdening of guilt. His quiet distress is arguably the abiding image of Operation Aderlass.

Hauke's case serves as an exemplar of the anti-doping

authorities and police intelligence co-operating for the common good. Which might serve as an odd opener for a chapter where we'll look at the many ways that athletes and their support teams look to sidestep the testers. But Hauke proved an outlier in that by admitting his guilt – how could he not? – he then divulged to the relevant authorities the methods that he and his fellow Aderlass disciples employed to beat the system. (Until that cool February in 2019, of course.)

'Max spoke at a USADA conference, where he explained some of the techniques to avoid being caught,' says Raphael Faiss, Research Manager at the Centre of Research and Expertise in Anti-Doping Sciences (REDs) at the University of Lausanne. 'One of the key methods involved playing about with the whereabouts system. He'd live on a high floor of an apartment block because when a doping officer would come and ring his bell, he'd have more time to drink salt water. That impacts your plasma volume, diluting the concentration of whatever PED he'd taken. He'd also say he'd been exercising hard so the doping control officer would have to wait two hours for his levels to settle [although as of April 2026, doping control officers will only have to wait 60 minutes to collect ABP samples, as per a change in WADA regulations]. Simple strategies but effective.'

We lightly touch on the whereabouts programme in chapter three and how it's hosted alongside an athlete's ABP in the ADAMS management system. Here's a deeper dive to uncover the whereabouts system's flaws. To the Machiavellian types it's open to abuse.

How does it work? Athletes in a registered testing pool must submit quarterly schedules where they provide a daily 60-minute time slot (between 6am and 11pm) of where they will be. They can update locations if their plans change via the app right up to the last minute. But if the athlete isn't where their whereabouts said they would be, that counts as a missed test. Three missed tests in 12 months equates to an anti-doping violation.

'It's also of note that an athlete may decide to indicate his or her 60-minute time slot at 5am. In some sports, training starts very early so these athletes can have this flexibility,' adds a WADA spokesman. 'And it must be stressed that an anti-doping organisation [ADO] can plan a test at any time. However, if the ADO goes to the athlete's home, for example, outside of the designated 60-minute time slot and the athlete is not there, unless there is evidence that the whereabouts filings are wrong, there will not be any consequences.'

Jonathan Taylor is head of the sports law group Bird & Bird in London and is one of anti-doping's most experienced lawyers. Taylor was involved in drafting the whereabouts system that was formally adopted by WADA in 2004.

'Various organisations were undertaking out-of-competition testing but there was a real issue that we needed athletes to be available. And we couldn't put a tracker on them!' he says from his plush office in London's legal quarter. So, WADA created the whereabouts system and, after a little refinement, it was accepted.

'I remember this guy, Rune Andersen, who was director of standards and harmonisation, who informed people from the US about the new system. USADA said we'll call the athlete an hour or so before we head over to take the test. We didn't want that as that gave cheating athletes time to mask their drugs.'

As has happened numerous times over the years, WADA suffered a backlash, with many sports protesting it didn't sit fairly with an athlete's human rights.

'I remember a football players' union saying, this is ridiculous. It's such an invasion of privacy to force us to tell you where we're going to be. I said, well, is it more of an invasion of privacy than following you into the toilet and watching you urinate into a cup? No, it's not. But we have to do that because if we don't, you could beat the test and the doping rules wouldn't work. If you only test in competition, the doping rules don't work either. So, we have to have the whereabouts system. They'd argue it's restrictive. And I'd say yeah, it wouldn't be a very good rule if it wasn't.'

Taylor maintains it is proportionate and, as time rolled by, says athletes became more accepting of it. 'The system should be a deterrent but it's really there so that the clean athlete can say, look, you can believe my results. I remember [Roger] Federer saying it is limiting but he wants a clean sport and he wants people to believe. Of course, the system isn't infallible, but if you are cheating the system, you will be looking over your shoulder.'

The whereabouts might have proved controversial but it has played a pivotal role in numerous doping cases, including in 2021 when the combined efforts of a number of authorities ultimately ensnared 100m Nigerian sprinter Blessing Okagbare with a growth-hormone package at her home. The whereabouts system informed the anti-doping authorities where Okagbare would be, leading to the targeted testing that caught her red-handed. Okagbare received a ten-year ban for a litany of offences.

If you miss three whereabouts tests in 12 months – reduced from 18 months in 2009 – under WADA rules you receive a two-year ban, reduced to one year if the athlete can show 'no significant fault or negligence'.

This can vary, though, by sport or case. Former UFC champion Conor McGregor was suspended for 18 months under the UFC's own anti-doping policy after missing three scheduled sample collections in 2024, while Brazilian cyclist Vinícius Costa was banned for 20 months at the end of 2025 for a similar infringement.

Whatever the sentence, it's three strikes and you're out. Mixing the metaphor, it's black and white. But there are grey areas. 'A simple way to avoid testing positive is simply not to answer the door when the doping control officer comes knocking,' says David Howman, chair of the Athletics Integrity Unit. 'Simply take the hit of a missed test. You're allowed two missed tests in a year. Do that when you're doped up and just ensure you're very careful for the remainder of the year. That tactic is being used a lot.'

Ironman athlete Joe Skipper is an experienced professional triathlete with multiple Ironman titles to his name. In 2023 he told *Triathlete* magazine that the paucity of testing in his sport means doping athletes could take a missed hit pretty much with impunity. The Brit revealed to journalist Shane Stokes that he was tested once in 2013, three times in 2015, five times in 2016 and three the following year. The high point was 2018 at ten tests. From there the numbers drop: four in 2019, just two in 2020 and 2021 (during the Covid pandemic, which limited resources and access to athletes) and six in 2022. To put it in performance context, Skipper has been ranked in the top 30 for the PTO (Professional Triathlon Organisation) world rankings since 2017 and in the top ten between 2020 and 2022.

'If we look back at 2020, I got tested on 2nd February and 7th March,' Skipper explained. 'I could have missed those tests [without sanction] as my next test wasn't until 2nd March, 2021. I was tested nine days later [on 11th March] and could have missed that one [and still only been on two missed tests because 12 months had passed since the theoretical 2020 missed tests].' Once the counter resets, and with limited testing in some sports, you can see why, as Howman said, some athletes are rolling the doping dice feeling the odds of success are on their side.

There are further flaws in the whereabouts system. The 2015 Cycling Independent Reform Commission (CIRC) report was a major investigation into doping, governance and anti-doping practices in professional road cycling. It was commissioned in the aftermath of high-profile cases like that of Lance Armstrong.

Within the 227-page report, the commission, similar to Matt Rendell's revelation in chapter three, tells of interviewing 'former riders getting up in the middle of the night and riding on a fixed bicycle in their room in order to get the blood circulating' to thin out their highly viscous blood after taking EPO (erythropoietin). Throw in further thickening from race dehydration and the riders had very real concerns that the low resting heart rate at night could lead to clotting, stroke or heart failure. Riders could not sleep easy.

The report also identified a nocturnal weakness in the whereabouts system in that you can be tested in any 60-minute slot between 6am and 11pm, but as a blanket rule, the doping officers won't come knocking at 5:59am or 11:01pm.

'The no-testing window from 11pm to 6am helps riders who micro-dose to avoid being caught. The CIRC is conscious of the principle of proportionality but the absence of night-time testing is a weakness in the current system and needs to be addressed.'

The CIRC report continued, 'The Commission was told of a team below the UCI WorldTour [see chapter three for more on lower-tier ambiguities] involved in doping. It was claimed that the manager and sports director brought a nutritionist into the team who advised a selected group of riders within the team on a doping programme. The instructions were to administer 1,000ml of EPO Zeta every second day after 11pm at night, and alternate in the winter with HGH [human growth hormone] and Lutrelef, a hormone. Their haematocrit levels were to be tested every third day, and amounts of EPO Zeta reduced to 500ml as the season approached. The nutritionist owned a gym, through which substances were procured from Eastern Europe. Other riders were said to have procured substances via a hospital and a pharmacy more locally. It was further explained that the team manager was also a senior person in a prominent anti-doping movement, and had later on introduced strong anti-doping clauses in the team contracts, including the imposition of significant fines for anyone caught doping.'

This was over a decade ago but, broadly, overnight testing remains off-limits. 'But athletes can be tested during that time if WADA has "serious and specific suspicion that the athlete may be engaged in doping",' a WADA spokesman told us.

This overnight freedom strikes at the heart of the whereabouts system. Though Taylor asserted that clearly it must infringe an athlete's life, it must also balance athlete welfare. It's a fine line between credibility and autocracy. Still, at the time, four-time Tour de France winner Chris Froome Tweeted, 'I for one welcome 24-hour testing. It may be an inconvenience but if it can help clean up the sport that I love, let's do it.'

Froome's comments came nine months before his wife, Michelle, gave birth to their first child. He may have felt differ-ently embarking on a six-hour training ride after repeated nights of broken sleep. It may sound trivial but awakening a family at 3am is deemed against normal standards of human decency. But not everywhere.

'In some countries, like Switzerland, you are now authorised to test the athletes 24 hours a day,' says Faiss. 'This makes a big change because the time window where the athletes would drink a lot to pee a lot to dispel the substances has been shortened a lot.'

For the discerning doper, it's all about shrinking that window of detection. Which is where diuretics come in. Those of you for whom alcohol and caffeine are (un)happy bedfellows are well aware of fluids with diuretic properties; in other words, they're fluids that increase the rate of urine flow (and sodium excretion) to dispense excess fluids from tissues. It's why beer breath is far from first-date friendly.

That's diuretics in a social context. In a clinical setting, diuretics are used for the treatment of various diseases and syndromes, including hypertension, heart failure, liver cirrhosis, renal failure, kidney and lung diseases, as well as a more general reduction of the adverse effects of salts and/or water retention.

As we've seen, professional sport keeps one eye on the money and the other on the medical, in search of (illegal) sporting application. And they found it with diuretics and that ability to crank up urine volume, more rapidly flushing out the trail of prohibited substance with what's called 'forced diuresis'. By removing water from the body, they're also a gift for athletes looking to shed weight rapidly, as you would for weight-category sports like boxing.

For both reasons, they've been banned in and out of competition since ahead of the 1988 Seoul Olympics, but that hasn't prevented their prevalence. In the latest (2024) WADA Anti-Doping Testing Figures Report, around 17% of adverse analytical findings (AAF) reported on ADAMS were diuretics or other masking agents, second only behind anabolic agents (37%) and ahead of stimulants (16%).

Within the S5 category (diuretics and other masking agents), furosemide racks up the most occurrences at 134. That's around 25% of AAFs followed by dorzolamide (20%) and hydrochlorothiazide (14%).

Furosemide, marketed as Lasix, is a loop diuretic used medically to treat fluid retention and heart failure, and its popularity is nothing new. According to the Anti-Doping Database, furosemide is the most sanctioned masking agent in sport, with up to 515 confirmed doping cases up to 2023. Thirty per cent of cases emanated from three countries – Russia, India and Kazakhstan – with weight-sensitive sports dominating usage. Wrestling, bodybuilding, boxing, track-and-field and powerlifting accounted for more than half the furosemide violations.

The Honest Sport Substack, run by investigative journalist Edmund Willison, reported in July, 2025, that there was a 'significant body of evidence that' drugs like furosemide and hydrochlorothiazide were being abused in professional swimming, like they had been in weight-focused sports such as gymnastics and boxing.

'This is unfortunately the most common use of diuretics; gymnasts trying to lose weight through water elimination, primarily in the thighs and buttocks,' the International Gymnastics Federation had warned previously.

These diuretics, known as 'water pills', were at the centre of further controversy in the pool. At the 2012 London Olympics, Enhanced Games' competitor James Magnussen's 4x100m medley relay mate Brenton Rickard tested positive for furosemide, followed a year later by another of Magnussen's countrymates, Kylie Palmer.

And in 2011, the 50m freestyle world record holder César Cielo, who was trained by Magnussen's coach Brett Hawke (now also part of the Enhanced Games set-up; see chapter 12 for more) prior to 2008, along with three of his Brazilian teammates, tested positive for furosemide at the same event.

American swimming endured similar diuretic issues with hydrochlorothiazide. But in every case, all of the swimmers were cleared of any intent to cheat with defences ranging from contaminated supplements to mistakenly confusing a relative's medication for laxatives, as was the case for American Emily Brunemann.

Manchester United's goalkeeper André Onana wasn't so fortunate. In February, 2021, the Cameroonian was banned for 12 months after a blood test showed up traces of furosemide. Onana protested his innocence, attributing the presence of furosemide to mistaking his wife's pregnancy medication for something else. The Court of Arbitration for Sport cut his ban to nine months.

Reducing chances of detection isn't solely down to diuretics. The doping athlete's drug and administration of choice matters, too. Here, the chemist's creativity goes a long way. Dr Grigory Rodchenkov is the former head of Russia's anti-doping laboratory who turned whistleblower. During Dr Rodchenkov's testimony to USADA, the Russian described how his 'steroid cocktail', called the 'Duchess', helped athletes beat the system. He explained that by mixing together steroids and alcohol you could accelerate absorption into the bloodstream and then muscle while reducing the window of detection.

'It was right round the time [Evgeny] Blokhin [FSB agent] entered our lives that I discovered the cocktail,' Rodchenkov wrote in *The Rodchenkov Affair: How I Brought Down Russia's Secret Doping Empire*. 'Steroid detection had become so sophisticated that we had to wean athletes off pills and injections, and we realised that if you consumed steroids dissolved in alcohol by swirling the mixture around in your mouth, the most risky – or detectable – long-term metabolites would not emerge. I'd remembered one important detail from the BALCO scandal: they never used pills. Buccal absorption – letting pills dissolve in your mouth – or transdermal lotion were the only low-risk and, hopefully, efficient way to administer steroids.

'I dreamed up the cocktail in my mind, a combination of methenolone, trenbolone and oxandrolone, dissolved in Chiva Regal whisky, and then mixed it up in my kitchen. Some athletes found the whisky too bitter, so my assistants, who learned how to prepare the cocktail, created a new version of the cocktail using vermouth. Irina Rodionova, a medical doctor, christened the cocktail the "Duchess" after her favourite yellow, pear-flavoured lemonade that we drank from heavy glass bottles as children in the 1960s.'

According to Rodchenkov, 36 Russian athletes were fuelled on the Duchess in the build-up to the 2014 Winter Olympics in Sochi.

Understandably, WADA and national anti-doping authorities aren't too keen on revealing the wash-out periods of powerful performance enhancers. But we do learn via their drugs and TUE forms that glucocorticoids – a potent anti-inflammatory that's legal out of competition – has a wash-out period of three days if taken orally, though this rises to ten days if using triamcinolone. Intramuscular injection of triamcinolone stays in the system for 60 days.

★

'Hauke told us that he was using blood transfusions and growth hormone rather than EPO because Dr Schmidt told him he'd be caught if he took EPO,' says Raphael Faiss, albeit he does stress that this was before the endocrine module of the athlete biological passport was added in 2023. 'Still, exogenous growth hormone is very hard to detect. You only need small doses to deliver a significant effect and it doesn't remain in your body very long. There's also evidence that athletes are returning to first-generation EPO products.'

Why they are resorting to old-school EPO is again down to how long it remains 'hot' in the body, leaving the athlete more vulnerable to being caught. 'EPO injections helped those with low levels create more red blood cells. With the original EPO, a patient would inject one to three times each week,' says Faiss. (Incredibly, in 'healthy humans' every second that passes your body produces around two to three million new red blood cells, driven by EPO. Each red blood cells lives for around 100 days, so each day the majority of people are creating 1% of their total – roughly 200-billion red blood cells daily. Those with kidney disease don't generate this amount. Hence, the creation of EPO to stimulate more red blood cells.) 'Over the years, new EPO products were designed that were longer-lasting so required fewer injections, maybe once every two to four weeks,' adds Faiss. That was great for the patient but not so much for the doping athlete due to the guilty evidence's longer half-life.

Recent cases of athletes testing positive for old-school EPO include that of Kenyan middle- and long-distance runner Esther Gitahi, who returned an adverse analytical finding that detected EPO in her urine after an April, 2024, 5km race in Boston, USA.

Gitahi wrote to the Athletics Integrity Unit explaining she'd been prescribed alfa epoetin injections to treat a condition called thalassemia, an inherited blood disorder. She argued that she sought a retroactive TUE but expert witnesses said she made up the condition of which her blood values showed no signs. Gitahi was banned for four years.

How athletes take EPO can influence detection time, too. 'Athletes take the same substances but in different forms,' the head of science and medical at the International Testing Agency, Neil Robinson, explains in the video 'Keeping the Light On' that's hosted on the ITA's website. 'When I began my doctorate, athletes were taking EPO subcutaneously. It's the best and cheapest way to make sure it works. But it's detectable. So, dopers went from subcutaneous to intravenous. It's less effective, offering fewer benefits but also less detectable.'

Blood doping seems medieval compared to EPO but, says Faiss, there's a good reason it's still used. 'Taking your blood out, putting it in the fridge and reinfusing it, compared to the quantity that you have in your own body, that's not a huge amount, so that's a challenge. Historically, we'd look for plasticisers, which are small plastic particles from the pouch that were detectable in the blood. But then athletes started using pouches that didn't release any plastic particles.'

Blood doping can be carried out in two ways. One is the method mentioned by Faiss, so the athlete's own blood is removed, stored in cool or frozen conditions, then later reinfused once the body has naturally replaced the lost red blood cells. This process, called an autologous blood transfusion, increases overall red blood cell levels and is hard to detect because it's the athlete's own blood. Hauke estimated that his autologous blood regime resulted in a 30-second improvement in a 30-minute cross-country skiing race.

Then there's homologous blood transfusion, where an athlete tops up their own blood with that from another person. This choice over autologous is due to avoiding a performance dip that comes from withdrawing your own blood; in fact, the athlete should see an immediate improvement. American cyclist Tyler Hamilton was stripped of his 2004 Olympic time-trial gold medal after failing a test for homologous blood transfusion at the 2004 Vuelta a España. The testing tool used by USADA 'detected the presence of mixed blood'.

Neither method is without risk, of course. Blood doping increases blood viscosity, making it thicker and harder to circulate through the vessels. This can lead to elevated blood pressure and, in severe cases, blood clots, heart attacks or strokes. Using another person's blood also carries additional dangers, including the risk of infections, viral transmission and allergic reactions.

Thousands of athletes and their support staff have barely paid lip service to those warnings. Operation Aderlass discovered that Dr Schmidt's athletes passed over 1,000 tests without ever being caught blood doping, while the same investigation revealed many Aderlass athletes would reinfuse blood just one hour before competition and then remove it straight after.

The vampiric lengths athletes and their support teams go to in search of peak performance is extraordinary. But do they actually need to cheat in the shadows when they know the answer is hiding in plain sight?

'There's no such thing as clean sport because you have TUEs, the therapeutic usage exemption certificates. You simply wander over to a doctor and say, "I've got these symptoms, I need this drug", and the doctor will write you a prescription there and then. Voilà – you're on a performance-enhancing drug. "Clean" sport doesn't exist. That's the reality. That's a fact.'

The words of Brett Hawke, who we'll hear more from in chapter 12 as the Australian is head swim coach at the Enhanced Games. The Australian's diatribe came off the back of me presenting the following hypothesis: if no world records are broken at the doping-friendly Enhanced Games, what does that say about 'clean' sport? And off Hawke flew.

If you find the idea of the Enhanced Games abhorrent, you can't deny Hawke has a point, as the TUE system is arguably the most controversial and most abused in anti-doping.

Like many simmering issues in the battle of anti-dopers vs the dopers, they came to a boiling point with the Russia state-sponsored doping scandal. In the case of TUEs, the subsequent hacking of WADA's database revealed a Pandora's box of secrets including the heavy use – and abuse – of the TUE system. I'll come back to that, but I'm ahead of myself. First, an explainer.

'A TUE is a medical exemption that allows an athlete to use a prohibited substance or prohibited method for a legitimate medical condition,' says David Healy, WADA's science and medicine manager. 'If they are then tested, they won't receive an adverse analytical finding and sanction.'

To see if you satisfy the conditions for a TUE, there's a 152-page guideline document to wade through. It's a cracking read . . . But at its core, the athlete has to tick off four main pillars: the athlete would endure significant health problems if the prohibited substance or method were withheld; no permitted and non-prohibited alternative treatment that would be effective; the medical need is not a consequence of prior use of a prohibited substance or method without a TUE; and no performance improvement beyond what is needed to restore normal health.

'The last one is particularly important as the system is about performance-enabling, not performance-enhancing,' says Healy. 'It returns you to the level you'd be at if you didn't have that medical condition. A good example is if you're diabetic. Though insulin is on the Prohibited List, clearly it's a life-saving drug, so that athlete would obviously be granted a TUE.'

(As an aside, Morten Horstrup of the University of Copenhagen, who popped up in chapter one and reappears in chapter 10, told me that they're seeing a disturbing rise in non-TUE insulin cases in female athletes. Why women specifically is that they enjoy the anabolic effects similar to steroids without suffering male side effects like hair growth. 'It's disturbing because while I'm not saying the risks aren't high with steroids, insulin can be fatal with just one dose.')

Healy delivers another stark and rather eye-watering example to hammer home the idea that TUEs legally level the performance playing field. 'Say an athlete has been in an accident and they've had to have an orchiectomy to remove both testicles. From then on they'll have to undergo testosterone therapy.

'It's rare we'd give a TUE for exogenous testosterone but we would in the case of organic hypogonadism. We'd then ask the national anti-doping organisation to monitor the athlete's testosterone levels. Again, it's all about bringing the athlete up to the physiological level seen before the incident or illness.'

The process of securing a TUE firstly requires sign-off from a medical professional, be it a doctor or specialist physician. You then contact anti-doping. If you're competing at national level, this might be your national anti-doping organisation; if you're an international, you go through the sport's international governing body. They'll guide you to the TUE application, which the athlete and the doctor then both sign. If the anti-doping organisation or international federation feel the TUE form is robust enough, they then send it to an independent panel made up of three physicians to evaluate the application.

'We recommend to the anti-doping organisations that they are sports physicians and, ideally, one will have an expertise in that particular area. So, if you're applying for a "prohibited drug" to treat a lung condition, we'd suggest a pulmonologist. It's also beneficial if one of the physicians has a sound knowledge of that sport because the context of a drug and sport can be nuanced, especially when assessing the performance-enhancing element of the substance.'

If the committee sanction the TUE, the athlete's free to compete, though WADA 'reserves the right to review and overturn any TUEC [therapeutic usage exemption committee] decision'. Athletes can also apply for a retroactive TUE – i.e. after the event – but that could lead to a sanction if not granted and PED traces show up in their system.

On the face of it, it's a relatively compassionate system that keeps the athlete's dreams of success alive despite outstanding health issues. But this is professional sport where compassion is snuffed out by the dual forces of competition and commercialism.

That Fancy Bears hacking episode revealed that many high-profile athletes had sought a TUE in the name of enabling performance. They included tennis legend Rafael Nadal, swimming great László Cseh and golfer Justin Rose. There was no suggestion that either athlete had done anything wrong.

But a subset courted controversy, of which Sir Bradley

Wiggins' case proved the most debated as it shone a light on the gap between what was legal and what many felt was unethical in elite sport. The British rider received multiple TUEs for triamcinolone, a powerful corticosteroid that was administered by injection shortly before major races, including the 2011 and 2012 Tour de France – the latter of which he won – and the 2013 Giro d'Italia. The drug was justified medically for severe allergies and asthma, and the TUEs were properly approved under the rules in force at the time. No anti-doping violation was ever proven.

The controversy centred on timing and effect. Triamcinolone can reduce inflammation, accelerate recovery and cause rapid weight loss – advantages that are particularly valuable in endurance cycling. Critics argued that its use immediately before grand tours blurred the line between treatment and performance enhancement, especially given cycling's history of doping.

The case was compounded by Team Sky's 'no needles' policy, which appeared inconsistent with injected corticosteroids, and by missing medical records. A UK parliamentary inquiry later concluded there was no proof of rule-breaking but suggested the drug was likely used to enhance performance rather than treat illness. The Wiggins case ultimately led to stricter rules on corticosteroid use.

It didn't help Wiggins' cause that the CIRC report quoted one rider whose opinion was that 90 per cent of TUEs were for performance-enhancing purposes, while a doctor commented that it was 'impossible to lose the weight that some riders achieve without assistance and that the TUE is taken advantage of to enable this practice'. By way of an example, the doctor explained that losing 4kg in four weeks for an already svelte cyclist would result in a 7% increase in power-to-weight ratio, a potential game-changer, especially in the mountains.

Healy says that corticosteroids remain one of the most commonly applied-for TUEs. 'That's not surprising as it's used to treat musculoskeletal injuries,' he says. This marries with research undertaken by a team including Healy that showed the most frequently observed substances under the TUE umbrella were glucocorticoids (0.5% in Rio, 2016 Olympic Games) and stimulants (0.39% in Tokyo, 2020 Olympic Games).[22]

'They're "popular" but the system evolves all of the time. There used to be an abbreviated TUE, an ATUE, that was specifically for beta-2 agonists, like inhalers, because we would see so many of them. But we see less of them now because we changed the threshold rules.'

Healy also says the number of TUE applications for ADHD drugs like methylphenidate is on the rise. These fit within the 'stimulants' category. He suggests that's down to greater awareness of the condition. That wasn't internationally recognised sports law expert Richard McLaren's view in the McLaren Report, commenting that 'there may be abuse there'.

While methylphenidate helps improve brain function in the ADHD population, it could also supercharge an athlete's performance by masking the fatigue endured during intense exercise. A 2022 review of ADHD medications and exercise found a significant boost in athletic prowess in six of the nine studies.[23]

If an athlete is seeking a TUE for ADHD, it'd be granted for up to four years at a time. 'How long exemptions are for depends on

---

22   https://bjsm.bmj.com/content/58/17/966

23   https://pmc.ncbi.nlm.nih.gov/articles/PMC8755863/#:~:text=calculated%20using%20I2.-,
Results,medications%20(p%20%3C%200.05).

the condition, of course, but unless it's chronic, it's generally for the duration of the treatment,' says Healy. A female athlete on a course of drugs to combat infertility – which might contain the substance letrozole that's on the Prohibited List, as men could hijack it to suppress the feminising effects of anabolic steroid use – could receive a TUE for up to 12 months.

One of the longest TUEs concerns human growth hormone, which is granted for younger athletes. Take footballing superstar Lionel Messi. It's well-documented that the Argentinian was diagnosed with growth hormone deficiency as a child and prescribed the human growth hormone drug somatropin. It's entered the annals of footballing history that one of the provisos of the 13-year-old prodigy and his family moving to FC Barcelona was that the Catalan team would pay for his treatment. Clearly it paid off. If the pre-pubescent Messi was making a name for himself in 2026, he'd be granted a ten-year TUE.

The TUE system is another area where a loophole's lengthened into a noose around WADA's necks that's tightened by insufficient resources. Healy says they receive applications that require nearly 4,000 TUECs each year. 'Like a lot of areas of anti-doping, a national anti-doping organisation might not be the best funded, so trying to find three physicians every time to review TUE applications, it's not easy. You've got to manage the workload.'

That not only means each committee adjudicating on several TUEs at a sitting, but also being pragmatic about who they test. 'I've seen TUECs in some countries where they test 60- and 70-year-old bridge players,' says Healy. 'They're often seeking retroactive TUEs as they're often on blood-pressure medication that contains a prohibited substance.'

Scepticism surrounds the TUE set-up, but there is evidence that if athletes are abusing the system, they're in the minority. Healy and then WADA Medical Director Alan Vernec undertook a study in search of a link between an athlete receiving a TUE and winning an Olympic medal.[24] 'The data showed that the number of athletes competing with valid TUEs at the selected Games was less than 1 per cent,' Dr Vernec commented at the time. 'Furthermore, the analysis suggests that there is no meaningful association between competing with a TUE and the likelihood of winning a medal.'

Overall, the study found that 2,062 medals were awarded throughout the five studied Olympics, with only 21 of these medals being won by athletes with a TUE. The inference? The TUEs were mainly prescribed to legitimately 'unhealthy' athletes.

Geography is another potential fault-line in global anti-doping, shaping who gets tested, how often and how effectively. On paper, the rules set by WADA apply globally. In practice, terrain and politics intervene.

In vast or remote countries, athletes often train far from major cities. Endurance runners in Kenya are based in high-altitude regions such as Iten, where poor roads and limited infrastructure historically made no-notice testing difficult. Similar issues have arisen in parts of Ethiopia and Eritrea, where geography and politics complicate access.

'There are many barriers in parts of the world in terms of transporting samples to laboratories,' says David Howman. 'You need to sort it within a certain amount of time, especially blood. It's within around 24 hours. If not, samples can be invalid. It's why we [AIU] helped to set up a blood-testing lab in Kenya.'

Political barriers matter, too, with conflict zones or sanctioned

---

24 https://bjsm.bmj.com/content/54/15/920

labs making routine out-of-competition testing unrealistic, even if athletes continue to compete internationally.

And then there's the great unknown: gene doping. This was the subject of media attention many years ago, off the back of the completion of the Human Genome Project in 2003, the year WADA banned gene doping.

The misuse of gene therapy techniques to enhance athletic performance rather than treat disease became a hot topic. Instead of taking a drug, an athlete would alter how their body produces certain proteins. For instance, increasing erythropoietin (EPO) to boost oxygen delivery, IGF-1 to stimulate muscle growth or supercharging genes linked to endurance and recovery. But to date, there are no proven cases of gene doping in sport, largely because the science is complex and risky.

'Despite great developments in gene therapy, there are still huge unknowns,' says Professor Yannis Pitsiladis. 'You'd need the appropriate people involved and the appropriate resources, meaning it'd have to be somewhat systematic – supported by governments, maybe – rather than someone doing it in their garden shed. But if you get it wrong, you could easily die.

'At the moment, I don't see it as a priority. Ask me in three years' time and that might change. It's something WADA need to keep an eye on. But no more than that.'

Gene therapy is at the cutting-edge of science. The Whizzinator is not. But on visiting London's WADA-accredited laboratory Christiaan Bartlett told me about the weird and wonderful methods athletes had looked to in order to game the system, including 'falsifying their urine'.

How they achieved this falsehood came down to a device called the Whizzinator. Its byline tells you all you need to know about how athletes might abuse it: 'The original synthetic urine simulation kit'. It features a lifelike prosthetic in five colours, an advanced heating element and a belt to hold synthetic or real urine. It's 'mainly used for personal needs or pranks', plus it gives you the tools 'you need to feel at ease when experimenting with an alternative lifestyle'.

American footballer Onterrio Smith suffered the ignominy of being the most famous Whizzinator case after said appendage was found in the former Minnesota Vikings running back's suitcase at Minneapolis Airport. Smith admitted ownership – arguably it'd been very hard not to – and was later suspended by the NFL for a series of anti-doping indiscretions.

While Smith proved a marketing dream for 'the leading brand in urine simulation technology', he's not the most famous urine swapper. That title goes to Diego Maradona and his famous 'knob of God'.

Manchester United's maestro Eric Cantona once said of Maradona, 'In the course of time, it will be said that Maradona was to football what Rimbaud was to poetry and Mozart to music.' Unfortunately, off the pitch, the Argentinian was more akin to Pablo Escobar, gripped by a cocaine addiction.

In 1990, he helped Argentina to the Word Cup final after beating host nation Italy in the semi-final. They lost the final 1–0 to Germany, the European side enacting revenge for the South American side's 1986 3–2 triumph.

Just one year later, when playing for Napoli, he was randomly selected for a drugs test and failed. Traces of cocaine were found in his urine. Maradona was banned for 15 months and his career spiralled. And so did his life.

His addiction was the worst-kept secret in football but, according to Jonathan Wilson on the excellent *It Was What It Was* footballing podcast, he'd escaped testing positive by his own version of the Whizzinator.

'He'd have a plastic penis with a bladder containing someone else's urine,' Wilson explained. 'He'd pop it into his tracksuit bottoms and con the testers by squirting the clean sample into the specimen jar.' Remarkable. But there was more to come.

'Maradona's fake penis was held in a museum in Buenos Aires for several years. Then in December, 2003, they took it on a nationwide tour and it went missing. On someone's mantelpiece there is a fake penis of Diego Maradona. I want to track that down.

'When it came to the sample that tested positive for cocaine, there was no doubt in his mind that this was Italy's vendetta after Argentina knocked them out of the World Cup. Or it could have been he'd taken mountains of cocaine for years and eventually got caught.'

Both Smith and Maradona learned their urinary-swapping craft from the Belgian Michel Pollentier. At the 1978 Tour de France, Pollentier slipped into the yellow jersey for the first time in his career after winning the 16th stage atop the iconic climb of Alpe d'Huez. Unfortunately for Pollentier, a doctor had just uncovered a fellow rider seeking to pass off someone else's urine as his own. He demanded Pollentier lift his shirt to reveal a condom placed beneath his armpit connected to a plastic tube containing 'clean' urine. Pollentier – and his clean condom – were immediately removed from the race.

Urine swapping is less common these days as, since 2003, WADA has made direct observation compulsory by a same-sex doping control officer. (Smith sidestepped this laser urinary focus as the NFL is independent of the WADA framework, operating its own anti-doping and substance policies.) But it does still happen, albeit in a more natural form.

'I'm certainly aware of examples of a doping officer rocking up to an athlete's house for an out-of-competition test and that athlete decides that his or her brother, sister or friend might be a safer bet to urine test on their behalf,' says David Howman. 'They might look similar and the chaperone might not notice the difference. That's particularly possible when you're testing somebody in their home country and you don't know the individual athlete.'

In June, 2022, a doping officer from the Anti-Doping Association of Kenya (ADAK) asked middle-distance runner Michael Saruni to head to doping control after competing in the 800m final at the Kenyan trials. He never showed up. Instead, the ADAK panel stated later, Saruni arranged for a lookalike to impersonate him and provide a urine sample in his place. He locked himself inside a toilet cubicle while a doping control officer observed another individual approach the stall. When asked to identify himself, the individual fled, leaping over a perimeter fence. Whether Saruni and his toilet lookalike are friends remains to be seen, but Saruni was banned for four years.

Where do these litanies of crime leave us? Confused? Anti-doping systems such as the whereabouts programme, testing protocols and TUEs were built to protect fairness and athlete health, yet they operate in a world where margins matter and scrutiny is uneven. For every safeguard introduced, athletes and support teams have found ways to work around it – sometimes crudely, sometimes with striking sophistication. And sometimes with the Whizzinator. Ahh, the Whizzinator . . .

It's almost bizarre that drugs to mask the drugs are as prevalent as the performance-enhancing drugs themselves. But that, for many, is the game of hide-and-seek that they call professional sport. Ultimately, the actions of the likes of Max Hauke exposed a simple reality: anti-doping is an exercise in managing risk, not eliminating it.

UNDERGROUND LABS TO INTELLIGENCE-LED ENFORCEMENT

The Russian state-sponsored doping scandal was one of the most systematic and far-reaching violations in sporting history. At its core was a scheme to shield elite athletes from positive tests. During the 2014 Winter Olympics, officials ran a covert night-time operation inside the WADA accredited anti-doping laboratory. Using a hidden 'mouse-hole' in the wall, FSB agents secretly swapped contaminated urine samples for clean ones that had been collected months earlier. As revealed in chapter four, bottles thought to be tamper-proof were opened using a refined technique developed by the security services. Positive tests outside Russia were avoided through advance warning, manipulated testing schedules and selective targeting of lower-level athletes to create the illusion of enforcement.

In 2019, WADA declared Russia non-compliant and imposed a four-year ban from major international events. That sanction was later reduced to two years by the Court of Arbitration for Sport.

During the ban, Russia was barred from competing under its flag, name or anthem, although athletes who could prove they were clean were allowed to compete as neutrals at events including the Tokyo 2020 Olympics and Beijing 2022 Winter Olympics.

WADA's Intelligence and Investigations department was set up in June, 2016, in the wake of the scandal. Günter Younger is its director and has been from the start. He looks functionally fit, with a whisker-free bald head and piercing eyes. If he ever leaves WADA, he's a villain shoe-in for the Bond franchise.

'I'm actually seconded from the cybercrime division at the Bavarian Landeskriminalamt [BLKA] in Germany,' he says. 'When WADA created this department, they were under attack from many people accusing them of corruption. I'd already done some work for WADA, so when they invited me to take on the role, my boss said they'd "loan" me, but if there was any potential damage to the reputation of the Bavarian police I'd be brought back. In fact, I still have that option. Many still question the independence of WADA, but when you talk about independence I can just walk out the door and return to my original position. But I've never needed to in the ten years I've been here.'

Younger's the perfect fit as WADA seeks to spread its enforcement net. He held numerous senior roles at the BLKA that combats drug trafficking and organised crime. In 2006, he was deployed to Europol's serious organised crime department before joining Interpol's drug unit in 2008. He returned to the BLKA in 2011 before his WADA move. He's in charge of both the intelligence and investigations units, and the department has 15 staff ('nearly 10 per cent of WADA's near-200 total').

'Since 2016, this department has been instrumental in supporting almost 500 athletes, officials and coaches to co-operate with our partners,' he says. 'They've been charged with either anti-doping violations or even criminal charges, which I think is quite an impressive number for a small team.'

The intelligence unit mainly comprises source managers from law enforcement, who are qualified at managing confidential sources. 'How to assess them, how to work with them, how to speak to them. One of our key tools is the "Speak Up" platform, which we launched in 2017. This is where athletes, their support personnel and anyone else can provide information regarding possible anti-doping violations in a confidential manner.'

While the intelligence department is all about gathering information from sources – be it whistleblowers, testing data or alerts from customs, and analysing trends and anomalies – intelligence is more about gathering admissible evidence, like financial records of drug transactions and messages between user and supplier. It's about really digging into what actually happened and who might be responsible.

'If someone comes to you and says Germany has a weight-lifting problem, obviously, that's far too general and you can't investigate that. But if someone says Günter Younger, a weight-lifter from Germany, is doping, that would be more specific and what we call "actionable intelligence". That then goes to the investigation unit. This unit is also composed of former law enforcement officers, plus scientists and forensic experts. They run the case.'

Whether a file progresses is down to WADA's triage system that looks to prioritise the most serious and credible cases. These are ranked by risk, taking in factors like the threat to clean sport, involvement of doctors or suppliers, cross-border elements and time sensitivity. The higher the risk, the quicker it rises.

From there, intelligence is routed. Some are passed to national anti-doping bodies or international federations. More complex cases are escalated to the investigation team, while supply-chain cases are shared with law enforcement. Others remain under development. Files are continually reviewed, says Younger, and a single new detail can quickly elevate a monitored lead into a full investigation.

There's continued interplay between both departments, though he says there's a physical wall between the intelligence and investigation units to avoid an investigator ever meeting the source. That's because there is a conflict. The investigator wants to run the case; they want to use the evidence; they want success. But for the intelligence officer, their objective is to protect the source.

'An example,' says Younger. 'An informant gave us a document which contained evidence of a sample cover-up. The intelligence officer asked who had access to the document. The guy replied only him and the man he was accusing. That meant if we gave it to the investigator, the accused would know exactly who the source was, putting him or her at threat.

'So, we didn't give the form to the investigator; instead, we said this is the evidence, it exists but you need to find another way of sourcing that information. They are intelligent people. They find ways. Ultimately, the best whistleblowers [are those] that you get a lot from but don't have to involve too deeply. It's why it's so important for us that our investigator only sees the intelligence report and talks to the source manager. They never talk to the source.'

Whistleblowers are essential and have been integral to numerous cases, including the BALCO scandal. Trevor Graham, a US sprint coach, sent an anonymous syringe containing a previously unknown substance to USADA in 2003 that was later identified as the designer steroid tetrahydrogestrinone (THG). Graham said he acted out of ethical, competitive and personal reasons. In a complex and controversial case, his actions saw many athletes receive bans and be stripped of their medals, including two of his former disciples, Marion Jones and Tim Montgomery.

Kara Goucher speaking out about doping practices at the Nike Oregon Project led to coach Alberto Salazar's ban, while Floyd Landis' admissions and evidence were central to the downfall of Lance Armstrong. Sport has a history of brave individuals exposing wrongdoing. But, says Younger, there are many 'informants' who cause more harm than good.

'I say to my team, "Whistleblowers can be your biggest asset but also your biggest enemy." Because sometimes people come to us with information and their motivations aren't pure. So, the first thing our confidential source manager will ask is, "Why are you telling me this? Give me your motivation. I want to understand why you have come to me." That's critical for trust, which is needed on both sides. But if you earn my trust, I will do everything for you. I will protect you.'

Younger says his team have enjoyed many successes, but Operation LIMS and how it helped sanction Russia was the greatest. It was also the most complex investigation he's ever worked on, both in and out of anti-doping, and the most traumatic.

'I had my suitcase packed and said to Olivier Niggli [Director General of WADA] that we're dead in the water if this doesn't come off. We spent a great deal of time in Russia and it was intimidating. But my psychologist says I must talk about it as much as possible to lessen the trauma!'

In 2015, the Russian Anti-Doping Agency (RUSADA) was deemed non-compliant with the WADA code following revelations of the state-sponsored doping programme at the 2014 Sochi Winter Olympics. One of the conditions for reinstatement required Russian authorities to hand over the Laboratory Information Management System (LIMS) database from the Moscow anti-doping lab, which contained raw testing data from 2012 to 2015, the period at the heart of the doping scandal.

A source manager had gotten hold of a copy of the data from the Moscow laboratory. It became clear that Russia's manipulation of test results and the reach of their programme was even greater than first thought. But WADA's lawyers said a copy wouldn't be permissible evidence in court.

'We'd located the safe containing the gold but we didn't have the key,' says Younger. 'For it to stand up, we needed the raw data, the original data. We discussed the situation with the chair of the Compliance Review Committee [CRC], Jonathan Taylor, on how we could get hold of the original data. He said, "Let's reinstate Russia." In return, we ask for the data from LIMS.

'The idea was a risky one but had two advantages, the first one obviously being we get hold of the data. But Russia would also fall under a new compliance programme, which was far tougher than the old system.'

These changes gave greater independence and authority to the CRC to 'assess signatories independently', while sanctions such as event bans and mandatory oversight became formalised, reducing reliance on negotiation and speeding up enforcement.

'So, we agreed to reinstate Russia thinking that either they play ball and hand over all the data, which is great but unlikely; they don't agree to the deal; or they hand over manipulated data, which is what happened, and if they do that, they'll be screwed as we'll get them under the new rules.'

Who would blink first? 'It was a very clever move, which didn't land as a clever move in the court of public opinion. At that time, it seemed like the whole world was against WADA and the decision we made.' Many leading athletes contacted WADA saying they believed it'd be a disaster for clean sport if Russia was reinstated.

A letter signed by British athletes, including 2014 and 2018 Winter Olympic skeleton champion Lizzy Yarnold, addressed to then WADA president Sir Craig Reedie read:

'Two of the conditions directed by the Russia Roadmap – accept the outcomes of the McLaren Investigation and permit access to the Moscow Laboratory – have not yet been met, and to readmit them despite this would be a catastrophe. We play our sports by the rules, and we expect the institutions that govern us, and which are there to protect us and our competition, to play by the rules too.

'The Roadmap clearly outlines what Russia must do to be allowed back. To ignore these conditions, ignores the wishes of the athletes you are there to protect. Athletes will no longer have faith in the system. It will undermine trust in the essence of fair play on which sport is formed.

'We, the athletes, insist you hold the line on the Roadmap. Do not U-turn. Do not fail Clean Sport.'

To global outrage, Russia was reinstated in September, 2018. Behind the scenes, Younger was delighted. 'I couldn't believe it when Jonathan [Taylor] phoned to say they had signed. I was convinced they wouldn't.'

Younger says RUSADA had taken their eye off the ball and were shocked when WADA turned up to dissect their computers and both servers – the 'hot' server and the 'cold' server; one had altered data, the other didn't. Hard drives were taken. RUSADA were under the impression they had control over handing over data. 'I think that's when they realised they had a big problem. They were so desperate to hide incriminating detail from us that they'd return to the laboratory in the evening and alter even more data.'

In all, WADA's forensic team examined 24 terabytes of data, representing around 24 million documents and the cases of over 800 athletes.

'Even Dr Rodchenkov was surprised at the success of our investigation. Most of the samples had been destroyed but we still uncovered samples and found anti-doping rule violations. After retesting and our forensic work, a total of 286 athletes were charged or sentenced. It showed we took the right approach.'

Russia and its anti-doping agency were again sanctioned under the new rules, this time hit with a four-year ban in December, 2019. Russia appealed, and soon after the Court of Arbitration for Sport reduced that to two years, stating that the sentence reflected constraints in international law. 'That was a bit disappointing, but that's how it goes,' says Younger. 'We respected and accepted the ruling.'

Operation LIMS instilled confidence in the department to extend its reach. In recent years, they've forged stronger links with global law enforcement and national anti-doping agencies to target the criminals further up the performance-enhancing drug chain.

'We've helped law enforcement in some really big raids and, in return, we really want the list of client names. One operation we were given more than 11,000 names. We can then share that with the national anti-doping organisation and say, "Look, you might find someone that is interesting – a doctor or coach." That's how we discovered the doctor [Mark Schmidt] behind Aderlass. It turned out he was responsible for over 30 athletes. Find the doctor and then see who the athletes are.'

In 2023, co-ordinated police raids, with assistance from Europol and WADA, led to the arrest of 19 people and the dismantling of ten warehouses across Poland, Slovakia and the Czech Republic that contained underground laboratories that were illegally producing dietary supplements and counterfeit drugs.

The authorities seized around 550,000 packages of illegal substances including banned anabolic and androgenic steroids, hundreds of packages of new psychoactive substances, significant amounts of cash and approximately one tonne of materials used in illegal manufacturing.

Between 2023 and 2025, says Younger, his department were involved in operations that saw over 500 kilogrammes of performance-enhancing drugs seized in Austria. 'Then we had around one tonne in North Macedonia; 3,000 kilogrammes in Serbia; eight tonnes in Germany and Denmark; one tonne in Portugal; another tonne in Slovenia; and we discovered a laboratory in Greece. We've been involved in around 140 operations with over 40 tons of seizures equating to around 800 million doses. And this is just from Europe. We're proving effective elsewhere, too.

'In a series of coordinated raids at the tail-end of 2025, Yemeni authorities seized almost 450kg of narcotics and performance-enhancing drugs, much of it made up of amphetamines and substances banned in sport.'

This case in particular highlighted the inseparability of sport and politics. Investigators believed drug manufacturers linked to Syria and Iran shifted production to Yemen following the collapse of the Assad regime in 2024, exploiting the country's ongoing conflict and economic instability. One newly built factory, equipped with modern machinery, was dismantled before it could begin exporting drugs abroad. The arrests included foreign specialists accused of providing technical expertise and funding.

Yemeni officials claim the trade has become a revenue stream for the Iranian-backed Houthi movement, allegations Iran strongly denies. Whatever the geopolitics, the operation underlines a growing reality: performance-enhancing drugs are no longer niche products for athletes, but lucrative commodities for organised crime.

These raids followed a WADA intelligence workshop in Saudi Arabia, part of its Global Anti-Doping Intelligence and Investigation Network (GAINN), which reframes doping as a public-health and security issue.

GAINN aims to strengthen the bond between national anti-doping agencies, law-enforcement agencies, customs and border authorities and Interpol. To share intelligence, expertise and best practice on identifying, disrupting and dismantling doping networks.

GAINN operates through several key areas: international workshops and training sessions; secure intelligence-sharing frameworks; and joint investigations across borders. 'The most recent phase of this programme has focussed on Asia and Oceania. We've held workshops in Thailand, India, Australia . . . and now we have ongoing operations in those areas,' says Younger. The next phase will take place in the Americas in 2026 to 2027 and will conclude in Africa between 2028 and 2029.

'It's an amazing project and having Interpol on board is needed. Sports integrity is a big issue. As well as doping, there's lots of corruption and match fixing.'

'We've also seen organised crime shift more and more to performance-enhancing drugs,' Younger adds. 'That's certainly the case in Europe. Why? Because of three main reasons. The first is profit. We've seen that there's the same money, if not more, in PEDs compared to classic societal drugs like cocaine.

'The second is deterrence. If you're caught with one kilogramme of cocaine, you could be looking at a prison sentence of five to six years. PEDs, you'll probably receive a slap on the wrist.

'The third reason is detection. Many police officers might be drafted for a case into cocaine. The same wouldn't apply to PEDs.' With GAINN, Younger adds, that is slowly changing. The fact that these gangs are hitting the profit margins of pharmaceutical companies adds weight, too. 'It's all about hitting the main players upstream. That will have an impact on the accessibility of buying PEDs whether you're an elite or amateur athlete . . .'

John Wesley's New Room in the centre of Bristol is physically, socially and emotionally distant from an underground laboratory in Yemen. It's the oldest methodist building in the world. Founded in 1739, the New Room became the cradle of the worldwide Methodist movement. In the 18th century it was a place where the religious society members would offer food and clothing to the poor, run a school for impoverished children and help the sick by running a free medical dispensary. Now, it's a museum, shop and café where researcher Josh Torrance, who used to work at the Bristol Drugs Project and who we met in chapter two, is scrolling through his smartphone for modern-day 'medicine'. It's not free and it's most certainly not to treat the sick.

'Buying drugs online has certainly increased the amount of people using IPEDs [image- and performance-enhancing drugs],' he says. 'Now you have online drug marketplaces, it really is at the press of a button. There are loads of IPEDs advertised on Telegram. It's a pretty safe way of ordering as it's extremely rare that the police would come knocking on your door. You're pretty much hidden behind VPNs [virtual private networks] and all kinds of encrypted layers of security. Ahhh, look at this guy . . .

'This vender does a whole load of PEDs including Selank and Semax. They're two different peptides combined in a nasal spray. The only people who've researched those products is the Russian government, so who knows how safe or not they are. This chap also sells steroids, of which he's offering 37 different options. You've got TRT [testosterone replacement therapy], you've got meta [methandienone] injections . . .

'What shall we go for? How about a bit of the steroid trenbolone? Okay, let's put it in the cart. That's £130 for ten 1ml ampoules of trenbolone injection. Just pay by PayPal and you're away . . .'

We don't follow through with the purchase, but many sports people do and insist their PED path was down to them and them only. In 2013, Italian rider Mauro Santambrogio tested positive for EPO at the Giro d'Italia and was suspended for three years. He said during the disciplinary process that he self-administered the drug without team direction. Ironman triathlete Collin Chartier insisted the same when he was banned in 2023 for taking EPO.

'You've got to be so careful if you're an athlete who decides to dope. Yes, there are oral IPEDs and pills, but they're generally at the milder end of the spectrum. Most are injections that users stick in their butts, which does dispel the misperception of old that only the part of the body you'd inject would grow big. But injecting can very easily go wrong. We see all kinds of infections, lumps and bumps. It's a big problem.

'The thing is, those guys on the street taking heroin and crack, they're really good at injecting drugs. They've been doing it for years and really know what they're doing. They can find their veins even better than a nurse can.

'Luckily, the supply of steroids, for instance, is generally quite clean, but there are always supply lines that are bolted down, mixed with something unpleasant to increase the profit margin. And then there are the actual facilities making these drugs. Quite a lot of them – at least the raw ingredients – are shipped over from India and that's relatively well made. But obviously a lot of people in this business aren't that fussed about sterile laboratory conditions.'

It's a dirty business. And one Dan Burke knows only too well. Burke is the intelligence and investigations director at USADA. Law enforcement is coursing through his veins. He took up his USADA role in 2025 after nearly 30 years in the federal government. 'Most of that was drugs and cybercrime,' he says. 'I started off working on child pornography cases, before moving into narcotics. Obviously, there were some pretty horrendous files, but it was also relatively easy from an investigative point of view. In the mid- to late-90s, cybercrime was in its infancy and we were way ahead of the bad guys. It was very busy but very rewarding.'

In the 2000s, Burke spent 'inordinate amounts of time' busting drug traffickers before he took up a position at the FDA (Food and Drug Administration) in the newly created office of criminal investigations. 'Part of their remit focused on online pharmacies, which were just starting to take off.' There he stayed for nearly 20 years, working on cases like combatting the trafficking of illegal fentanyl from China. 'In that time, I worked on several cases involving performance-enhancing drugs (PEDs), which is how I ended up at USADA.'

Burke's been aware of the baddies since birth. His father was an agent at the DEA (Drug Enforcement Agency). One of his first cases turned out to be battling a vast heroin-smuggling network that'd come to be known as the French Connection. The network operated from the 1950s, linking Marseille to New York, where largely Corsican crime groups supplied much of the US heroin market. It was refined in secret laboratories in southern France, then smuggled to the US using hidden compartments in cars, ships and other cargo. The operation was exposed through joint French and US police work, with a landmark 1962 seizure of around 52kg of heroin, then the largest in US history. Its legacy was cemented by 1971's neo-noir action thriller *The French Connection* starring Gene Hackman.

'My dad hated that film and I never understood why until I watched it recently, flying back from Europe. The agent's portrayed as real jerk, which made me laugh but not my dad. That said, I've got this great picture of him from the case on the front page of the *New York Daily News*, where he's arresting the Guatemalan ambassador to Belgian. Once he retired from that, he was one of the first drug programme coordinators for the National Football League.'

Burke's USADA role is heavily online, both in fighting crime and deterring potential customers. 'Let me share my screen as I'll show you the presentation I'm delivering to the team at TikTok later today. We're looking to partner with them for our TrueSport campaign, aimed at educating youngsters about clean sport and clean living. It's obviously a popular platform, especially for the young, and there's some captivating content on there. There's also a lot of videos about PEDs, including steroids.'

They're proving popular, especially among young men. In fact, according to a 2023 report by the Centre for Countering Digital Hate (CCDH), entitled 'TikTok's Toxic Trade', content posted to hashtags promoting steroids, peptides and selective androgen receptors (SARMs) was seen 117 million times over a three-year period, with 89 million of those views by males aged 18 to 24.

'There's one drug I'm particularly concerned about on there. It's dinitrophenol and it's dangerous as hell. It was originally used as ammunition.'

Dinitrophenol, or DNP, first came into widespread use in French munitions factories during World War I, where it was combined with picric acid in the manufacture of explosives. The effects on exposed workers quickly revealed both its potency and its danger; labourers experienced rapid weight loss, severe fatigue, excessive sweating and dangerously high body temperatures. Before protective measures were introduced, numerous fatalities were recorded.

'It's still classified as an explosive in the United States but it's crazy stuff. It can lead to rapid weight loss and we've seen it used by many athletes, especially in wrestling. The problem is, if you slightly overdose you become hypothermic and your organs start to shut down. You cook from the inside and you die. There have been a lot of cases in the United Kingdom of kids dying from it because they wanted to drop a load of weight.'

Over 30 men and women, average age 21, died in the UK between 2017 and 2023 from taking DNP. The tragic toll included Vaidotas Gerbutavicius from London, who took 20 pills in March, 2018, and died within an hour of being admitted to hospital, and bodybuilder Jack Knapman, from Northampton, who 'took a substantial quantity' of the drug, leading to severe toxicity and cardiac arrest. In 2015, Interpol tagged DNP with a rare Orange

Notice warning over its 'serious threat' after information sharing from a WADA-accredited laboratory in Sydney, Australia.

In the world of performance sport, according to the Anti-Doping Database, only one athlete has been sanctioned for using DNP, Canadian runner David Freake in 2019. A urine sample after the Ottawa Marathon also showed up traces of EPO, ephedrine and GW1516, resulting in a four-year ban. Freake passed away unexpectedly at the age of 39 in July, 2025.

'It's simply a drug that should scare people,' says Burke. 'We always have internal dialogue when it comes to speaking to the media about illegal substances, as we don't want to get the word out about a certain drug and people start using it. But this is so experimental, such a killer, that we had to.'

Education, says Burke, is an effective anti-doping tool. To warn athletes over the dangers, both mentally and physically. Chair of the Athletics Integrity Unit, David Howman, who's been involved in anti-doping for nearly 30 years, agrees that education serves a purpose – if the athlete lets it.

'Education works when the person's receptive to being educated,' he says. 'If you look at how many people cheat in sport, it's probably similar to how many people "cheat" in real life. There's no difference. Say 90 per cent of sports people are good and 10 per cent are bad (and their support teams). How can you educate them? If they want to break the rules, they will. And you're not going to change that by patting them on the back, giving them a book to read and tomorrow you'll be fine. It doesn't work like that. What are people doing to break the rules? And who are the people helping them break the rules?'

That's part of Burke's remit, especially in the digital world. But, over time, his job has become harder. 'Cybercrime used to be so easy as IP addresses linked to subscribers and their homes. We could easily subpoena the server, finding out who's paying for what and who's supplying who. Now the suppliers are cleverer, plus you have the dark web. It's very difficult.

'Things weren't helped when the EU brought in GDPR [General Data Protection Regulation] in 2018. That was one of the nails in the coffin in tracing the people behind online pharmacies who supply a lot of these PEDs. To set up an online pharmacy, I need a server to host my content. Then I need domain names. You find savvy online pharmacy operators have thousands of these to maximise search engine optimisation.

'Well, in the past, when I was working at the FDA, you could quite easily look at the domain name and locate who owns or leases it. Of course, it may have been falsified, but even if it was, there'd be patterns that we could start to identify. Overnight, GDPR took that ability away. Visit your high street chemist and you know who owns it. On a website, you don't have that luxury.'

Burke says he locked horns with ICANN (the Internet Corporation for Assigned Names and Numbers) due to a lack of responsibility. 'I said to them you can't have domain names like "buyheroinnow.com" or "buyopioids.com". And they're like, not our problem. It's regrettable.'

Burke's also restricted by his role and department having relatively little power, lacking the authority to subpoena, to compel testimony, to seize goods. That comes with collaborating with law-enforcement agencies.

'I'm more of a private investigator, as much of my work is down to interviewing. I might be able to image your phone or laptop, though that's voluntary. If the athlete agrees, I do then have the capacity to analyse it. The AIU [Athletics Integrity Unit] can oblige an athlete to hand over their phone, as do some national governing bodies. USADA does not.'

It's a little different to his FDA days, where he spent time in China as an undercover agent and discovered an online pharmacy operation run from a boat in Tel Aviv harbour. Then again, in his role at USADA, sometimes he comes across cases where the level of detective work is nominal.

'I don't remember the kid's name but he was a weight-lifter, and he spoke to our lawyer and the science just didn't make sense. He said he must have taken a tainted supplement, but I checked with our chief science officer Matt Fedorek and he said there was no chance it could be taken in powdered form, as it was an injectable. I went back to the kid and said this just doesn't add up, dude. And he's like, yeah, you're right. Case closed.

'Another low-level case we worked on recently involved triathlete Anthony McCauley, who we ultimately sanctioned for four years for possessing and using peptides. He was a recreational sportsman who'd completed several Ironman events. But he was also an affiliate for an online pharmacy, which he didn't understand was illegal in sport. It turned out he went on podcasts to promote all sorts of different PEDs, including GW1516. Real experimental stuff.'

We covered this novel drug in chapter one. Not only is it banned by WADA, it's also not legally permitted in medications or supplements, as it was pulled from clinical trials for accelerating the growth of cancer tumours in mice. McCauley extols its fat-loss credentials.

'Honestly some of the stuff the likes of McCauley and others are promoting, you have no idea where it's created. It might be a powder from China that's reconstituted in the USA, a label is slapped on it, you create a fancy website and away you go. I've seen vials that purport to contain PEDs and they've been full of mouldy water. And people are injecting that stuff.'

McCauley doesn't seem too concerned with the sanction. His Instagram features the bio 'Endurance and peptide coach', while many of the 826 posts (as of 10th January, 2026) extol the virtues of peptides. He also mentions his big goal for 2026 is the legendary Leadville 100 running race.

Looking ahead, Burke is concerned that gene doping, which has simmered for years, could take off as gene therapy enjoys further positive medical breakthroughs. He's also concerned that the scientist can only test for what they're looking for. 'When you look at how you can now make compounds based upon artificial intelligence, it's worrying and can turn anybody into not only a chemist but a sophisticated one. They might take an experimental drug, slightly change its composition via AI and it'll send the lab folks into a flux. They won't be able to test for it. AI is a real concern. Novel compounds and substances will go through the roof.'

Technology. A force for bad. But also good. Edmund Willison is the latest in a long line of investigative journalists who've shaped modern anti-doping and our perception of sport. David Walsh spent years uncovering Lance Armstrong's doping, work that culminated in the USADA case that brought down cycling's most powerful figure. Hajo Seppelt led ARD documentaries that revealed Russia's state-sponsored doping system, triggering those investigations by WADA. In the US, Mark Fainaru-Wada exposed the BALCO scandal, linking elite athletes to designer steroids.

Willison started off at ARD, working on a Kenyan undercover story before spending two years based in their Berlin office, then returning to London to work on the investigations team at Al Jazeera. In a freelance capacity he's regularly written on doping in sport for British newspapers, including *The Times* and the *Mail on Sunday*.

On 1st January, 2024, Willison launched his Substack, giving him greater scope to publish his work, including a three-part series on Jamaican sprinting and a deep-dive into Pep Guardiola's eight-year battle to clear his name from a nandrolone case when playing for Italian side Brescia in 2001.

He's a big sports fan and while, like all of us, he'd prefer our superheroes to be clean and fuelled by talent and commitment, the motivation behind his work stems from telling the whole story.

'I'm interested in doping because we have all these analysts, TV pundits and journalists talking about every facet of performance without mentioning doping. How can you present a full picture if you're not taking into account this huge driver of performance? I'm more interested in that than the ethical perspective.'

Key to filling in the gaps and to Willison's work is open-source intelligence. It refers to the analysis of public information, data and resources to produce actionable intelligence that can be used to aid investigations.

'I was inspired by Bellingcat,' says Willison. 'They've done some amazing investigations.' Bellingcat is an award-winning group of full-time investigators and volunteers founded by British citizen journalist Eliot Higgins, who became an expert in military weapons during the Syrian civil war by analysing hundreds of YouTube videos of the conflict each day. 'He did this from the comfort of his home while looking after two young children during a period of unemployment.'

One of Bellingcat's highest-profile cases exposed the Russians behind the Skripal poisonings, including secret-service officer Anatoliy Chepiga. Digital forensics were core to the Skripal case and Bellingcat's work as a whole.

'A lot of my work involves social-media searching, wading through private data and public databases,' says Willison. 'An athlete won't dope alone, so you'll find what the coach or doctor are doing via Instagram. You might wonder why an athlete would mention a doctor if they're doping them. Why not keep them in the background like [Michele] Ferrari? I think it's because, for some athletes, it's so ingrained into what they do that they're just not guarded about the relationship.

'Instagram is a really useful platform for this work. And Facebook, though mainly for older stuff. People forget what's on there. But yeah, Instagram is good for the contemporary stuff. And often people get tagged. A fan will take a picture with an athlete somewhere and you piece together what might be happening.

'It creates a huge source of information that you can build matrixes from. Who's this guy's trainer? Where's his coach based? In Florida. Then you see a picture of the coach at an anti-ageing clinic. Look on their website and they're selling testosterone replacement therapy. Why's that coach there? He's young. For me, simple steps like that crank up the probability that his athlete is doping.'

It's all about asking the right questions and knowing where to look for the answers. 'Say it's a cyclist. Who's the coach? Who are the soigneurs? What former teams were they on? What former doctors were involved with those teams? Were there previous doping scandals? Read the tribunal decisions from documents, see the names mentioned. Cross-reference that against Instagram and the next thing you know you have a rough idea of what's going on and who's involved.'

Willison says it's not rocket science. It's just that he's one of the few journalists spending time uncovering this information. 'But you do learn tricks along the way,' he says. 'Simple stuff like sometimes you'll receive a redacted document. If you copy the document and paste it into Word, sometimes you can read the redacted passage. It's less common now but it used to happen a lot in tennis. Then there's metadata in documents. Just like tags of who created the document, when it was created. All these little things can always lead to something.'

On his Substack, Willison explains how he used open-source intelligence to unpack the unusual case of US Paralympian Roderick Townsend, who tested positive for the growth hormone-releasing peptide capromorelin yet escaped a doping sanction. Initially flagged by USADA, Townsend claimed the positive result came from capromorelin in pet medication prescribed for his terminally ill dog, Winnie, and that he had inadvertently continued to use the same oral syringe to administer his own vitamin D after the dog died. USADA accepted this explanation and concluded Townsend bore 'no fault or negligence', allowing him to compete and win high jump gold at Paris 2024.

'By looking through photos that Townsend posted that month, as well as the posts he was tagged in, it soon became clear that Townsend had been training with a strength and conditioning coach called Mr King in Arizona during the track-and-field off-season,' says Willison. 'King and Townsend posted videos and photographs of themselves training together several times and the day before Townsend's drug test.'

Through Willison's research, he discovered that 'in 2021, Mr King was a personal trainer at a fitness and wellness centre in Arizona whose wellness department offered testosterone therapy and peptide therapy (tesamorelin) involving the same class of substances that Townsend had tested positive for (capromorelin). This treatment, while legal in the US, is prohibited for professional athletes subject to the WADA Code. In a YouTube video, King had also spoken about the peptide ibutamoren.'

After his open-source work, Willison stressed, 'There was no evidence that Townsend had knowingly doped and there was no evidence that King had ever supplied any of these substances to Townsend, or any other athlete, but we did think that our research showed that USADA could have taken the case to the scrutiny of independent arbitration, rather than settling the case themselves.

'Before publishing we reached out to Townsend and King. Townsend did not respond, and King said by email that he had no association with the wellness department, that offered hormone therapy, at the centre he worked at in 2021. He wrote that he had only been a trainer at the fitness centre.'

The USADA chief executive Travis Tygart told Willison that he wouldn't be reopening the case and that the agency were aware of Townsend's association with King.

'That isn't necessarily fair to infer on someone when all the other evidence in the case, you know, points to a different direction,' said Tygart.

As an acclaimed investigative journalist, Willison operates to a high standard and is bound by libel laws and source protection. On paper, that makes him an ideal candidate to collaborate with anti-doping agencies. 'They [WADA] don't seem that interested. It's a shame as their reputation is terrible.'

Alongside official investigations, journalists like Willison have played a key role by asking questions that testing programmes cannot. Using open-source data, social media and public records, investigative reporters have highlighted blind spots, contextualised decisions and, at times, pressured authorities to look harder at uncomfortable cases. Their work has forever been an important part of how doping in sport is exposed, examined and understood.

Did the Russian case mark a turning point in how anti-doping is enforced? It certainly seems that investigation and intelligence is expanding. 'Data', 'documents' and 'networks' are becoming buzzwords. That shift has since shaped a broader strategy. Anti-doping now overlaps with policing, cybercrime and organised crime investigations, targeting suppliers, doctors and distributors as much as athletes. It seems that catching dopers increasingly depends on understanding systems, not just substances.

WHAT PRICE FOR CLEAN SPORT?

UKAD press release, January, 2025. Whistleblowing has become one of the most effective tools in the fight against doping. In 2025, whistleblowers submitted 185 reports of suspected doping to UK Anti-Doping (UKAD), spanning 25 different sports. Intelligence generated through those reports helped lead to two individuals being charged with anti-doping rule violations.

'Seeing yet another year of consistently high reports coming in has been positive, it shows that individuals feel safe coming to us and that they want to protect the integrity of their sport,' said Mario Theophanous, head of intelligence and investigations at UKAD.

Sports law specialists Morgan, April, 2025:

'The miserly approach taken by WADA and other anti-doping organisations towards whistleblowing is difficult to understand. It may be that WADA and others have taken the view that by severely limiting the extent of the benefits offered in exchange for "substantial assistance", they can protect themselves from possible criticism for allowing former dopers back to competition earlier than they otherwise would be permitted.

'If that is the reason, then it is a very short-sighted view. For a start, the advisers and lawyers of athletes who have been through an unsatisfactory substantial assistance process will often counsel other athletes against whistleblowing. Whistleblowers face serious risks with little to no reward, while the substantial assistance process feels designed to frustrate rather than encourage cooperation.'

Two sides of the same coin. We know which side Günter Younger, WADA's director of intelligence and investigations, is on. In the last chapter he extolled the virtues WADA's 'Speak Up' platform, where anyone can report anti-doping activities. Launched in 2017, it's a digital system that includes apps for all the main smartphones. A core principle of the policy is the protection of the confidential source: 'On launch, we were overwhelmed with over 200 reports in the first couple of months. The amount of people sending us information is increasing year on year. It's a strong programme.'

Many national anti-doping organisations operate their 'Speak Up' equivalent. Many label theirs 'Report Doping', including Australia, the UK, Belarus, China and France. Lithuania tweak it to 'Report Violations', the USA's is 'Play Clean Tip Centre', while Denmark's is an abrupt 'Stop Doping'. The International Testing Agency has its own whistleblowing channel, too, in the form of 'Reveal'. Many international sporting federations have their own, albeit many link straight through to WADA's Speak Up platform.

Younger's proud of a system he says has an 80 per cent positive feedback rate from whistleblowers and that none of their whistleblowers have ever been disclosed in the public domain. 'Of course, that's as it should be. It's the same in sport as in the police force. As soon as the source is known, there's little choice but witness protection. And believe me, nobody in the world wants to be in witness protection. You give up your family, you give up your friends, your social life. You live in a foreign country. You can never go back. And still, every day you wake up with a fear that someone could find you. That's a terrible way to live. So, the preferred way is to protect the whistleblowers by ensuring they don't become public.'

One source who bypassed privacy for the intense glare of the public eye was Dr Grigory Rodchenkov. The Russian's popped up a few times in *Dope* as he was the head of Russia's national anti-doping laboratory. He was also the inadvertent star of American documentary maker Bryan Fogel's 2017 film *Icarus* that started off as Fogel acting as a doping guinea pig to expose the performance impact of PEDs, but morphed into a geopolitical thriller when Rodchenkov revealed the scale of the state-sponsored doping programme.

The 2022 sequel, *Icarus: The Aftermath*, focuses on Russia's attempts to discredit him and Rodchenkov's new reality of shifting from safe house to safe house, protected by his own security team. He reflects that telling the truth didn't bring relief, just a different kind of prison – one defined by secrecy, protection and loneliness. Whistleblowing cost him his country, his career and his freedom, leaving him isolated and permanently displaced. 'I will never be safe again,' he says.

'I was in Moscow and said to him privately, "Come forward now and we will find a way to protect you," meaning we find a way of getting the information we need without involving him,' says Younger. 'But he said, "No, I must do what I have to do." Soon after, he went public. I still have contact with him from time to time because we had some cases where we needed his statement. So, he's very collaborative. But I think he took the wrong decision on going public. We've worked with many Russian whistleblowers who still live in Russia. They are very safe.'

Younger says sporting whistleblowers are a different breed than those he encountered in his law enforcement days, who 'were usually driven by two things: sentence reduction and money . . .'

Younger says that since WADA launched, no legitimate whistleblower has ever wanted money. They want justice. 'If someone did come to me and say, I have information but I want money for it, we would say no. We [WADA] have a policy of paying a reward based on the outcome, but upfront? Not a chance. It's the same in policing. When money's involved, you must be careful because you could easily pay for misinformation. You see, in sport there is the third group, the biggest group, who simply love sport and are motivated by fighting for clean sport.'

Younger is full of appreciation for legitimate whistleblowers. That their values are to be admired by all. But does that include the system itself?

Renée Anne Shirley is 70. She's spent the last few years caring for her mum, who passed away in 2025 at the age of 96. She's also one of the most infamous whistleblowers in sport, who was branded 'Judas' and a 'traitor' by her country.

Between 2003 and 2007 she was senior advisor to Jamaica's minister of sport, Portia Simpson-Miller, who became prime minister in 2006. 'That was when I got my first taste of anti-doping,' says Anne Shirley from her Kingston home. 'I was sat in her office, a little bored and I saw a piece of paper on her desk. It was a signed declaration.'

More precisely, the signed Copenhagen Declaration, which was presented at the 2nd World Conference on Doping in Sport in 2003 and laid the groundwork for governments to harmonise anti-doping standards around the world.

'I said to the minister and the cabinet, do you know what you've signed? Has somebody sat you down and told you what all this is about? This thing talks about setting up a whole anti-doping system and programme. I don't think they realised the work involved. So, she said to me, come to the next sport council meeting and talk to the prime minster. I did, and things took off from there.'

From a standing start, Anne Shirley scraped together funding and employed her legal know-how to shape Jamaica's anti-doping system. She was elected one of the vice chair people for the first session of UNESCO's 'International Convention against Doping in Sport', which runs every two years to support the global implementation of anti-doping programmes. The Jamaican Anti-Doping Commission was formally established in 2008.

Between 2009 and 2012, she served as CEO for the Jamaican Rugby Football Union, before returning as executive director to the Jamaican Anti-Doping Commission in 2012. The role proved short-lived.

'I was becoming increasingly disillusioned with the system.' She recognised WADA and national anti-doping agencies were underfunded but says that when there was money available, too many officials preferred to go shopping than working. 'My eyes were opened to decisions on who was tested and when.'

She felt the frequency of testing by her own commission was risible but no one was listening. 'I was working 18-hour days and staying at the commission offices until two o'clock in the morning. The security team knew me very well. I was trying so hard to put proper systems in place but kept coming up against a hostile board. I wrote to important people in government but they didn't even look at my letters. No one wanted to know about the shortcomings.'

While Anne Shirley suffered, Jamaica ran off with 12 sprint medals at the 2012 London Olympics: four gold, four silver and four bronze. The fastest man in the world, Usain Bolt, won three of those golds – 100m, 200m and the men's 4x100m relay, the latter annulled in 2017 due to reanalysis of teammate Nesta Carter's sample testing positive for methylhexaneamine – with Shelly-Ann Fraser-Pryce claiming the other in the 100m.

This followed five sprint golds four years earlier in Beijing – again, Bolt won two individual titles and the relay; Fraser-Pryce won the 100m in a time of 10.78 seconds – 0.53 seconds faster than her previous season's best – and Veronica Campbell-Brown sprinted to 200m gold.

Sprinting is woven into Jamaica's cultural fabric with lightning-fast runners becoming local heroes even before they've graduated to the elite ranks. The Inter-Secondary School Boys and Girls Championships ('CHAMPs') is the heartbeat of Jamaican sprinting, attracting thousands of fans and intense media coverage. Sprinting offers global visibility for a nation of fewer than three million and an island half the size of the Scottish Highlands. Both Beijing and London cemented Jamaica as a sprinting powerhouse – a source of pride and a symbol of independence.

Anne Shirley continued her battle to improve the system but, beaten down and 'on the verge of a nervous breakdown', in February, 2013, she met with JADCO board members and they agreed that she should step aside. Six months later, scarred by her experience, she wrote a letter to the Caribbean's oldest newspaper, the *Gleaner*. It generated little attention. That changed when she sent the same letter to *Sports Illustrated* in 2013, soon after the culmination of the 14th IAAF World Championships in Moscow where Jamaica once again lit up the track, winning four of the six medals available in the men's 100m and 200m, plus gold in the 4x100m relay. Fraser-Pryce won both the 100m and 200m, while the women also triumphed in the 4x100m relay.

The piece acted both as a warning and a lament: Jamaica's success on the track, she argued, was undermined by an anti-doping system that was under-resourced, conflicted and dangerously complacent. This complacency laid the foundations for the stormy lead-in to the championships, as Jamaica was hit with news that 'was the equivalent of a category-five hurricane crossing directly over the island': five of their elite track-and-field team had failed doping tests, including former world-record holder Asafa Powell and 2004 relay gold medallist Sherone Simpson.

Anne Shirley proceeded to detail alarmingly low levels of out-of-competition testing by JADCO, particularly in the build-up to the London 2012 Olympics, when not a single out-of-competition test was conducted in the final three months before the Games, and only 11 between January and the Games starting on 27th July.

(This doesn't mean they weren't tested at all. This from John Leicester of the Associated Press in October, 2013: '[Before London], track-and-field's governing body, the International Association of Athletics Federations, says it extensively tested elite Jamaicans, including Bolt more than 12 times last year. History's fastest man has never failed a drug test.')

'The current programme, while improved, makes a mockery of Jamaica's posturing and flames suspicion more than it douses it,' wrote Anne Shirley. 'Out-of-date testing kits and limited staffing resources resulted in a total of one out-of-competition test since March.'

She fleshed out basic operational failures – vacant senior roles, the absence of a whereabouts officer, unpaid bills, missing financial records and committees that existed in name only – and raised concerns about a broader culture of denial.

'I urged the authorities in Jamaica to get more serious about anti-doping before a scandal hit us,' she wrote. 'I quietly tried to point out the presence of Jamaican threads linked to the BALCO case, via the testimony of Ángel (Memo) Heredia about his contacts with elite Jamaican athletes. My position is that these threads, no matter how thin, should not be brushed aside as malice, but treated seriously, as they represent a potential threat to the integrity of our athletes and our nation . . . But despite my efforts I could not get any member of the JADCO board or member of Jamaica's Cabinet to take it seriously. They believe that Jamaica does not have a problem.'

By November, 2013, the entire 11-commissioner board of JADCO had resigned after political pressure. They'd lost their jobs. Anne Shirley lost her liberty and future. 'I started to receive death threats in the middle of the night,' she says. 'I switched phone numbers several times. It got so bad that I had to leave Kingston and live in the middle of the island.'

Where, she says, she was set adrift. 'I'd burnt my bridges at JADCO, so contacted the team at USADA and said I need to get out of here, even if it's just for six months. Is there a project I could work on somewhere? I don't care where – Africa, Asia . . . I just need to feel safe. Everyone came back with the same reply: yeah, yeah, we'll help you. But nobody came through. Nobody.'

She recalls speaking at the Tackling Doping in Sport Conference at Wembley Stadium in London in March, 2014, where she presented on the subject, 'Daring to Speak Out: The Lonely Road of a Whistleblower'. She spoke about how the local Jamaican press labelled her as someone who's 'clearly demented' and who exaggerates the truth in order to grab attention and money. She told of how pressure was placed on her family to 'shut her up' and that most of her true friends worry about her personal safety.

'It was a very intense time and hard to escape,' she says. 'Even at that conference, the organisers pulled me aside and informed me that the Home Office had contacted them saying that the Jamaican government was going to refuse me a visa. The organisers told me that the Home Office saw no reason to deny me. Obviously, if I was denied a visa, that'd hurt me for the rest of my life. All because I attended an anti-doping conference in London and spoke the truth.'

The pressure didn't end there, she says. 'I'm in the airport lounge at London with a journalist friend of mine. When I land in Jamaica many hours later, there are pictures of me sitting in the airport all over social media. That was the kind of stuff I faced.'

Anne Shirley says she became unemployable to many companies who didn't want to recruit her and jeopardise government contracts. 'I'm at a crossroads. I had to give up the consulting work to care for my mum. I'm a methodical person and ordinarily would have had plans in place by now for my retirement, for my future. I'm so low-key, many people in Jamaica don't realise I'm still alive.' She says reading and meditation have replaced sport in her life. 'I just can't believe in professional sport anymore, even if the testing system is allegedly stronger.'

Jamaica's Ministry of Culture, Gender, Entertainment and Sport (MCGES) pronounced in June, 2021 that JADCO was now fully compliant with the WADA Code. 'What this means is that Jamaica's credibility can no longer be questioned when it comes to doping in sport,' said the MCGES' Olivia Grange. In January, 2023, WADA called for 'more education, testing and collaboration to strengthen anti-doping in the Caribbean'.

Over a decade on, after all that she's been through, does Anne Shirley regret penning what she calls 'that innocuous letter' to *Sports Illustrated*? 'No, I don't, even if it has been very stressful and my mother said I should have just kept quiet. I've missed out on lots of opportunities but I did the right thing.

'But would I recommend speaking out to others? That depends whether you really think anyone wants to hear what you're saying. The authorities, sponsors, even the public, do they want to hear about the practices of their country's athletes? Other countries' athletes? Fine. But not your own. Just don't expect that being brave will turn out to be a worthwhile venture. I just hope you don't become as disillusioned with sport as me from writing this book.'

Anne Shirley has spoken to fellow whistleblowers but, respecting their confidentiality, doesn't say who. 'I hope I help in some small way. One has forged a new path in broadcasting, so that's good. But there are many from the outside who look like they're just drifting. Take those two Russian whistleblowers. They've been hung out to dry.'

Yuliya and Vitaly Stepanov helped to expose the Russian doping scandal. Yuliya was a middle-distance runner who competed on the international stage, while Vitaly was an adviser at RUSADA, Russia's anti-doping agency. Yuliya had first-hand experience of the state-sponsored system, beginning her doping programme in 2007. For years, she ran fuelled by testosterone, anabolic steroids and EPO before abnormalities in her biological passport saw her banned for two years from February, 2013.

In 2010, despite his wife's doping regime, Vitaly first approached WADA. According to a 2018 report by WADA, at the time Vitaly had yet to tell his wife that he was in contact with the agency; and that, he 'had no concrete evidence whatsoever to support his statements, that they were his words and his words alone'.

Jack Robertson, a chief investigative officer at WADA, said the agency was restricted by how much they could investigate under the 2009 Code, but told them to contact the German investigative journalist Hajo Seppelt.

In December, 2014, Yuliya's secret recordings of her conversations with Russian athletes, coaches, doctors and sports officials on doping were published in Seppelt's documentary, *The Secrets of Doping: How Russia Makes its Winners*.[25] Following the broadcast, the couple faced credible threats to their lives.

'That's why they snuck out of their hotel under the secrecy of darkness and got themselves on a plane to Germany,' says Spencer Harris. The Brit is professor of sport management at the University of Colorado and has been a close friend of the Stepanovs since

---

25 https://www.youtube.com/watch?v=iu9B-ty9JCY

2016. 'It was crazy, but for the first three or four weeks they were living in Hajo's Berlin flat. Nobody seemed to know what to do with them.

'It was like the whistleblowing policies were written on the back of a cigarette packet. I think things have tightened up a lot since then, whether it's from WADA or other agencies, but it still seems pretty perfunctory. When you get into the real complex issues of keeping people safe and being able to live, I'm still not sure that's properly addressed.

'Certainly, when we look back at their time in Germany, things get a little entrenched in the weeds. The intelligence agent told them to get the heck out of Germany as they weren't safe. He said head to the US and everything would be taken care of.

'Well, they did. That was predicated on what the intelligence agent said. They had conversations that all would be sorted and that included the ability to live in the United States as a green-card holder or even a citizen. But that hasn't happened.'

Without a visa or citizenship, they can't leave the United States so they are stuck. The Stepanovs now have two sons and they live in an undisclosed location. But over ten years on since risking their lives, the couple feel forgotten, helpless and abandoned. 'For many years, Vitaly felt it was fine,' says Harris. 'That they're not owed anything and nobody needs to do us any favours. We're just asylum seekers, like many other hundreds of thousands of people. We'll be seen when our time comes.

'But over the last year that's changed, Vitaly's been far more assertive, bordering on aggressive at times. He's like, what the hell are you guys doing? You promised us X, Y and Z and you've delivered nothing. That's been levelled at various leaders in sport, and I think rightly so.'

A WADA spokesman said in 2024 that when the Stepanovs first contacted them nearly 15 years previous, they weren't equipped to deal with the situation. That it was an unprecedented situation for the agency and it needed to adapt quickly.

'Apart from not having the authority to carry out investigations, the rules in place at that time meant WADA would have had to provide the information to RUSADA and/or the International Athletics Federation (IAAF) – two organisations that were accused of protecting doping cheaters,' the spokesman said. 'It is fair to say that WADA and the entire anti-doping community learned a lot from that experience. The landscape today is completely different as WADA went well beyond what was expected of it by building what is now considered to be a flagship confidential source programme.'

As we've seen, anti-doping agencies have limitations. They're not the government or a police force. They don't have the powers of arrest, search or seizure. That's down to law enforcement. WADA's strength lies, said the spokesman, in its strong relation-ships built with many collaborators, in particular with public authorities, customs agencies and law enforcement around the world. 'Whistleblowers' courage to come forwards is never taken for granted by the agency.'

Harris isn't convinced. When I tell him about WADA's 80 per cent whistleblowing approval rating, he simply answers, 'That's convenient. He can spew whatever figures he likes. The feedback is confidential so we'll never know.'

Harris says USADA's chief executive officer Travis Tygart raised a Private Members' bill to the US Senate, concerned not only with the current delay in their asylum application but also that changes to scheduling policy could see their wait extended beyond 2030. 'It got nowhere,' says Harris. 'I wrote a joint letter with Travis from the University of Colorado and USADA to the immigration services asking for their case to be expedited. But they just wrote back to the Stepanovs, saying sorry, your circumstances don't permit expedition. We've written to presidents and Travis has employed various lawyers for legal advice on how to accelerate the case. But again, nothing.'

He says there remain options including challenging the Department of Justice (DOJ) in court, to explain why the Stepanovs' case has been delayed. 'But that carries risk. You could then have the DOJ come after you and expedite your extradition to Russia. These aren't the times to do that.'

During the fallout from the Russian doping scandal, two former senior RUSADA figures died suddenly. Former executive director Nikita Kamaev died in February, 2016, of a reported heart attack. He'd contacted a journalist shortly before his death, offering to speak out about Russian doping. 'This was death by "invisible inoculation", a familiar FSB practice,' Dr Rodchenkov wrote in *The Rodchenkov Affair*. 'They wanted to bury him as soon as possible.' Vyacheslav Sinev, the agency's general director between 2008 and 2010, also died of unknown causes in the same month.

Back in America, the couple's time has been bookended by Donald Trump's presidency. 'Trump wins the 2017 election and turns the immigration process upside down overnight. Historically, there'd be a digital queue, so if you're 600th in line, your case will be looked at once the 599th case has been seen. That changed immediately to a "last in, first out" system, so as more papers and cases come in, they're seen first while the people who've been waiting for a long time disappear further into the bottom of the filing cabinet. Typically, more applications come in each day than are processed, so the backlog keeps growing.' Now, Harris says, is not the time to shout about their case from the rooftops.

Despite the ever-present threat to their lives, the Stepanovs look to live as normal a life as possible. That means unlike Dr Rodchenkov, they didn't accept the offer of falling under the witness protection programme.

'When they came to the US, they were conscious that they didn't want to live in the shadows,' says Harris. 'They didn't want to change their identities. As far as they possibly could, given the enormity of the situation, they wanted to live a normal life.

'They have modest expectations of quality of life and what they want from it. If you forget about immigration issues, they are content with their place in their community. They have a network of folks that they socialise with; they have a running and training regime that they're happy with; and they hang out as a family over the weekends and do fun things that they enjoy.'

They also work. Harris's first interaction with them came in 2016 when they met on a drive to Boulder for an anti-doping symposium. 'We decided there must be a way of utilising them in the university system, so we proposed a programme of educational talks where they could share their experiences with higher education institutions across Colorado. We won a grant and so spent a lot of time driving together around a very large state.'

Now, says Harris, Yuliya has a day job and is currently working with WADA on various projects as a remote contractor. In the past, Vitaly's also worked at USADA, and the IOC has provided some financial support, but everything is piecemeal. There is little sign that 16 years after Vitaly first contacted WADA that things will change.

'Some cases are just too big for sports agencies. They're not equipped to run through all of the implications. Vitaly would go so far to say they wish they'd never met him because he's brought them a problem that they don't want to deal with. It's a cynical view but you could view the whole system as a façade. That when it comes to it, how much do you want to catch the dopers? It's a massive inconvenience.

'Okay, that's arguably too far and I don't feel that's where WADA is at, but at the same time, those ideas can co-exist. It's vital for the anti-doping system and its integrity that people like the Stepanovs blow the whistle and expose systemic schemes of this type. But at the same time, it's a huge pain in the ass for the authorities, especially when it's a state-sponsored programme, not just a coaching squad or an athlete.'

So, what can be done? Harris suggests a significantly clearer framework of what lies ahead for the whistleblowing athlete. 'As a result of their experience working with the Stepanovs, WADA gave out various grants including to Dr Kelsey Erickson at Leeds Beckett University, who focused on developing a whistleblowing policy. The policy is now more comprehensive, especially about understanding a whistleblower's emotional needs and thought processes, but WADA's policy still doesn't deal with the big issues, like what do you do when you're faced with a family who must move country? Who's working with the different state agencies and the government to make sure that these people are taken care of?'

Before leaving Leeds for the United States in 2019 to take up a new role at USA Cycling, Dr Erickson and her team undertook research that lifted the lid on the serious dilemma whistleblowers wrestle with: a battle between the morality of loyalty and morality of principle.[26] 'This dilemma has been referred to as the

---

26 https://www.tandfonline.com/doi/full/10.1016/j.smr.2018.12.001

fairness–loyalty trade-off,' read the paper. 'They are considered basic moral values but they conflict at times, including in potential whistleblowing situations.'

Before their 2018 work, there was limited research in this area but, of note, the authors did reference a 2014 study that highlighted differences between how athletes from individual and team sports approached whistleblowing, with 'rugby players demonstrating more hesitation [to blow the whistle] in comparison to their track-and-field counterparts' due to a reluctance to report their teammates' actions.[27]

'Doping whistleblowers must choose between reporting the doping athlete to protect the rights of athletes at large to compete in doping-free sport or staying quiet to protect the doping athlete's athletic career, reputation and well-being, given the social consequences associated with being labelled a "doper". Importantly, someone gets hurt regardless of the final choice. Ensuing from the true moral dilemma, individuals were hesitant to blow the whistle on doping despite being personally opposed to engaging with doping substances and/or methods.'

To highlight the emotion and complexity of whistleblowing, Erickson interviewed three whistleblowers before knitting together their answers in a composite creative non-fiction story. It's a fascinating read into the whistleblowing experience . . .

Step One: 'It's not black and white.'

'A lot of things that make sense from the outside are completely jumbled and messy when you're in it yourself. You don't see it as "wrong" straight away. You just think this is how things are done.'

---

27 https://pubmed.ncbi.nlm.nih.gov/24673128/

At this step, the interviewees reveal whistleblowing rarely begins with a dramatic revelation like spotting a teammate injecting their buttocks with testosterone or an athlete undergoing a blood transfusion. Instead, it starts with a creeping sense that something isn't quite right. The three athletes describe noticing small, unsettling details like unusual medical routines, whispered conversations and sharp improvements in performance that defy logic. At first, these signs are easy to rationalise. In high-performance sport, unusual behaviour is often normalised as 'doing what it takes', especially in the sporting world that, like the western world in general, is increasingly medicalised.

This step is further defined by ambiguity and denial. Athletes are deeply embedded in sporting systems that are built on trust, loyalty and shared sacrifice. Questioning those systems can feel like questioning teammates, coaches or even oneself. Many only fully recognise the wrongdoing in hindsight – often months or years later – when distance from the incident or situation affords clarity. By then, the realisation can be shocking – not just that doping was happening, but that it was happening around them, unchecked.

Step Two: 'People need to know.'

'You sit there for hours thinking, "Is it worth it? I've put this much of my life into this already." You know what the right thing is, but you also know what it could cost you.'

Once the 'illegal act' is acknowledged, the athlete faces one of the hardest decisions of their lives: whether to report it. This is the point at which their moral conviction comes face-to-face with personal risk. Speaking out threatens careers built over decades, financial security, friendships and identity. Athletes fear retaliation, being ostracised or, worse, being assumed guilty by association.

This stage is often prolonged and emotionally draining. Many whistleblowers hesitate, test the waters anonymously or approach multiple organisations before committing. The process is rarely empowering. Instead, it's marked by anxiety, uncertainty and a sense of isolation, especially when responses from authorities are cumbersome. For some, like Dr Rodchenkov, the decision to speak up only comes when silence feels more damaging than disclosure.

Step Three: 'It has totally changed my life.'

'The whole process isn't a case of report it and stop. It's a case of report it, and that affects my life until now. It doesn't end when you speak. That's when it really starts.'

Reporting doping is far from the finish line. It is the beginning of a new life.

Whistleblowers frequently describe lasting personal and professional fallout. Take Emma O'Reilly, one of the soigneurs at Lance Armstrong's US Postal team. She came forward in 2004 to reveal that she knew of his doping, even helping the Texan to cover up needle marks on his arms as well as disposing of syringes. Armstrong branded her 'an alcoholic' and 'a whore' before later apologising. Careers stall or, like O'Reilly's, end. Public narratives simplify complex situations, leaving whistleblowers exposed to criticism, abuse or disbelief.

There is no relief, with many experiencing prolonged stress and vigilance. Even when investigations succeed, recognition is rare and closure elusive. Yet alongside the cost, some describe a sense of moral clarity – a release from carrying a secret that conflicted with their values. This final stage underscores the paper's central message: whistleblowing isn't necessarily a moment of courage, but a long-term condition, one that demands far greater protection and support than sport has traditionally offered.

Ultimately, the paper concludes, choosing to report doping is an active step towards ensuring clean sport and benefits the sporting community as a whole. But that comes at a cost to the doper (you might say valid) and the whistleblower, who might endure reputational damage and emotional distress.

This isn't helped by a sport's culture, with further research by Dr Erickson revealing that of more than 400 British and US elite athletes and coaches surveyed, fewer than half felt their sport actively encouraged them to report doping. The study also discovered that nearly a quarter of the athletes surveyed feared they would be labelled as a 'snitch' if they expressed their suspicions, while fewer than a quarter of coaches (23 per cent) and athletes (19 per cent) surveyed felt that the public reaction to those who've reported doping in sport would encourage them to do the same.

Can sports do more? We examine the anti-doping success, or not, of individual sports in chapter nine. But, says WADA's Günter Younger, it's not just those participating in sport that can do more, but those reporting on it, too.

In October, 2025, Germany television company ARD's doping editorial team announced that WADA 'is hunting whistleblowers'. Based on internal WADA documents seen by ARD, 'The official inquiry by the intelligence and investigations department is being conducted with the consent of president Witold Bańka and director Olivier Niggli. It's called "Operation Puncture".'

The aim, the news report continued, is to expose possible

whistleblowers who passed on information about suspected doping cases among 23 Chinese swimmers. The account released by the state broadcaster explained that WADA had requested various anti-doping organisations to provide data that could help identify possible leakers in relation to the Chinese file.

'All organisations have an obligation to protect whistleblowers,' Minky Worden, director of global initiatives at Human Rights Watch, responded. 'This is especially important where China is concerned because China is known to retaliate against whistleblowers.'

That was followed up by Jens Sejer-Andersen, founder of the sports policy watchdog organisation Play the Game: 'There is an obvious contradiction between having a whole department to support and encourage whistleblowers, on the one hand, and on the other starting to chase whistleblowers that WADA regards as challenging their interests.'

For an organisation whose credibility was hit hard by the Chinese 'contamination' case, pursuing those who leaked what many thought a cover-up wasn't a great look.

'No, we are not chasing whistleblowers,' says Günter Younger. 'We were asked by ExCo [WADA's 16-member Executive Committee] . . . We want to understand how the leak took place because one of the concerns of the Athlete Council [a committee of 20 members elected by athletes that "represents the voice of athletes"] was: How can we be sure this will not happen again? We want to find out the motivation behind the leak.

'Human rights is mentioned [in the news story], but what about the human rights of minors, especially those like in the China case that were proved innocent? How traumatic it is for them, their friends and their family when they are named by the media.'

Younger's referring to swimmers who were under the age of 18 at the time of the 2021 scandal. 'To publish the names of the minors in the media is, for me, unacceptable. But that was Mr [Hajo] Seppelt's decision.'

Younger then directs attention to Operation Refuge, a WADA examination of doping among minors (those who are under the age of 18). Between 1st January, 2012, and 1st September, 2023, there had been 1,518 adverse analytical findings reported against 1,416 minors, with diuretics, stimulants and anabolic steroids being the most detected substances. In 2024, a 14-year-old Russian swimmer became the youngest ever athlete to be banned by RUSADA after testing positive for a derivative of the anabolic steroid Dianabol. There are currently 17 minors in Russia suspended by RUSADA. Previously, there have been several child doping cases in swimming, including a 13-year-old in Germany.

'You should not name minors,' Younger says. 'And we are not in the business of chasing whistleblowers.'

Nor should they. Whoever they are. As whistleblowers can be anyone. You have athletes like cyclist Toby Atkins, who revealed that his manager offered him PEDs when competing for an Italian under-23 cycling team, and the retired French rugby player Laurent Bénézech, who blew the whistle on the doping culture in French rugby in the 1990s. But then there are scientists, coaches and, says USADA's intelligence and investigations director Dan Burke, 'angry parents who often tip off USADA about cheating high-school athletes. We don't really have jurisdiction over them.'

Whistleblowing remains one of the most effective yet most costly tools in anti-doping. While agencies increasingly rely on confidential reporting to uncover systemic abuse, the personal consequences for those who speak out can be severe and long-lasting, ranging from professional isolation to exile and insecurity. The cases of Renée Anne Shirley and the Stepanovs show that that the system designed to protect these principled people struggles when their disclosures become politically inconvenient or structurally complex. Clean sport depends on their courage, but sustaining that courage requires clearer protections, realistic expectations and a willingness by institutions to stand by those who take the risk of telling the truth.

WHERE CONTAMINATION COLLIDES WITH STRICT LIABILITY

'The family feud goes on,' announced the MC. Camera shutters fire off, the athletes trade insults, the crowd are edgy. So far, so normal for the obligatory face-off. This is boxing theatre. Stoking the competitive fires before a punch is thrown. Then, from his inside pocket, Chris Eubank Jr plucks an egg and cracks it across his opponent Conor Benn's face. An already volatile Benn, with his father Nigel beside him, loses control and both boxers are held back by security guards. Stare-downs build tension. Slap-downs fill the front pages. They also send ticket sales through the roof. Eubank Jr knew that. But substance lay behind the sensational.

This was February, 2025, over two years since their original fight was called off after Benn tested positive for clomifene. Clomifene is a fertility drug but can be used by men to boost testosterone levels. It led to a two-year battle with doping authorities before Benn's suspension was lifted after the World

Boxing Council accepted the 'reasonable explanation for the failed test' – elevated egg consumption of 'around 35 to 40 eggs' that week. Eubank wasn't convinced.

'Did I cross the line? During this whole process I think many lines have been crossed. So me throwing an egg at somebody who absurdly claims that was the reason why he failed two drug tests, I think that's light. I think he deserved the embarrassment of what happened. If I had an opportunity to do it again, I would.'

'There's no holes in the truth,' Conor Benn replied. 'There's nothing to hide.' Benn insisted that strict liability, when an athlete is punished regardless of intent, should not have applied in his case.

'How can that be strict liability if that's in our food?' said Benn. 'You can't stop that.'

This strict liability is the most contentious issue in the anti-doping framework. In Benn's case, he argued it was down to consumption. But the majority of cases that, in the public eye at least, push the boundaries of plausibility are down to contamination with (according to the Anti-Doping Database) clenbuterol, one of the most significant contaminants, involved in nearly 500 anti-doping violations. To understand why, we head to the Wild West.

Bradley Johnson was born and raised in Lubbock, Texas. It's on the fringe of the Permian Basin, the highest-producing oil field in the US. It's estimated that 30 billion barrels of oil have been extracted since the 1920s. Above the black gold, roaming the arid land are cattle. In Lubbock you either end up in oil or agriculture. Dr Brad Johnson, who grew up on a farm, chose the latter.

Johnson holds numerous titles at Texas Tech University, but the top line is that he's an expert on meat science and muscle biology. For over ten years he's been USADA's go-to expert when it comes to cases where an athlete's defence has centred on meat contamination.

'Yes, I know a lot about clenbuterol,' he says. 'I recall when Alberto Contador was stripped of his Tour de France title after testing positive in 2010, though that was before I got involved with USADA. If I remember rightly, that was around the time of the incident involving the young footballers from Mexico . . .'

More accurately, the 2011 FIFA U-17 World Cup held in Mexico. The home country won for the second time, but that proved a footnote to the revelation that more than half of the players subject to doping controls – over 100 from 19 of the 24 squads involved – tested positive for clenbuterol due to contaminated meat.

FIFA ordered meat samples to be collected from team hotels, and 30 per cent of these showed the presence of clenbuterol. The Mexican government subsequently made a number of arrests and closed down several slaughterhouses.

'That's because although clenbuterol increases the yield, it will never be approved for use in meat animal production because the residues are high enough to cause human health issues,' says Johnson. 'But there's a huge black market in many Latin American and South-East Asian countries.'

Contador's contamination defence didn't hold up partly because though the Spanish authorities have seized clenbuterol when investigating illegal practices in farming, the problem is nowhere near as prevalent as it is in countries like China or Mexico.

'Much of my work involves education,' says Johnson. 'Recently, a bunch of US athletes competed in Indonesia. I know first-hand that Indonesia has used illegal compounds to accelerate meat animal production, so we contacted the hotel the players were staying at, ensured they checked the provenance of their meat and told the players to eat in the hotel only.

'Likewise, I've worked with teams from the NFL [National Football League] and MLB [Major League Baseball]. Some athletes are understandably risk-averse when it comes to food and contamination, so pay due diligence. But every athlete must be on their guard. Which can be hard because there is a ravenous desire for meat from many elite competitors because they demand protein.'

So prevalent were the cases of athletes returning positives for clenbuterol, including a string of Mexican boxers including Canelo Álvarez, Luis Nery, Francisco Vargas, Rey Vargas and Julio Cesar Martínez, that in 2021 WADA amended the Code: 'For cases of clenbuterol, ractopamine, zilpaterol or zeranol or its metabolites at a concentration at or below 5ng/mL, WADA-accredited laboratories shall report the result as an "Atypical Finding" and the Results Management Authority shall conduct an investigation to determine whether that finding may be due to ingestion of contaminated meat.'

WADA's often seen as dogmatic and blinkered, but in cases like this, you could argue anti-doping authorities are caught between a rock and a hard place. How do they know that an athlete doesn't specifically partake in training camps in countries where contaminated meat is a real issue, using its known illegal farming practices as a convenient excuse?

'I've often thought about that,' says Johnson. 'It's the same with countries like the Dominican Republic and Colombia, who allow the use of the steroids boldenone and nandrolone in meat animal production. I was involved in a tennis case where European players were training in Colombia and they tested positive. They were let off. But did they simply go there to take boldenone?'

If athletes head to contaminated climes for a ready-made excuse, it could be worth their while. 'We've undertaken many studies on clenbuterol in rodents and other animals and measured significant muscle growth,' says Morten Hostrup, associate professor of physiology at the University of Copenhagen. 'Then at the end of 2025, we published one of the few studies into its impact on humans. The results were significant.'[28]

That is an understatement, especially seen through the lens of sports like boxing where raw power counts, for after just two weeks' use of clenbuterol, the participants piled on an average 1kg of muscle mass.

How? Clenbuterol is similar to adrenaline, says Hostrup, in that it stimulates a fight-or-flight response. 'But unlike adrenaline, which has a half-life of a couple minutes, clenbuterol's is around 30 hours.' In evolutionary terms, it means when that lion comes chasing, your nervous system is so aroused, your heart rate so pumped that you can just keep running and running hard. 'Your muscles react quicker and your reaction times improve.'

Whether that's enough to escape the savannah with your life intact remains to be seen. But if you do, you'll be that bit leaner thanks to clenbuterol clinging on to receptors in skeletal muscle. That not only stimulates protein synthesis for muscle gain but also reduces protein breakdown for muscle preservation. It's a double win. Or a big loss in WADA's eyes, as this powerful performance enhancer is also associated with elevated cardiac risk.

To deliver its muscular benefits, athletes take it in pill form. A clenbuterol inhaler works solely on opening up the lungs. 'Bodybuilders and good studies out of California give us an idea about their regimes,' says Hostrup. 'It's usually for around eight

---

28 https://pubmed.ncbi.nlm.nih.gov/40946331/

to ten weeks but in cycles of maybe two weeks where they're gradually increasing the dose. In our study, we had our athletes take 80 microgrammes [μg] a day for two weeks. That's what bodybuilders might start on, but they'd slowly raise that to 200μg daily for two weeks. They'd then stop or reduce it, before cranking it up again. This rise is needed because your body readily tolerates these lower levels, meaning reduced gains.'

But nail the protocol and bodybuilders and power athletes will fly. Unlike endurance athletes. Hostrup says his research suggests that though clenbuterol also boosts fat burning, it actually impairs performance of marathon runners, triathletes and road cyclists because it 'suppresses mitochondrial function' in the muscle. These are the cells' energy powerhouses that fuel aerobic activities. 'It's one reason why the current regulations would have accepted Contador's explanation. He wouldn't have been suspended.'

Boosting the efficiency and yield of meat production is satiating the world's increasing demand for high-protein food. But not without controversy. 'Growth promoters are political,' says Johnson. 'In the US, we can't export the majority of our meat to the European Union or UK because around 90 per cent of US cattle receive a steroid hormone implant that contains trenbolone. On our farm growing up, we used anabolic steroids as growth promotors. That's why it became my academic interest.' And, latterly, his sporting interest.

'Around ten of the 25 or so cases I've been involved in have involved trenbolone. I remember my first case was a female weight-lifter. She had elevated trenbolone levels in her urine and claimed it was from beef she'd consumed the day before.' Trenbolone is a 'good' choice for female athletes compared to a steroid like testosterone as it delivers significant muscle growth without the masculine side effects. 'But when I did the maths based on the pharmacokinetics of trenbolone deriving from food, she'd had to have consumed nearly 20 kilogrammes of ground beef the day before. Even for an athlete I'd say that is impossible.'

Johnson's calculations are helped by the predicted norms set out by JECFA, the rather creative acronym for the Joint FAO/WHO Expert Committee on Food Additives. The FAO is the Food and Agricultural Organisation based in Rome, while WHO is the World Health Organization out of Geneva.

'JECFA works out the maximum residue levels of a compound like trenbolone once the animal's been treated. Those figures are pivotal in anti-doping cases. We can work out that if an athlete consumes meat, they should have this amount of trenbolone in their urine.'

Several assumptions are made that impact these residue figures, including point of administration. 'The trenbolone is mixed into a compressed pellet and injected into the back of the cattle's ear. The steroid then dissolves into the bloodstream. Traces of the trenbolone are consistent throughout the cattle, though might vary slightly depending on the cut of meat due to the number of receptors for the substance to bind to. But there's not a huge difference across the carcass. After around 200 days, the animals are "harvested", whereby the ears are removed immediately to prevent potential contamination.

'JECFA sets the maximum residue level as two parts per billion. Or two microgrammes per kilogramme of muscle. In reality, it can be as low as one part per trillion, which won't really be detectable.'

In short, if the farmer follows standard trenbolone practice and an athlete registers an anti-doping violation, the contaminated meat excuse is flimsy. 'That's why a couple of cases I've had recently, the defence has focused on misplaced pellets – that instead of injecting the cattle's ear, the implant must have entered the muscles from which rib-eye and loin steaks are cut.

'It's similar with oxtail. Recently, we've had an inordinately high number of trenbolone cases, including US sprinter Erriyon Knighton. Are ranchers putting the implants in the tail? That's been an athlete's defence. It's doubtful. But the area of residue levels across different cuts of meat does demand further research.'

The situation's further complicated by processing. 'A hamburger made in the United States and sold through the likes of Costco and Walmart could comprise meat from ten different animals, some of them from outside the US,' says Johnson. 'I've had cases where the athlete's said they'd consumed two or three hamburger patties the day before and that's where the contamination must have come from. It does make finding the source of that product, the exact ingredients, much more difficult. It's the same with other, what I call, "mixed-in meats" like salamis, sausages . . .'

Picking apart the provenance of a sausage would be near impossible. It's hard enough with any perishable item, says Johnson. 'An athlete is responsible for what they put in their body, so when it comes to food, you'd have to provide evidence of where and what you ate in the form of receipts or restaurant bills in the days leading up to the test. But are those receipts legitimate? We've certainly had cases where they haven't been.

'But the bigger problem is that once the meat's gone, that lot number is gone. We can only presume what's left in the cooler at the restaurant was similar to what the athlete consumed. But it might not be?'

After Erriyon Knighton notified USADA of the suspected source of his positive test, investigators went to the bakery and collected a sample of the oxtail he'd eaten. Analysis of that sample returned a positive finding for trenbolone metabolites. USADA also secured the bakery's purchase receipt for the meat, with the manager confirming the shipment had arrived before Knighton's adverse test in April, 2024.

The receipt and packaging showed the oxtail originated from the SuKarne meat processing facility in Nicaragua. An independent arbitrator concluded that Knighton had established the source of the substance and that he bore no fault or negligence. He was free to race, finishing fourth in the 200m at the Paris Olympics. Come September, 2025, CAS upheld appeals from both World Athletics and WADA, and handed him a four-year ban.

'It's much easier to trace contaminated supplements,' says Johnson. According to a 2025 survey by Sport Integrity Australia, one in three sport supplements – around 35 per cent of 200 – bought online contained at least one substance prohibited by WADA that would have resulted in a suspension. It's not a recent issue, with 2004 research by German doctor Hans Geyer discovering that 14.8 per cent of 634 supplements purchased were contaminated with hormones, stimulants and other prohibited substances.

'Contamination is a concern; in fact, the thought of it makes me sick,' says professional cyclist Rory Townsend. 'The other day I was looking at buying collagen supplements as I'm heading back to the gym [collagen supplements can potentially help muscle repair and rebuild]. I contacted one brand as I was interested in their grass-fed collagen; I asked them if they batch-tested their collagen. Occasionally, they said, but it felt too risky, so I left it.' Townsend says he's also raced in China and avoided all meat because of contamination worries.

Supplement contamination generally occurs for two reasons:

accidental or intentional. Accidental contamination often arises when manufacturing equipment isn't cleaned to the required standards, leaving residues from previous products. 'We've also seen examples where manufacturers have "exploited" their supplements with prohibited substances,' says Professor Olivier Rabin, senior director of science and medicine at WADA. 'It makes them more effective, so more popular.'

In November, 2010, South African rugby players Chiliboy Ralepelle and Bjorn Basson tested positive for the banned stimulant methylhexaneamine after they beat Ireland. After the positives were reported, both the team's head coach and its doctor stopped the team from taking any further supplements because of concerns that the entire team might have taken a contaminated supplement

'We've stopped all supplements until we get to the bottom of this, both our own supplements as well as those that players take individually,' said Dr Craig Roberts, now of Chelsea FC. 'But it's the proverbial minefield. We do send all supplements to independent labs to be tested, but even then there are areas that are not entirely accurate.'

After testing, it emerged that the two players had taken the supplement 'Anabolic Nitro Nitric Oxide Extreme Energy Surge', which had been contaminated with methylhexanamine. The supplement had been reportedly provided by the team's strength and conditioning coach trainer, Neels Liebel. The players were consequently found to have been at 'no fault' and avoided suspension.

In 2022, two-time tennis Grand Slam winner Simona Halep received a four-year ban after testing positive for the blood-booster Roxadustat, reduced to nine months by the Court of Arbitration for Sport after accepting that contaminated collagen was the likely source. And then there's the curious case of three-time Olympic champion LaShawn Merritt, who sought forgiveness for his 'foolish, immature and egotistical mistake' when buying a male-enhancement supplement that was 'contaminated' with a prohibited substance. His 21-month sanction was cut to 12 months, with USA Track & Field's chief executive Doug Logan's words ringing in his ears: 'Personally, I am disgusted by the whole episode.'

Rabin also raises concerns over zilpaterol, which has become a recognised concern in horse racing. It's used legally in cattle feed in some countries, but it's strictly prohibited in racing. The most common risk is feed-chain contamination, where equine feed or raw ingredients are inadvertently tainted during manufacture, transport or storage alongside cattle products.

Trainer Aidan O'Brien had to withdraw his four runners from the £2.5-million 2020 Prix de l'Arc de Triomphe after he elected to have them tested on the eve of the race when it became apparent that he had a contaminated batch of feed. The horses returned positive tests for zilpaterol. O'Brien settled his case against Glanbia Foods Ireland at the high court in 2023.

'We also see more of these cases because the level of detection in WADA labs has improved massively,' says Rabin. 'We've gained about a factor close to 1,000 over the past 20 years. There's also the fact that we're exposed to an increasing amount of chemicals in the air, which can cause issues.'

This 'air contamination' strikes to the heart of the 2021 Chinese swimming case involving 23 athletes that we dig into in the next chapter. But it's one reason why amendments to WADA regulations from 2027 will serve reduced suspensions in contamination cases involving 'environmental contamination'.

WADA recommends athletes take supplements that are third-party tested. These products will feature the testing company's respective logos, and include NSF Certified for Sport, Informed Choice and Informed Sport.

Athletes take supplements to perform. They take medication to partake. As we've seen, that often requires a therapeutic usage exemption (TUE) certificate to avoid a positive test. But that doesn't cover legitimate medicine containing small amounts of a prohibited substance that's not declared on the label.

In August, 2025, British former pro cyclist Lizzy Banks, whose *palmarès* includes two stage victories of the Giro d'Italia Women, made an impassioned plea for how contamination cases are managed after losing a two-year battle to clear her name. In July, 2023, Banks tested positive for traces of the diuretic chlortalidone. On 26th April, 2024, UK Anti-Doping (UKAD) cleared Banks, accepting that the contamination likely stemmed from a tablet she took for asthma. On 4th June, 2024, WADA appealed her case to the Court of Arbitration for Sport, ruling that she had failed to prove the source of the contamination and so banned her for two years.

'This case demonstrates the high bar set by the application of the "strict liability" principle,' UKAD pronounced, 'and the challenges in identifying and establishing unintentional violations.'

The 'will they, won't they?' sanction left Banks in turmoil. I reached out to the British athlete but received no response. Thankfully, Banks, normally so communicative, chronicled the case on her website, lizzybanks.co.uk, where she said the ordeal left her fighting suicidal thoughts.

'I desperately want and need to move on from this now, to put this torrid chapter to bed, forever. To try to rebuild my health and career, to be able to work again and to rediscover the person I used to be before this process sucked the life and happiness from me,' Banks wrote.

Banks detailed how, after the initial shock of notification, she became engulfed by fear, terrified that every medication, food item and even water might contain a banned substance. She stopped taking medications necessary for her health, fluctuated between panic and despair, and endured severe deterioration in her mental health. The emotional and financial strain was significant, as Banks and her husband drained life savings (over £40,000 by their reckoning) on legal and scientific investigations, all while she was barred from competition and income.

On her website, Banks castigates WADA's processes – that they appealed without first providing her with the basis for their challenge, leaving her and UKAD uncertain of the case's found-ation. CAS then promptly ruled against the British athlete, asserting that she'd failed to prove the specific source of chlortalidone, despite overwhelming scientific and contextual evidence pointing to contamination.

'I'm not sure yet whether I regret having carried on the fight,' she wrote. 'I am so empty right now that I barely know what I feel anymore. But this is what they do to people like me. They crush us. They expect that we will just walk away and they will never have any consequences. But there must be consequences.'

Banks suggested UKAD, British Cycling and the French, German and US anti-doping agencies agreed with her and called for influential bodies and authorities to help make the change happen.

'I implore these bodies to stand with me that rules surrounding contamination must change. The rules and the system are simply not good enough and as it stands are not fit for purpose. Unless we fight for it, nothing will ever change. I have done my bit and now it is your turn.'

Banks' changes fell into four categories. The first was easing the burden of proof, that athletes shouldn't be required to provide the exact source of contamination when strong scientific evidence shows the substance level is incompatible with intentional use. Banks believes the law should allow panels to conclude contamination on the balance of probabilities, rather than demanding an almost impossible 'smoking gun'.

Secondly, and one of her strongest criticisms, was WADA's ability to appeal a full exoneration long after a national anti-doping body has cleared an athlete. She suggests tighter limits on WADA's appeal window; a requirement that WADA clearly sets out its legal basis before launching an appeal; and greater deference to well-reasoned national decisions, especially where scientific experts are aligned.

Thirdly, Banks highlights what she sees as inconsistencies and legal errors in CAS reasoning, particularly where WADA submissions are treated as de facto law. She suggests clearer precedent rules; greater transparency in how panels interpret the WADA Code; and clearer explanation when departing from earlier CAS decisions.

Finally, that the human rights and welfare of an athlete is given more consideration. She sees the current system as creating prolonged uncertainty and psychological harm.

Ross Wenzel is WADA's General Counsel. He's based out of the Agency's European office in Lausanne, Switzerland, and has overarching responsibility for WADA's legal affairs. 'The Lizzy Banks case was one that we didn't defend with particular enthusiasm but it related to an extremely important point of principle, which is based on definitions on the Code,' he says. 'You cannot get a "no fault finding" if you don't show where the substance came from. In that case it was WADA's view that she hadn't shown where the chlortalidone came from. It's why we appealed against UKAD's decision. It was an important case for the system.'

Sports lawyer Jonathan Taylor was more bullish about 'protecting' the Code. 'Everyone says she's innocent, but she couldn't prove how it got in her system. Ultimately, the athlete is in charge of what goes into their body. If they can't, then how can I judge whether or not they're telling the truth? This case was vital for the integrity of the Code. Some would say she's the innocent sacrificed on the altar, of making sure it's effective for everybody.'

The case also highlighted a disconnect between WADA and national anti-doping authorities. Disparate voices in the united fight to keep sport clean.

'There are common issues with signatory decisions,' says Wenzel. 'One of the most common, like the Lizzy Banks case, is contamination and whether the source of the substance was established. Sometimes, the athlete's story isn't robustly questioned. That can be testing factually through interview and cross-examination, or from reaching out to third parties that could be relevant to the case, like from a scientific perspective.

'This rigour varies. At the Beijing Olympics, an athlete tested positive. They then contested that the substance must have been in a cream his teammate gave to him. Remarkably, the anti-doping authority accepted that explanation without even reaching out to the athlete who's said to have given the cream to them. When we did, the athlete said it was untrue. That was a simple case for a sophisticated authority. For anti-doping organisations that don't have the resources, you can imagine deficiencies in testing the athletes' explanations are significant.'

The case also focused the spotlight on sanction length. Under the WADA Code, sanctions for doping depend on the substance involved, the athlete's intent and their history. Four years is the standard ban for intentional use of non-specified substances such as anabolic steroids, EPO or blood doping. Two years applies where the athlete can show the violation was not intentional. Specified substances (often stimulants or contamination cases) can result in reduced bans, ranging from a warning to two years, depending on fault. Contamination or 'no significant fault' can cut sanctions further, sometimes to months or no ban at all. Multiple offences can lead to longer or lifetime bans. Sanctions often include disqualification of results, loss of medals and prize money.

There's flexibility in this framework, highlighted in the Anti-Doping Database, for cases where the defendant argued contamination. Between 2016 and 2025, there are ten categories of sanction, ranging from 49 athletes suspended for four years to five with no sanction. In between, you have 51 athletes banned for two years, four athletes for 18 months, 13 athletes for one year, 17 athletes for six months, four athletes for four months, seven for three months and six for two months, while five were admonished via a public warning.

'It's important to assess the fault properly,' says Wenzel. 'We see too many athletes that we say should be getting four years for steroid or non-specified substance getting two years based on irrelevant considerations, like it was their first doping violation.

Wenzel says cases were far simpler when he first worked in anti-doping 15 years ago. That complexity and length of cases has gone through the roof. 'Some of the cases run to thousands of pages.

These days, the business of athlete defence – and it really is a business now – is much more sophisticated. The arguments, factually and scientifically, are sophisticated. It was rare that defence teams filed more than one exchange of submissions before CAS. Now it's two or three. Multi-day hearings at CAS are common.'

We'll stop Wenzel there as to understand the business of athlete defence, you must understand the legal pathway from a positive sample to the final verdict. Here, we'll bring in Richard Harry, the chief executive officer of the not-for-profit that's one of the most important links in the anti-doping chain that you've probably never heard of: Sport Resolutions.

'We manage and administer processes that you read about on the back pages all of the time, but nobody knows what we do,' he says from their London offices. 'Is that a conscious thing not to blow our trumpet? Maybe. If you're in dispute and it's newsworthy, sensitive or involves big money, you must know that when you come here, your case will be dealt with sensitively and professionally. This is an athlete's safe place.'

Sport Resolutions is the intermediary, an independent body that provides arbitration, mediation and tribunal services, including safeguarding issues, selection and eligibility disputes, contractual disagreements and anti-doping cases.

They work with national sporting bodies such as Sport England, Scottish Rugby and UKAD, along with international federations, too. 'We were involved in the LIV Golf dispute with the PGA and ran the processes in the Jannik Sinner and Simona Halep cases in tennis. And plenty more.'

Harry and his team play a key role in settling anti-doping disputes by administering the National Anti-Doping Panel (NADP), appointing legally qualified arbitrators and experts to hear cases brought beneath the umbrella of the WADA Code, ensuring proceedings are fair, impartial and conducted according to proper legal standards. Sport Resolutions doesn't act as a prosecutor, regulator or advocate for any party – its role is to provide a neutral forum in which disputes can be heard and decided.

'Here's how it works,' says Harry. 'If UKAD receive an adverse finding, a metabolite of nandrolone or whatever, then they'll write to the athlete. If there's then a need for a hearing, they'll formally write to us and say, "We're formally charging Richard Harry, could you please start the process?" We then sit between UKAD and the athlete, picking who is on the independent panel.'

Each panel has three experts. 'The chair is always someone with a legal background. The WADA Code is pretty impenetrable, it's legal heavy, so you need a competent lawyer. We also look to recruit an expert in the particular area. If UKAD inform us that their biological passport is showing suspicious markers, we'll ensure we bring in an expert in pharmacology or chemistry. We also use psychiatrists, ex-doping control officers and ex-athletes who also have a legal background. We've pioneered case-specific doping panels.'

Once the decision's made – no fault, reduced sanction or full sanction – the athlete can appeal. Where that takes them depends on their sporting status. 'If it's a domestic athlete, that'll be back to us. If the athlete competes at international level, the appeal goes to CAS.'

One of Banks' complaints lay at the glacial progress of her case, the brakes slammed shut when WADA and CAS intervened. Harry, who set up the Welsh Rugby Players Association in 2003, is aware that the longer a case drags out, the deeper the strain on an athlete.

'We look to shift things along and, once the hearing is finished, we aim to give the parties involved a written decision in three weeks. That's something we stipulate to the expert panel in their terms and conditions. It might be they spend three weeks doing 16-hour days, but it's imperative we turn this around quickly and accurately. We are talking about someone's career. That differs to when a case elevates to CAS, where it can take up to three years to adjudicate, if not more.'

A swift turnaround also keeps costs down, helped by the panel members charging as little as 10 per cent of their standard rates due to it being not-for-profit. 'We also offer every single athlete or respondent access to free legal advice. We call it "equality of arms". It ensures there's a fair balance afforded to all the parties involved.'

That's been a key tenet of Sport Resolutions since its foundation in 1997 off the back of one of the gravest injustices in the history of sport. In 1994, British middle-distance runner Diane Modahl was unceremoniously sent home from the Commonwealth Games in Canada after failing a doping test, or so it was alleged.

'She contested that she'd never doped in her life and that there must have been a terrible mistake. But this was before WADA, the WADA Code and international standards, and the anti-doping system was like the Wild West, if you like

'She engaged lawyers, and it was unearthed that her positive urine sample came about from a random drugs test at a meeting in Portugal in June. The sample was then left next to a laboratory window in the summer sun. If you don't store urine properly, it degrades. Or gives a false positive. She had irrefutable proof of this and was cleared of any doping offence by an independent panel in 1995.'

Modahl then sought damages from the British Athletics Federation (BAF), who'd imposed the four-year sanction, alleging bias on the part of its disciplinary committee. A six-year legal battle ensued that bankrupted both Modahl and the BAF.

'The whole thing was a mess,' says Harry. It was against this backdrop that the Sports Dispute Resolution Panel, later renamed Sport Resolutions, was created by a representative umbrella group of sports in the UK. As for Modahl, she retired in 2002. In 2012, Modahl and her husband, Vicente, founded the Diane Modahl Sports Foundation, its mission to help 'young people from disadvantaged areas across the north-west of England, enabling them to make the most of themselves in sport, education and employability'. In 2018, Modahl was awarded an MBE for her services to sport and young people.

Modahl told Sport Resolutions that they spent £480,000 in proving her innocence, selling their house and losing earnings from performance and coaching. The 'equality of arms' is important, but arguably money – and plenty of it – is the more powerful currency when it comes to anti-doping defence.

'The Richard Gasquet case is a classic example,' says Harry. 'In 2009, the French tennis player tested positive for cocaine at a time when you could receive a ban of two years.' One of the more interesting changes to the 2027 WADA Code, in effect from 1st January, 2027, is that first-time violations for 'Substances of Abuse', such as cocaine and ecstasy, that are detected out of competition and unrelated to sports performance now carry a fixed period of ineligibility of just two months. A second violation results in a four-month ban, reduced to two months if the athlete enters an approved substance of abuse treatment programme. Back to Harry. 'Gasquet argued that the traces of cocaine must have stemmed from kissing a woman, identified as "Pamela" in the hearing, after withdrawing from a tournament in Miami and hitting a nightclub.

'Because he was successful and in a wealthy sport, he had the resources to not only find the girl who he'd kissed, but also invest in scientific experts who could show that if she'd just taken cocaine and kissed Gasquet it'd have resulted in the dose that showed up in his sample.'

The International Tennis Federation's tribunal panel said that Gasquet consumed no more than 'a grain of salt' of the drug and a long ban would be an injustice, imposing a retroactive ban of two months.

'I'm not saying he was spinning a yarn at all, but imagine if you were a player of nil means. Would you have been able to afford to fly back to Miami? To source and pay for that expert? Basically, if you have loads of cash, you can throw the kitchen sink at it.'

Or an uppercut. In February, 2015, Tyson Fury and his cousin Hughie both tested positive for the banned steroid nandrolone, blaming the positive on eating uncastrated wild boar, though they were not charged until June, 2016. In 2017, both fighters accepted a reduced and backdated two-year ban from UKAD after a lengthy legal battle.

It was reported that if the case had dragged on longer, UKAD would have had to declare bankruptcy. Chief executive Nicole Sapstead said at the time, 'Our legal decisions are not made for financial reasons.' But the agency spent nearly £600,000 on the Fury case. That was over 7 per cent of its annual £8-milllion budget.

In November, 2015, it was reported Tyson Fury earned nearly £6 million from fighting Wladimir Klitschko. The 2024 rematch against Oleksandr Usyk profited Fury another £60 million. The

British fighter and his family moved from Morecambe to the Isle of Man in December, 2025. The Isle of Man is known for its favourable tax system, with income taxed at 21 per cent compared to the UK's 40 per cent higher-rate band.

Money matters at each step of the legal framework, right up to sport's equivalent to the Supreme Court, the Court of Arbitration for Sport. This is the end game where decisions are rubber-stamped or overturned.

According to its 2024 accounts, CAS's budget equated to around £23 million, funded primarily by contributions from the parties involved in disputes (57.1 per cent), the International Olympic Committee (32 per cent), FIFA (10.4 per cent) and 0.5 per cent from other sources. From 2019 through to 2024, CAS disputes rose significantly, from 609 to 917. Of those, 322 were due to employment-related issues, 155 were contract-related, 47 transfer issues and 41 lay in anti-doping.

'Of course, money plays a role. Money plays a role in every dispute.' That's Professor Dr Ulrich Haas. Haas has been chairman of arbitration on more than 200 sports-related tribunals at CAS.

'At CAS, each dispute has three arbitrators,' he explains. 'The respective parties choose one each and then the chairperson is appointed by the institution itself.' The arbitrators are paid on an hourly basis dependent on the value of the case, from around £280 an hour for cases below £2.3 million up to £470 per hour for cases above £14 million.

He says that on average it takes between three and nine months for a verdict, with contamination cases often at the upper end due to their complexity. 'This is relatively fast for the legal system due to CAS being based in Switzerland, where the arbitral awards are only reviewed by the Swiss Federal Tribunal. Switzerland's also a good base because it's arbitration friendly. Some parts of the world are far more hostile.'

That timeline's a sprint compared to the marathon that was the Pechstein dispute. 'This was a rare case that reached the European Court of Human Rights. If ever a case reaches that level, it could go on for years.'

It did; in fact, the Claudia Pechstein case is the longest doping dispute in sport. In 2009, the German speed skater was banned for two years after abnormal blood values suggested blood manipulation, despite no positive drug test. Pechstein denied doping and argued the values were caused by a genetic blood condition.

She challenged the ban through CAS and later the German courts, raising issues about scientific evidence and the independence of sports arbitration. Although CAS upheld the sanction, years of litigation followed. In 2020, Pechstein reached a settlement with the International Skating Union, which acknowledged errors in handling the case.

But Pechstein continued fighting to restore her reputation as a clean athlete, scarred by how the accusations affected not only her career but her mental health. She experienced 'suicidal thoughts' during the ordeal.

Finally, in March, 2025, over 15 years since those abnormal blood values, Pechstein and the world governing body of speed skating officially confirmed the closure of the dispute, noting that both parties had decided to resolve the matter 'in a spirit of reconciliation' and with the intention of focusing on the future of the sport. In its statement, the federation acknowledged 'Pechstein's sporting achievements and expressed its willingness for the athlete to contribute to the development of future generations in speed skating'.

Episodes like Pechstein's and countless contamination cases leave an athlete vulnerable. Anti-doping laws must be strict to support clean sport, but strict liability and burden of proof are often more than an athlete inconvenience. They can be life-threatening, as in the case of Lizzy Banks, and aligned with the absurd.

In 2025, USADA chief Travis Tygart warned elite competitors: 'Watch out who you have an intimate relationship with.' He cited the 2020 case of American boxer Virginia Fuchs, cleared after showing that trace metabolites in her sample were consistent with sexual transmission from her partner. Tygart called on WADA to raise minimum reporting levels for substances that could be transmitted this way, like clostebol and ostarine, so athletes aren't unfairly penalised for tiny traces. 'I think it's a pretty ridiculous world we're expecting our athletes to live in . . . The onus is always on the athletes. We as anti-doping organisations need to take some of that responsibility back.'

WHEN ANTI-DOPING MEETS POLITICS

'The governance around anti-doping globally of late would appear to be found lacking in many ways. While the system isn't perfect, if the anti-programmes are used with real intent and purpose, they can be very powerful tools to deter doping. Unless global anti-doping programmes are adequately resourced, they will remain nothing more than lip-service agencies wielded around and abused by powerful sporting groups as a public-relations tool rather than truly deterring doping. Doping and image-enhancing drugs form a heady cocktail that the media and savvy marketing executives cannot resist when promoting or selling particular sports and their personalities.'

The words of Dr Robin Parisotto, stem scientist at the Canberra Hospital, Australia. Parisotto is a key figure in modern anti-doping, having played a pivotal role in the development of the athlete biological passport. He later became one of the expert witnesses relied upon in cases that ended up at the Court of Arbitration for

Sport. He says that fundamentally, sport and anti-doping hasn't changed in the past 25 years.

'It remains hard to believe one way or another that exceptional performances are "clean" as a result of freak physical prowess or artificially enhanced. The whole sporting hierarchy should be engaged to "own the problem". While it would be naïve to think that the problem will ever be resolved, all stakeholders should participate in managing the problem.

'One thing is clear: doping will always be part of sport. Every available resource should be made available and be undertaken in an environment free of personal, corporate, commercial and political interference. These are utopian and lofty ideals but what is the alternative? A drug free-for-all?'

Utopian and lofty indeed. In recent times, heavyweight battles haven't been confined to the boxing ring. The two biggest anti-doping agencies in sport, WADA and USADA, have publicly fought over a number of issues. But it's the Chinese swimming scandal that took top billing. The case centred on 23 swimmers testing positive for trimetazidine, a heart medication that's abused by athletes because it stimulates metabolism and increases blood flow. Both result in improved endurance.

Sun Yang, who in 2012 became the first Chinese male athlete to win a swimming Olympic gold medal, served a three-month doping suspension in 2014 for taking trimetazidine, while teenage Russian figure skater Kamila Valieva received a four-year ban after testing positive for the same substance at the 2022 Beijing Winter Olympics.

CHINADA (China Anti-Doping Agency) reported those 23 athletes returned 28 adverse analytical findings at a January, 2021, training camp that took place in a city 300km north of Beijing.

They included Olympic champions Zhang Yufei, Wang Shun and Yang Junxuan.

After investigating the incident, CHINADA attributed the positives to the kitchen of the hotel where the athletes were staying, stating that traces of the doping agent were found in the extractor fan, spice containers and drain, and so the athletes escaped sanction. WADA had the right to appeal CHINADA's decision but, after reviewing the case, accepted the explanation, meaning the swimmers were allowed to compete at the Covid-delayed 2020 Tokyo Olympics.

It was only three years later that the episode came to light. In April, 2024, German broadcaster ARD broke the story in a documentary, *Doping Top Secret – The China Files*, while *The New York Times* ran with it in print. 'That a doping pill ends up in whole or in part in a pot of soup, from there onto plates and then in the stomachs of athletes does indeed sound very contrived,' ARD filmmaker Hajo Seppelt said.

There were calls of a cover-up, with the chief executive of USADA, Travis Tygart, pulling no punches, 'It's crushing to see 23 Chinese swimmers had positive tests . . . It's even more devastating to learn that the World Anti-Doping Agency and CHINADA secretly, until now, swept those positives under the carpet by failing to fairly and evenly follow the global rules that apply to everyone else around the world.'

The man credited with bringing down Lance Armstrong called WADA's decision 'a devastating stab in the back of clean athletes and a deep betrayal of all the athletes who compete fairly and follow the rules'.

WADA defended its verdict, though appointed a prosecutor, Eric Cottier, to conduct an 'independent' report into the case. Cottier concluded WADA showed no bias towards China and the decision not to appeal the swimming cases was 'indisputably reasonable', though he flagged up that CHINADA deviated from recognised anti-doping practices by neither informing the swimmers they had tested positive nor provisionally suspending them.

Even then, WADA had to defend its choice of prosecutor. For 17 years through to 2022, Cottier was the attorney general of Vaud, the home canton of the International Olympic Committee where WADA has its European office in Lausanne. During the last 13 years that Cottier was chief public prosecutor, the Vaud police commander was Jacques Antenen, who also worked with WADA from 2018 until December, 2023, as supervising auditor of the doping watchdog's investigations team.

'I think it's highly problematic and it's totally unnecessary,' Swiss anti-corruption expert Mark Pieth said of WADA's selection process. 'It shows they don't have the awareness of possible conflicts of interest.'

In a global sport governance game of tit for tat, WADA filed a lawsuit against Tygart and USADA over the cover-up claims. Soon after, the US government withheld its annual payment (£2.8 million) to WADA – about 6 per cent of WADA's annual budget – after WADA refused to drop its libel case against Tygart, while stressing it'd also lost confidence in the agency after the China scandal. WADA dropped the lawsuit soon after, though 'remain convinced that lawsuit would be successful on its merits'.

Forwards to the present and the scars remain raw. 'What signal does this send out to the athletes?' Tygart tells me. 'There were 23 positive tests for a potent performance enhancer, where the default sanction is four years. In our opinion, WADA also had a credible witness who came to them nine months before the positives and told them that the Chinese sports system is systematically using three drugs including trimetazidine. What did they do? Nothing. It's incredible.

'At the end of the day, with the information that's publicly known, they should have got four-year suspensions. That decision affected 96 medals from the 2021 and 2024 Olympic Games.'

WADA insist the science trumps Tygart's scepticism, albeit there is ambivalence in the Cottier report, specifically the input of the scientific expert appointed by Cottier, Professor Xavier Declèves, who wrote: 'On the basis of these pharmacokinetic data alone, it is not possible to rule out intentional (or unintentional) intake of trimetazidine for doping or therapeutic purposes in the weeks leading up to the competition. Environmental contamination with low doses of trimetazidine during the hotel stay is also possible and can neither be ruled out nor affirmed with certainty on the basis of scientific data, but I see no scientific argument of a pharmacokinetic nature in favour of one hypothesis over another.'

'Professor [Olivier] Rabin's conclusions were more towards ruling out anything but contamination,' says Ross Wenzel, WADA's general counsel. The Cottier report highlighted that the therapeutic use of trimetazidine increased in China during Covid-19 due to its anti-inflammatory effects on the heart, suggesting that hotel employees could have contaminated kitchen utensils via trimetazidine, their 'hands were soiled' by urine, saliva or sweat, 'even though the presence of trimetazidine in these excreta has not been studied'.

Rabin suggests you can never be 100 per cent sure of contamination cases, but he felt the likelihood was 'super high'. 'Of course, it would have been a much easier contamination case if they'd found a kitchen worker crushing his pill of trimetazidine every morning before swallowing it. That would have left no doubt, but it didn't happen.'

As for WADA's president Witold Bańka fending off Tygart's bias claims, 'One of the biggest decisions by CAS [under Bańka's watch] was to sanction Sun Yang, the biggest star in China, for eight years [reduced to four years on appeal]. I received a huge number of death threats from his Chinese fans. There was no cover-up, there was no bias towards China, our people did a good job.' Bańka says accusations of lacking independence come with the territory; in the past, he's been called a CIA agent working for the US by Russia.

It was an unedifying washing of laundry in public, and critics argue it did nothing to instil athletes with confidence in a system designed to protect them. USADA are vocal that WADA isn't fit for purpose and hasn't been for a long time.

'Prior to joining USADA [in 2002], I worked for a law firm [Holme Roberts & Owen], who worked a lot with WADA in their early days,' says Tygart. 'My partner, Richard Young, was – is – the godfather of anti-doping and we worked on the first draft of the WADA Code [that came into being in 2003]. I have blood, sweat and tears invested in the WADA system.

'For years, it did a wonderful job. It brought the world together; it established uniform laws; it oversaw and harmonised laboratory accreditation. It was fit for purpose in a lot of ways. But there was a defining moment in 2016 where WADA recommended that Russia should be banned from the Rio Olympics. That was arguably its bravest moment, but it backfired. It upset the IOC.'

At the time, the International Olympic Committee didn't heed WADA's advice. Instead of a blanket ban, it'd be left to international sports' governing bodies to decide if Russian competitors were clean and allowed to take part. 'From that point on, I feel that WADA went from a strong and effective watchdog to the lapdog of sport and the IOC.'

Tygart reflects and corrects the timeline, that the foundations began to crumble in 2013 when WADA elected IOC vice president Craig Reedie as its new president, taking over from Australian John Fahey, who'd served since 2008 after formerly being Australia's minister of finance.

'I'll never forget my board asking what this would mean for us. I said, "Well, we're going to be an island because WADA will now be run by the IOC." We're not going to have the backing of WADA like we once did.

'Take the Lance Armstrong case. They were with us. They were instrumental in extracting blood-testing evidence from the UCI, and they helped pay the costs [over $1 million] when Floyd Landis appealed to CAS.

'I said to the board, "Look, they're not going to do that anymore." They're going to shun us. I said, "This is an existential moment for us to decide, are we going to go the same route as them to be service providers? Or are we going to continue to be the regulatory defender of the promise of clean sport?"'

Tygart suggests that 'sport' and its stakeholders didn't take too kindly to anti-doping agencies having the power to shape its past, present and future. In the case of cycling, that equated to erasing Armstrong's record seven Tour de France titles.

The major problem with WADA, says Tygart, is that there's an inherent conflict of interest, that of both policing and promoting sport. 'Professional sport clearly has an interest in putting bums on seats, and exposing its dark side isn't great for business. It's bad for the brand. But up to 50 per cent of WADA's Executive Committee have a direct or formal connection to the IOC. How independent can you be with that set-up?'

A snapshot of the IOC-containing WADA committee as of 1st January, 2026, is Jiři Kejval, IOC member and president of the Czech Republic National Olympic Committee; Dagmawit Girmay, IOC member and board member of the Ethiopian National Olympic Committee; and Nenad Lalović, IOC member and president of United World Wrestling. WADA's vice president, Yang Yang, is also a former IOC member.

'In 2000, the US Olympic and Paralympic Committee, who would also like to control its brand, did a courageous thing and said that anyone who's on their board cannot simultaneously sit on the USADA board. It's such an obvious but needed thing to have done. And for WADA to do. Imagine if the president of USA Cycling was sitting on our board during the Lance Armstrong case? Do you think he would have voted to expose Lance? Not a chance. Therein lies the conflict.'

Tygart says the USADA model is a more athletic-centric one with around 50 per cent of ex-athletes on the board. That includes track-and-field legend Edwin Moses, who won 400m hurdles gold at the 1976 and 1984 Olympics, winning 122 consecutive races between 1977 and 1987, and Kara Goucher, the Olympic middle-distance runner who helped to expose the culture of abuse, including doping, of the Nike Oregon Project. 'We do what's right by athletes,' says Tygart. 'We focus on the athletes.' But not all US athletes.

'I truly believe that collaboration is possible with a lot of people in the US, but it must be based on mutual respect,' says Bańka. 'Remove the emotion and look at the facts of what USADA is doing. In 2024, they collected around 7,500 samples from fewer than 3,000 athletes. That's not even in the top-six of national anti-doping agencies around the world.'

In the past, Travis Tygart testified before Congress and said that the NCAA [National Collegiate Athletic Association] is a joke. He said they had no whereabouts system and no out-of-competition testing, and this was a serious problem for the world, as it created "doping holidays" for foreigners going to the US to train.

'When you realise that almost 90 per cent of American athletes are not competing under the World Anti-Doping Code, it's not great. This is a gap that must be addressed. America deserves a strong anti-doping system,' says Banka.

This lack of unification is a perennial bugbear for WADA and the cause of much political friction. US professional sports, like the National Football League (NFL), National Basketball Association (NBA), Major League Baseball (MLB) and the National Hockey League (NHL), aren't signatories to the Code because they have Collective Bargaining Agreements (CBAs) with the unions that represent their athletes. Under such CBAs, the professional sports leagues and players' unions negotiate anti-doping testing protocols. From the US perspective, this creates a fairer system where the athlete has rights; from WADA's perspective, inconsistencies and leniency are pervasive.

The 2020 suspension of American footballer Luke Gifford was a case in point. Gifford, then playing for the Dallas Cowboys, received a two-game ban for returning a positive test for a stimulant or masking agent. This compared to a 25-game suspension under MLB rules and 20-game ban in the NHL.

'The US is arguably the greatest sporting nation with fantastic athletes and they deserve to have a strong, robust anti-doping system,' says Bańka. 'My wish, my dream, is that instead of politicisation, instead of attacking us, they have the will to strengthen the system and to make sure that NCAA signs up to the WADA Code.' Bańka concedes that the major US leagues are more problematic because they are private businesses.

Where both WADA and USADA suffer – in fact, every national anti-doping organisation suffers – are claims of impartiality from their respective funding models. WADA's 2025 budget nestled just under $57.5 million that, like previous years, was split roughly 50/50 between public authorities, like national governments, and the Olympic Movement, led by the IOC, with the IOC insisting on board members.

USADA, says Tygart, receives around a third of its annual budget of $23.5 million (in 2024) from the US Olympic and Paralympic Committee. Then again, who else would fund the system and look impartial? Private business? Would that be impartial? If testing, investigations or sanctions were funded by private companies with commercial interests in outcomes, credibility would immediately be questioned. Even more so than it is currently. But that's not to say private industry isn't involved in the future of anti-doping; in plugging the funding gaps that have left many experts exasperated.

Yannis Pitsiladis is one of the world's leading geneticists. Following 15 years at the University of Glasgow, where he collated the largest-known biobank from world-class athletes, in 2013 he was appointed professor of sport and exercise science at the University of Brighton. It's there that I first interviewed Pitsiladis, as I'd heard rumours that he was undertaking research that could transform anti-doping.

'I'm still working on it,' Pitsiladis says from his new home of Hong Kong, where he's now professor of the department of biology at the University of Hong Kong. He's a scientist with a politician's demeanour. 'Honestly, James, as well as this role, I'm on WADA's Health Medical Research Committee and am also a member of the IOC's Medical and Scientific Commission, but I think when it comes to the integrity of sport, we are at rock bottom. Don't listen to the hype about how wonderful we are at catching the cheats. Bullshit. We're low. Any lower and we'll be underground.'

To understand Pitsiladis' frustration, you must understand its context, namely the potentially game-changing test that's been his life's work. 'Essentially, we're looking at the genetic markers of doping, which falls under the umbrella of "omics". This is cutting-edge technology that's used in biomedical research in an effort to treat conditions like Alzheimer's.'

Omics comprises four key disciplines: genomics, which examines every cell in the body; metabolomics, every single metabolite that's produced in the body; proteomics, every single protein in the body; and transcriptomics. 'This is the switching on and off of genes,' says Pitsiladis. 'This is what we're mainly focusing on. It's basically a way of looking at messenger RNA [ribonucleic acid].'

Pitsiladis' test examines the genetic imprint of injecting a blood-boosting drug like EPO. While a drug is taking effect, thousands of messenger molecules transcribe instructions – in the case of EPO, an increase in red blood cells. Unlike blood and urine tests that measure the short-term markers of doping, Pitsiladis' 'breakthrough' delves much deeper, isolating the genetic fingerprint.

'One of the key benefits [over the current anti-doping testing tools] is that genetic testing extends the window of detection. If an athlete's micro-dosing EPO, markers might show up in their body for hours. If a doping control officer shows up after then, forget it. You won't find anything. With our omics test, we're comfortably looking at four weeks.'

Pitsiladis adds that it solves issues that plague the biological passport, such as differentiating between altitude and micro-dosing. 'It'll work like the biological passport, which in principle is excellent. The problem is, the markers it tests for are useless. This is a modernised version and will be much more effective.'

Pitsiladis says his work's focused on blood samples but, in the near future, he'll look to extend its reach to the more practical and more affordable dried blood spot testing. 'It could work for saliva samples, too.'

He's also seeking to explore 'multiomics', bringing together the four strands of omics for 'the most powerful diagnostic tool available to us in modern medicine and modern biomedical science'. To that end, Pitsiladis sends me his PowerPoint presentation on 'ZANES', which stands for 'Zeus Anti-Doping and Next-Generation Expression System'. ('Zeus' is tagged on as life-sized statues of the Greek god of the sky were erected at the Ancient Olympics to dissuade athletes from cheating.)

ZANES is a testing platform that 'is a paradigm shift from reactive detection to proactive biological intelligence'. It'd integrate omics, automation and artificial intelligence in an effort to clean up sport. 'It'd also act as a major deterrent to dope,' says Pitsiladis. 'You will be found out.'

Pitsiladis oozes enthusiasm and is optimistic that this year (2026), he'll receive around 170 million Hong Kong dollars (around £17 million) to pursue his multiomics dream, 'To come up with a test that'd kill all other tests.' His confidence is founded on the government already investing over 60 million Hong Kong dollars in helping Pitsiladis create what he feels is the most sophisticated genomics laboratory in the world.

It's a far cry from his days at the University of Brighton where

WADA repeatedly rejected funding applications. The last time we spoke at length, he received notification that his bid for $750,000 had been rejected. At the time, I contacted Professor Rabin, who suggested that research like that undertaken by Pitsiladis is 'very expensive'. And significantly more than current funding projects.

As a snapshot of WADA's '2025 cycle three approved projects', James Hopker and his team in England received the most at $201,633 for further work on the performance modelling we examined in chapter four. The least, $30,000, headed to China for work by Jianghai Lu and his team on metabolic profiling of steroids.

Politically, the research pot needs to be shared equitably – donating a significant chunk of the budget to several scientists from one continent could threaten future contributions from other parts of the world.

'WADA is hamstrung by [lack of] money,' says Pitsiladis. 'That limits the research, especially because they tend to fund studies by laboratories that have a link to WADA. It's not focusing on the best research, but research that fits the business model.

'Coming to Asia has been an eye-opener. Here, they want to know if this will be the best and what its impact will be. Then they might mention money. But they don't talk about grants of $50,000 here or $30,000 there. If you're not pitching for millions of dollars, they laugh at you. They say you're not serious about your work.'

Pitsiladis suggests it's not solely money that's impaired his anti-doping research, and that inertia in the WADA hierarchy stifles progress. 'Do the guys at the top really want to change the rules, to deck out the WADA-accredited labs with new equipment and have to retrain their scientists? I'm not saying they're corrupt – I don't think that at all – but I just feel they're archaic in their views.

'They're good people, but many of the people in the most important positions have been there since WADA was created in the early 2000s. That doesn't make sense when though some things have improved, for the most part they're not very successful. At the end of the day, I don't think WADA or IOC really care about innovative tests like omics, though I hear they've just signed an agreement with British company, Nanopore. That's surprising. We'll see if they're serious about genetic testing for anti-doping purposes. But what I know is that if it wasn't for the support of Hong Kong government, I might have given up.'

Even the money Pitsiladis is talking about is a drop in the ocean of professional sport.

Take the Premier League, whose last record TV deal was £6.7 billion for Sky and TNT to show up to 270 live games a season. The importance of England's top footballing league is hammered home by the inflated rewards for underperformance. The 2023/24 season saw Sheffield United finish bottom on 16 points, winning just three league games out of 38 and meaning they returned to the Championship after one season. It was a demoralising blow for the club with over 130 years of tradition but one somewhat softened by a parachute payment of £49 million.

Parachute payments are a series of solidarity payments the Premier League makes to relegated clubs, for up to three years, to help them adapt to reduced revenues back in the Championship, including significantly less TV money. Because Sheffield United failed to win promotion in the 2024/25 season, they received another payment of £40 million. If they aren't promoted in 2025/26, they'll enjoy a final parachute payment of around £20 million.

Those figures please the finance department, but it's expenditure that fires up supporters. Splashing the cash is a sign of intent. A sign that you want to challenge for big honours. It's why Liverpool spent over £400 million to defend their title in the 2025/26 season, with £220 million of that securing the services of Alexander Isak and Florian Wirtz. Manchester United's net spend between 2021 and 2026 came in at nearly £700 million. Chelsea's expenditure kissed £2 billion between 2014 and 2024. When it comes to tempting talent in search of success, the money flows. When it comes to policing integrity, things dry up.

'Investing in anti-doping isn't an asset on the balance sheet,' says sports lawyer Jonathan Taylor. 'Teams much prefer spending money on their commercial arms that deliver millions in broadcasting contracts. Arguably, you can't blame them, but it's a necessary fiscal evil for them.'

But not that evil. A joint investigation by Simon Briggs of *The Telegraph* and Edmund Willison, that involved Freedom of Information requests to UKAD, revealed that English football invests just 0.04 per cent of its revenue in catching drug cheats. That included '£0 (nil)' from the Premier League's reported turnover of £3.65 billion for the 2023/24 season and 0.3 per cent of FA revenues, amounting to £1.55 million.

The FA released a statement stating doping in English football remained rare, with just one Premier League player sanctioned since 2015 – former England international Jake Livermore, who tested positive for cocaine. Ultimately, Livermore received no punishment after it was ruled the offence 'only occurred as a result of the severe impairment of Mr Livermore's cognitive functions and judgement' due to recently losing his son in childbirth. The case involving Chelsea's Mykhailo Mudryk, who was charged with a doping offence after testing positive for the banned substance meldonium, had not concluded at the time of writing.

'The Premier League insists that anti-doping efforts are not its responsibility,' the report read, 'and should be left to the FA, the body that regulates the sport in this country.'

'Football only signs up [to the WADA Code] because it wants to be in the Olympics,' one legal expert told me. 'Why does it want to be in the Olympics? Because for most countries, at a national level, your funding depends on the sport being in the Olympics. So, the national federation in Africa says to FIFA, we've got to be in the Olympics because we won't get any public funding unless we're an Olympic sport and we get Olympic medals. So that's the lever. It's also not a great look if you're not signed up to the Code.'

That's not to say UK footballers aren't tested. Between 1st April and 30th June, 2025, according to UKAD's quarterly report, of the 1,994 tests, 404 were in football. That was the highest for any sport, followed by 298 in rugby union and 188 in athletics. Football wasn't the only sport to come out of Briggs' and Willison's investigation in a bad light, with rugby and cricket attributing around 0.1 per cent apiece of their revenues to UKAD.

Further question marks hung over English football when *The Times*' Matt Lawton revealed that most out-of-competition drug testing takes place at club training grounds and UKAD doesn't retain data regarding how many tests are conducted at a player's home; clubs provide the FA with their training schedules and a player has to provide their whereabouts only if they know they're not going to be at training; and a player does not have to provide their whereabouts on a day off or during the close season.

Is that an issue in a team sport that's based on skill? Would steroids assist a Cruyff turn? It's a lame argument. The game at the highest level is more physical than ever, where recovery between games is ever more important. And though football has never endured its Lance Armstrong moment, that doesn't mean it's immune from PEDs. 'Doping corrupts sport when stakes are at their highest,' Lawton warns.

No sport's reputation has suffered quite like road cycling. The Festina affair of 1998, where vials of drugs were found in the boot of soigneur Willy Voet's car en route to the Tour de France, catalysed a chain of events that saw riders and teams thrown off the race. Things got so bad in Germany that organisers cancelled the Deutschland Tour after losing a major sponsor due to cycling's poor image. The Tour de France wasn't shown for years after broadcasters lost faith in the sport. 'Repeated violations of the doping rules can result in a decline of the whole sector,' read a 2015 paper looking at the economics of corruption in sport.

Forwards to the present day and major doping stories in cycling are rare. 'Sports that have endured crises come through it stronger,' says Jonathan Taylor. 'You mustn't waste a crisis in sport.'

Cycling still has its doping cases and, as we've seen throughout this book, the best-resourced riders and teams could simply be aping a creaking system. But for their part, cycling's international governing body, the UCI, invested 17.3 per cent of its revenue on anti-doping.

'A decent percentage of prize money goes towards anti-doping,' says professional rider Rory Townsend. 'And I know that Cycling Ireland were fined when Irish rider Jesse Ewart was banned [for three years in 2024] for taking EPO.'

Townsend believes that the sport is in a stronger position than it's been in a long while due to the testing procedures now in place – he was recently tested twice in a week and this is for, as he says, 'an average-level professional rider' – but he's experienced enough to recognise that some riders will always seek to bend the rules. 'Still, I do find it a little disrespectful when people ask me if I've ever doped. I guess that's the assumption people have about our sport, which is a shame.'

Athletics is another sport that's suffered its share of doping scandals that have tarnished its reputation. 'That's why Seb Coe says the creation of the AIU is one of his proudest achievements,' says Jonathan Taylor. The AIU, Athletics Integrity Unit, was established in 2017 off the back of the McLaren Report into the Russian state-sponsored doping scandal. It's now seen as one of the strongest integrity bodies in world sport, reflected by World Athletics assigning almost £6 million of its £40-million income (15 per cent) to the AIU to implement anti-doping in the sport. In 2023, the AIU also collected another £3 million from other sources including the Label Road Race Programme, which includes contributions from the world's leading marathons, athletes and their representatives, and shoe companies such as Adidas, Nike, Asics and On.

David Howman has been the AIU's chair since its beginnings. He was also WADA's director general for 13 years up to 2016. He suggests that the AIU's reputation is helped by both operational independence – though they are financially dependent on World Athletics – and a transparency that builds trust and affords scrutiny.

'But arguably our greatest strength is that we are one of the few anti-doping organisations that are really committed to catching the best athletes,' he says from his New Zealand home. 'I'm not pointing fingers elsewhere, but maybe some sports' anti-doping programmes just aren't that rigorous.

'If you want to catch the cheats, you can. It takes time and effort, as you've got to work out what they're doing to beat the rules, and then you work out the best time to test them. With micro-dosing or cocktail dosing, if you're not tested within 24 hours of taking those banned substances you won't test positive. So, you must maximise your resources and your intelligence. That's what we do.'

Howman points to the Ruth Chepng'etich case as an exemplar. In October, 2024, Chepng'etich set the world record of 2:09:56 at the Chicago Marathon, becoming the first female athlete to run under two hours and ten minutes. That year, Chepng'etich was subject to out-of-competition testing by the AIU 15 times and to in-competition testing four times.

After her performance in Chicago, the AIU subjected the Kenyan to an increased level of testing during her preparation for the 2025 London Marathon, the AIU report detailing that they tested Chepng'etich six times between 28th February and 26th March, 2025. On 3rd April, 2025, the WADA-accredited laboratory in Lausanne, Switzerland, reported that analysis of Chepng'etich's out-of-competition sample in Kenya from 14th March tested positive for the masking agent hydrochlorothiazide.

Chepng'etich identified several supplements and over-the-counter medicines that she'd been taking and handed over eight different products that she had in her possession. These included carnitine, multivitamins and energy products. They were sent to the Lausanne laboratory that proved they couldn't have been the source of contamination.

The AIU's forensic team discovered screenshots of testosterone vials on her WhatsApp messages, with testosterone-themed messages covering 2022, 2023 and 2025. Fighting a losing battle,

Chepng'etich conjured up a new story to explain the prohibited substance, stating that on the evening of 12th March, 2025, she was experiencing symptoms of sweating, weakness and tachycardia. She knew her housemaid had experienced similar so asked her for the medicine she'd been taking. Chepng'etich provided an image of the blister packaging of the medicine, which clearly identified as 'hydrochlorothiazide', claiming she forgot to disclose it on the form.

The AIU had 'serious reservations about the credibility of the new version of events' and, in the context of the sport's anti-doping rules, such 'recklessness' is considered 'indirect intent, for which a four-year sanction applies'. An automatic one-year reduction was applied after Chepng'etich admitted the anti-doping rule violation within the 20 days required. Other global stars sanctioned by the AIU include Christian Coleman, the 2019 100m world champion, banned for 18 months due to whereabouts failures; and 2019 400m world champion Salwa Eid Naser of Bahrain, banned for two years for the same offence.

And then there are Chepng'etich's Kenyan teammates: Asbel Kiprop, 2008 Olympic 1,500m gold medallist, four-year ban for EPO in 2019; Ruth Jebet, 2016 Olympic 1,500m gold medallist, four-year ban for EPO in 2018; and Wilson Kipsang, former marathon world-record holder, four-year ban for whereabouts failures.

Howman is scathing of the entourage around these athletes, stating that up to 25 people could be instrumental in persuading an athlete to cheat. 'As an aside, those are the people who should be punished and are not. You don't have the jurisdiction to do that. That said, athletes are more vulnerable in countries where poverty is part of a problem. Sport provides an avenue to escape that poverty. In Kenya, you could be number 200 in the country over a 10km road race, but if you win a lower-grade race around the world, you could win $10,000. That's sufficient to sustain your whole family for a year.

'You'll be staggered how many athletes are training in the Rift Valley. And not just Kenyans. There are a number of other East African runners there, and we've been looking pretty closely at Ethiopia, Uganda, that sort of region, to ensure that our testing and our regime isn't confined to Kenya. But poverty does play a part.'

Tennis doesn't suffer from a lack of money, but the sport and WADA did have their integrity called into question with the case of the sinned or sinner. In 2024, Jannik Sinner returned two positive tests for clostebol, a prohibited anabolic agent commonly found in certain topical medications in Italy. He denied any intent to dope, his defence centring on 'inadvertent contamination'.

Investigators accepted that the substance entered his system during a massage from a member of his support team who had used a clostebol-containing spray to treat a cut. Expert evidence showed the quantities detected were consistent with transdermal transfer, not performance-enhancing use.

The ITIA (International Tennis Integrity Agency) concluded that Sinner bore 'no fault or negligence', meaning he was not sanctioned and did not receive a suspension. WADA wasn't happy with the ITIA's ruling and appealed against the decision to the Court of Arbitration for Sport, arguing that even though Sinner had inadvertently been contaminated, he must take responsibility for his team's actions.

In order to avoid a protracted legal battle, Sinner accepted an offer from WADA of a three-month ban.

Many in the tennis community weren't happy. Nick Kyrgios,

the 2022 Wimbledon runner-up, called the situation 'ridiculous' and said the sanction was too lenient, while Switzerland's three-time Grand Slam champion Stan Wawrinka posted on X that he didn't believe in clean sport anymore.

Britain's Tara Moore, banned for 19 months after testing positive for nandrolone and boldenone at a tournament in Colombia in a case where she also 'bore no fault or negligence' because contaminated meat was ruled as the source, wrote on social media, 'I guess only the top players' images matter. I guess only the independent tribunal's opinion on the top players is taken as sound and right. Yet, they question them in my case. Just makes no sense.'

There was scepticism not just at the decision but also the timing of the sanction, from 9th February, 2025, to 4th May, 2025, meaning Sinner didn't miss a Grand Slam. 'I do think a lot has been put into when the ban would take place, to impact Jannik's career as little as possible,' British tennis player Liam Broady told BBC Sport. 'The ban ends the day before the Rome Masters, which is the biggest tournament in his home country and the perfect preparation for him to then go and play the French Open. I don't think he loses any [ranking] points or his number-one spot either, so it's an interesting ban.'

Many suggested special treatment for one of the faces of tennis, but this was rejected by WADA. 'This was a case that was a million miles away from doping,' says the agency's General Counsel Ross Wenzel. 'But I understand the perception. It certainly wasn't part of the reasoning. With external counsel, we came up with what we felt was the right sanction proposal. It was accepted, not negotiated.

'We approached Sinner's team [with the proposal of a three-month ban] in December, 2024, when the WADA Executive

Committee had assembled in Saudi Arabia. Discussions resumed and Sinner's team accepted the sanction. Once there is an agreement on the outcome, it's important that you don't delay. You can't let the athlete play for two or three events before the ban kicks in.

'We contacted Sinner's team. Sinner was in the Middle East [for the Qatar Open] and we reached an agreement around three in the morning. The next morning, he withdrew from that competition. Again, I get the perception but there's a saying that a sanction should be blind to the sporting calendar. If it lands in the off-season, that's the luck of the draw.'

Wenzel said what's termed 'case resolution' isn't rare, with 67 agreements struck between 2021 and the start of 2025. He also said the Code is set to change from 2027, meaning cases where athletes weren't deemed at fault, like Sinner, could be punished from a reprimand to a two-year ban. Sinner would have received a reprimand. Which arguably is inconsequential when talking about an incident from 2024.

Novak Djokovic was quick to slam the decision, suggesting it was unfair and, 'It appears that you can almost affect the outcome if you are a top player, if you have access to the top lawyers.'

For his part, Sinner's lawyer Jamie Singer told the BBC that the swift resolution came down to not throwing the kitchen sink at it. 'From day one, [Jannik] didn't challenge the science. He didn't challenge the test. Didn't challenge the rules. He accepted, even though it's a trace – a billionth of a gramme – that he was liable for what was in his body.'

Singer was also aware that the timing was as good as it could possibly be. 'We can't get away from the fact that you can't choose when these things happen,' he said. 'So the fact that WADA approached us and in the next three months there are no Grand Slams, that seemed to me to make their offer more compelling.'

Sinner shrugged off the controversy, reaching the final of the French Open before winning Wimbledon. Sceptical boos at Roland-Garros had dispersed into loud cheers by the time he'd become the first Italian to win a Wimbledon singles title. This is professional sport, where fans have short memories and stakeholders rack up large profits. Politics and sport should never mix? Impossible.

'I would assume that every anti-doping organisation and sporting federation would regard a successful anti-doping programme as one that has uncovered few cheats ensuring that their patrons, backers and sponsors keep "turning up and paying up". For any particular sport to expose widespread doping would be an anathema to their image and probably existence so it cannot be too strong. You will note some cynicism here but at best anti-doping worldwide efforts constitute a "limited hangout" situation, if not by design, then simply because of the lack of will and resources devoted to the matter.'

Dr Robin Parisotto, 2025

WHY DOPING DOESN'T STOP AT ELITE LEVEL

'Did you see the race in Spain a year or two back? It highlighted that recreational athletes aren't averse to taking performance-enhancing drugs. And I guess why would they not be? Sport reflects society. Certainly in the western world, we're a pill society.' The words of Raphael Faiss, research manager at the centre of Research and Expertise in anti-Doping sciences (REDs) at the University of Lausanne.

Faiss's amateur anecdote concerned a 2024 cycling event in Villena, Spain, where the field comprised a mix of juniors, masters and amateur racers. Word got out that anti-doping officers were in town – rare for an amateur event – resulting in only 52 of the 182 starters crossing the finish line, leading to suspicions from spectators and racers alike.

Álvaro Marzà, who finished in the top ten, called the mass dropout 'a fucking joke' in a post on Instagram. 'Anti-doping control in Villena = punctures and withdrawals! It is not a mathematical formula. It is pure reality. Let's see if measures are taken because this is a fucking joke. By the way, I have passed control!'

One anonymous racer commented, 'We all know who is and who is not [doping]. We are fed up with these exhibitions and that when there are controls, curiously the same as always, they do not finish the races to avoid the control, but of course without evidence we cannot accuse, but everything is clear.'

There was no Spanish Inquisition, so these dropouts could have been coincidence. Doubtful. Competitive sub-elite cycling events like Gran Fondos regularly see amateurs charged with performance-enhancing drug offences. In February, 2024, 35-year-old Italian Fabio Cini won the Ricordando Marco Pantani amateur race, before testing positive for stanozolol. (The event's namesake, Marco Pantani, won the 1998 Tour de France but later retested positive for EPO. He died of a cocaine overdose in 2004.) He was banned for four years.

Fellow Italian Gianbernardino Velotti won his age group at the Italian national championships. It transpired the 34-year-old was fuelled by EPO, leading to an eight-year ban. The sanction was so high because his victory came just days after a three-year ban ended for refusing to submit an anti-doping sample.

The Gran Fondo curse struck again at the start of 2026, with the UCI provisionally suspending 41-year-old American Matthew Clark for an unspecified 'anabolic agent'.

It's not just amateur cycling that's been tainted by the needle. In 2017, recreational rugby union player Michael Lowis tested positive for drostanolone and trenbolone. The 40-year-old was banned for four years. Incredibly, his Clevedon teammate, Dean Ashfield, received his own four-year sanction a year later after using the same steroids as Lowis, plus clenbuterol. Ashfield was tested after scoring a try in a 46–12 Somerset Cup semi-final win over Bridgwater & Albion.

In 2025, Radio France reported that '800 amateur athletes die suddenly during their sporting activities, and the Academy of Medicine clearly implicates doping', though I couldn't verify the source of this information.

Many club-level sanctions go unnoticed because they're redacted or anonymised on UKAD's list to protect privacy. That doesn't apply for the elites, but those on the front line know.

'I've seen many performances that are suspect,' says triathlon, marathon and endurance-sport coach Hywel Davies. Davies is a top-ten Ironman finisher and former teacher based in the Midlands. 'Take an 80kg-plus 55-year-old guy running two-and-a-half hours for the marathon. His body's ripped, like a bodybuilder's physique. He dropped his 5km run time from around 17 minutes to the low 15s in a year. I know a few like that.

'He's on testosterone treatment, claiming he needs to get back to normal levels. I know a few like that. They know they'll never get tested. I coached a guy who was on TRT [testosterone replacement therapy] and he went from running 19-minute 5ks to low 17-minute 5ks, while being a smoker. It was unreal. TRT abuse is rife in the 40-plus age groups. It makes a massive difference to strength and power.'

Davies formerly excelled in indoor rowing and cycling, where he'd compete against his good friend Dan Staite. Staite was banned for two years after testing positive for EPO after the Roy Thame Cup, a national B event, in 2010. 'Dan and I were really good friends. We did a lot of two-up time trials together; we stayed at each other's houses training and I never suspected it. I just thought he's a really good cyclist who puts the work in.

'Then one year in the rowathlon [indoor row/bike/run] series he just rode away from me. I'd beaten him the year before but this time he put two minutes in me over ten miles. That was huge. Professional rowers, ex-Olympians, they couldn't get near him. I put it down to good training but it came out in the wash that he had an unfair advantage. It shook me that someone could cheat in this way, and for what – a first prize of an Easter egg?!' Staite said he doped due to curiosity.

That's the anecdotal, but what about the empirical? The little research in this area is compelling. A 2018 paper, 'The New Front in the War on Doping: Amateur Athletes', split athletic participation into three categories – bodybuilders, fitness enthusiasts and non-elite sports competitors – with doping motivations and substances varying across the group.[29]

Not surprisingly, bodybuilders were closely linked to anabolic steroids 'where males are commonly depicted as monstrously muscled or suffering from so-called rages and women as overly masculinised freaks'.

Fitness enthusiasts – those with whom you rub shoulders down the gym – were equally convinced of the merits of PEDs, with a survey of 500 German gym regulars revealing that 12.5 per cent reported using various doping products. A Dutch study had prevalence rate at 8.2 per cent. As for the non-elite sports people, a study of German amateur and recreational athletes found PED users ranged from 3.35 per cent to 10.55 per cent. The authors caveated that studies 'tended to focus on endurance athletes, as running, cycling, swimming and multisport events have large competitive fields with multiple levels of competition'.

Triathlon punches above its research weight when it comes to

29 https://www.sciencedirect.com/science/article/abs/pii/S0955395917301408?via%3Dihub

recreational athletes doping. In 2013, a study on the PLOS ONE platform – an open-access online publication – revealed that 'one in seven triathletes dopes'.[30] Those were the findings from a survey of 2,997 recreational triathletes at 2012 Ironman Frankfurt and Regensburg, and also the Ironman 70.3 at Wiesbaden.

Via a questionnaire at race registration – which the athletes filled in anonymously – the researchers assessed the percentage of triathletes that physically and cognitively doped. Physically this included performance-enhancing drugs like EPO, human growth hormones and anabolic steroids; on the cognitive front it comprised cocaine, beta blockers and methylphenidate.

Thirteen per cent of athletes confessed to physical doping, rising to 19.8 per cent at Ironman Frankfurt. Cognitive doping came in even higher at 15.1 per cent, hitting a peak of 16.4 per cent at Ironman Regensburg. Around 10 per cent admitted to both forms of doping. Remember, that's not elites. We're talking firemen, nurses, accountants, stockbrokers . . . Another informal survey around Challenge Roth suggested that around 11 per cent of age-group triathletes reported using substances like EPO, steroids or stimulants in the previous year.

(The caveat with all of these figures, of course, is the quality and credibility of the surveys. These weren't face-to-face, which is the ideal, and heightens the chances of an honest reply. Return to chapter two for more on creating a bulletproof doping survey!)

What rules are the recreational athletes breaking? Since WADA expanded the Code to include amateur and recreational sports people in 2015, anti-doping rules in amateur sport have been broadly the same as those at the top table of sport. That means any athlete competing in a sport or event that's signed up to the

---

30 https://journals.plos.org/plosone/article?id=10.1371/journal.pone.0078702

WADA Code is subject to those rules regardless of status, age or payment.

Like the elites, the key rules apply, including strict liability, where athletes are responsible for any prohibited substance found in their body, even if accidental; being tested in-competition and sometimes out-of-competition; and, as we've seen above, sanctions with bans ranging from months to four years or more, depending on intent and fault.

So, broadly, the rules are the same. The major difference is the frequency of testing and education. Amateurs are tested far less – if at all – which is why they're generally not clued up that the same rules apply to a Saturday league match or club event as they do at the Olympics.

As ever, money matters. According to its 2023/24 annual report, UKAD's net expenditure was just under £10 million. Around £1.91 million went on its contract with the Drug Control Centre, King's College London, plus £2.25 million on its athlete testing programme. That's a total of £4.16 million on testing with the remainder on essentials including education, intelligence and salaries.

Around 10,300 in- and out-of-competition tests were analysed at King's across 40 sports, but it's not public knowledge how many of those are amateurs. 'UKAD don't breakdown budgets per sport because we operate an intelligence-led testing programme, which means we gather information from a wide range of sources to determine when and where to test.'

King's wouldn't clarify the cost of the different tests 'due to its commercially sensitive nature'. However, a 2020 request of freedom of information to UKAD revealed, 'UKAD confirms that it holds the information requested of your request.[31] A standard

---

31 https://www.ukad.org.uk/sites/default/files/2020-05/200507%20FOI-262.pdf

urine sample test costs £440 + VAT and a standard blood sample test costs £419 + Vat.' This was several years ago, so it'd be unlikely if those prices hadn't increased. Whether inflation had gripped or not, you can see why UKAD direct much of their 'amateur' resources on credible tip-offs from competitors who might have seen a spike in the suspect's performance.

You might ask why should they need to divert precious resources to the recreational playing field? Victory doesn't pay the mortgage, fund mid-winter Dubai retreats or fuel that next Bugatti. So, what are the motivations behind recreational cheating? Why potentially damage your health and reputation for a pint-sized trophy or plastic medal?

'An academic friend of mine, Michael Shermer, has a fascinating insight into this,' says Joe Papp. 'He says that ego and pride are just as strong a motivator as money. Men especially are motivated by status and honour in their tribes, stretching back to our Palaeolithic ancestors. Even just being top dog in your local sporting club can be a real ego boost to a lot of guys.'

A dig into Shermer's research suggests that we are highly motivated by psychological factors related to where we stand in comparison to other humans. Sport brings this out in spades. 'The swelling pride of winning is the result of our dopaminergic neurons releasing dopamine,' write Shermer. 'This is the "reward" molecule related to learning, gambling, drug addiction and so on that gives us a burst of pleasure – and that can be as motivating, and sometimes even more motivating, than money.'

When Papp was drug trafficking, according to his attorney he brokered deals worth $80,000 to 187 clients, including cyclists, runners and triathletes. He served a six-month period of house arrest followed by two-and-a-half years' probation, that leniency down to Papp testifying at the Lance Armstrong and Floyd Landis cases.

'Out of nearly 200 clients, around 80 per cent were amateurs and 20 per cent professional, of which I think only four were women,' says Papp. 'There was a smaller group of younger guys; lads with the potential to compete at elite or international level. But the bigger group was male, late 30s/early 40s, with a good amount of disposable income, professional security and really wanting to see how far they could go.'

This echoed findings of the Cycling Independent Reform Commission (CIRC) report. To recap, the commission was set up in 2014 by cycling's international governing body to investigate the extent of doping in professional cycling. The report painted an unsettling picture of a sport losing control, of the embedded doping culture spreading beyond the elite ranks.

'The Commission believes that doping in amateur cycling is becoming endemic. This was confirmed by amateur riders, as well as professionals, managers and anti-doping personnel who had exposure to it. It has been caused by a combination of ease of access to drugs via gyms and the internet, the reduction in costs for substances, a spread of knowledge in means and methods of administration, and a lack of funding for regular testing at the amateur level.

'Masters races were also said to have middle-aged businessmen winning on EPO, with some of them training as hard as professional riders and putting in comparable performances. Some professional riders explained that they no longer ride in the Gran Fondos because they were so competitive due to the number of riders doping.'

This moneyed MAMIL (Middle-Aged Man in Lycra) matches Hywel Davies' experience. 'I know a couple of older athletes who took EPO,' says Davies. 'They invested a lot of money over the course of a few years – around £6,000. They achieved massive improvements, but their form was spikey and they suffered spectacular blow-outs when not taking anything. I think doping is a massive elephant in the room that no one's prepared to tackle.'

That's Calum O'Connor's experience. O'Connor grew up just south of Manchester on the edge of the Peak District, but now runs a cycling coaching company, Revolution Velo Coaching, in France. He's 37 and races at sub-elite level.

'I've certainly had suspicions of older riders who are either genetic freaks or on something,' he says. 'Why might they dope? There's certainly an argument that as you age, you see diminishing returns on your effort. Some riders won't be able to handle that. One of the most infamous age-related doping cases was Loïc Herbreteau and "Dr Mabuse".'

In 2007, Herbreteau won the French amateur championships, just six months after testing positive for a banned stimulant. But the sanction wasn't enforced until 2008. Then in 2022, Bernard Sainz, nicknamed 'Dr Mabuse', was sentenced to a year of house arrest for the 'illegal practice of medicine and inciting doping'. The case also involved Herbreteau, for putting athletes in touch with Sainz, and former actor Pierre-Marie Carlier, for introducing his son to Sainz.

'He still rides [at 50] at quite a high amateur level,' says O'Connor. Herbreteau won the 45–49 age group at the 2024 Gravel Cycling World Championships. 'I remember racing against him a few years ago and he finished in the top three. There was an interesting reaction from the crowd at the medal ceremony.'

A driver of the ageing amateur doper is the longevity movement. It's estimated that there are over 1,000 anti-ageing clinics in the US alone, focusing on wellness and hormone optimisation. 'The testosterone supplement industry is huge in the States,' says John Hoberman, chair of Germanic studies at the University of Texas, who's an expert on doping in sport. 'I could walk into a clinic and say, "Gee, doc, I think I've got low testosterone." He'll take my levels, and even if they're okay, there's a financial incentive for him to prescribe. Honestly, those clinics have grown like mushrooms. Testosterone replacement has become a de facto male entitlement.'

'Older' athletes have easy access to testosterone. On the surface, the doctor and individual agree it's for health reasons. But the inference is performance-enhancing, not enabling. The amateur peloton, it seems, is packed with Benjamin Buttons on a bike.

Papp adds that the affordability of doping is another key driver. A quick search online and you're presented with myriad websites offering EPO. One recommends 'a loading phase of average 6,000IU for weeks one to three, then supportive dosages of 4,000IU for weeks four to six. Weekly dosage is to be split into three equal shots and most specialists agree that one should not use erythropoietin for more than six weeks!'

'When I trafficked, I regret the degree to which I made it easy and inexpensive to get doping products,' Papp says. 'EPO used to cost $400 for four weeks of the lowest dose, which was prescription for anaemia. Once China started producing strong EPO, we could deliver a year's worth of strong EPO for around $1,000 and still make a huge profit.'

'American culture is very much focused on pharmaceuticals,' adds Calum O'Connor. 'I was in the navy and when we were stationed in bases over there, we were categorically told by the navy doctors to avoid supplements from their gyms and health shops because we might fail a UK armed forces drug test. You really didn't know what might be mixed in with the creatine.'

Ego and identity are great drivers. Both are relevant in research out of Leeds Beckett University, England, that looked at the reasons behind sanctions of UK rugby union players between 2009 and 2015. Forty-nine players and one coach received bans, with more than half involving those competing at 'sub-elite' level, so a good standard, maybe paid per game, but not a full-time professional.

Eight cases used substances for weight management, with four looking to increase mass. Three were adolescent athletes who stated that they felt under pressure to bulk up. That's arguably no surprise as their icons have grown significantly since the game turned professional.

In 1994, a year before rugby union went full-time, the England team's average weight hit the scales at 92.3kg. By 2014, that'd inflated to 105.3kg. On average, that's a two-stone increase. Between 1947 and 2015, the average weight and height of players in the team increased by 6.93cm and 20kg.

In 2013, then-teenager Sam Chalmers tested positive for steroids at a Scotland under-20 training camp. He'd taken Pro-SD, 'one of the most potent designer supplements available . . . many users reporting gains of between 8 to 12lbs in as little as three weeks'. The 5ft 11in, 12st 8lb stand-off said he felt under 'constant pressure' to put on weight and admitted his 'stupid mistake'.

Three of the players in that study blamed the strain of juggling demanding jobs and rugby commitments, and that the pressures of both were draining them, physically and mentally. Medication to boost sexual performance and recreational cocaine use were further explanations from the sub-elite.

There's external – in this case, paternal – pressures, too. In 2014, Welshman Philip Tinklin was sanctioned after admitting the supply of anabolic steroids. His 'clients' included his daughter, Sophie Tinklin, a competitive amateur boxer and former Welsh women's champion, who received a four-year ban after a tribunal concluded she must have known about the steroids in the household.

Tinklin wasn't a professional coach, but because he transported his five children – all amateur boxers – and others to Welsh Amateur Boxing Association events, he fell under the sport's anti-doping jurisdiction. Prosecutors argued that his 'family business' of handling and distributing prohibited substances placed him at the heart of a supply chain that had no place in sport.

When Gwent police raided his home, they found 722 tablets containing methyltestosterone, 1,948 tablets containing stanozolol and 36x10ml vials containing testosterone.

Philip Tinklin became the first person in the UK to receive a lifetime sports ban, due to supplying anabolics. Science says he shouldn't be the last.

Claire Traversa is a researcher at McGill University, Canada, who's become an authority on the phenomenon of skeletal muscle memory.

'My background is muscle physiology, so WADA approached me to look into this theory from an anti-doping perspective,' she says. 'They were interested in whether athletes might continue to benefit from doping long after they've stopped.'

At the heart of their concerns sit tiny but powerful myonuclei that nestle inside the nuclei within muscle fibres. 'Muscle cells contain multiple nuclei. These nuclei drive protein production. The more nuclei you have, the more proteins you can synthesise, the larger the muscle fibre can grow.' That is clearly advantageous for sport.

The concept emerged in the early 2000s when researchers observed that resistance training prompts satellite cells – skeletal muscle stem cells – to fuse with muscle fibres, forging new myonuclei. Lift weights, add nuclei, grow stronger. Not controversial. What raised eyebrows came after training stopped.

'When training ceased, muscle mass declined. You could see it visually and via ultrasound – the muscle cross-sectional area shrank. But the extra myonuclei didn't disappear. They stayed.'

This is where doping entered the frame. Steroids push muscle growth beyond natural limits, creating what Traversa calls a 'supraphysiological' state. 'You wouldn't see that number of nuclei in a clean athlete,' she says. In effect, dopers raise their transcriptional ceiling. To coin an well-known phrase from *Spinal Tap*, they dial performance up to 11.

That poses an uncomfortable truth, says Traversa. 'If someone doped years ago, whether amateur or elite, served their ban and returned clean, do they still retain that unnatural advantage? Meanwhile, an athlete who's never doped may never reach that level. Is that fair?'

Analysis by *The New York Times* found that of the roughly 11,000 athletes at the 2016 Rio Olympics, around 120 had previous doping sanctions but were eligible to compete. That's roughly one in every 100. Of the 974 medals awarded, 35 were won by athletes who had served bans, most notably in weight-lifting and athletics.

There's no evidence those medallists directly benefitted from past doping, but WADA is certainly convinced of the long-term impact of steroid abuse even once the regime has finished. 'One of the reasons why the sanction for steroids rose from two years to four years was due, in part, to this muscle memory aspect,' says Morten Hostrup.

Hostrup is currently undertaking research in a similar area, examining whether this muscle-memory phenomenon occurs after treatment with clenbuterol. The proposed mechanism is similar – myonuclear addition, hypertrophy and myocellular reprogramming. He's still working through the findings but 'the results are promising'.

Further research is probing whether blood doping leaves subtler fingerprints. While EPO's effects appear transient, emerging epigenetic research hints that endurance adaptations might leave longer-lasting molecular traces.

But the ease, accessibility and, in some quarters, normalisation of steroids are the major problem in the amateur ranks. A BBC State of Sport report in 2017 revealed that 13 per cent of 18- to 34-year-olds surveyed had taken steroids. Pain relief, injury recovery, improving performance, improving looks and copying the elites were the staircasing of why.

That's a concern, says Professor Marc Silver. Silver is a haematological expert of over 30 years. 'My whole life's work has been about making hearts work more efficiently, to take sick hearts and fix them,' he says. Which is why he's alarmed by a growing trend – that of young amateur sports people coming to see him, whose blood resembles sludge.

'I'm seeing younger and younger men on testosterone replacement therapy, who've clearly not undergone an evaluation. They might read about the risks in a publication like *Men's Health* but that doesn't worry them. Their only concession to the dangers is that they go and donate blood, not because they're Good

Samaritans but to reduce the red blood cell mass. That lowers viscosity, the thickness, of the blood. I've seen young athletes in my clinic whose haematocrit [the percentage of red blood cells in your blood] levels have been over 60. It's dangerous.'

That might surprise, as testosterone is a hormone widely known to crank up muscle growth. But it also stimulates bone marrow that increases red blood cell mass, increasing the body's capacity to carry oxygen to working muscles. The result? A harder, stronger workout for performance and/or image-enhancing reasons.

'The problem is, boosting red blood cell number increases haematocrit,' says Silver. 'When that rises above 52 or 53, there's a greater incidence of the red cells sticking together. Blood clots then form. If these form in the lungs, the consequences could be catastrophic. These youngsters need to be educated.'

Especially, says the 2015 CIRC report, if they aspire to become professional. 'If youth riders want to reach higher ranks, the incentives are there to dope at an early age.'

Body image and aesthetics also come into play. In fitness, combat and endurance sports, drugs are often used to look leaner, stronger or healthier, not purely to perform better. This blurs the lines between doping and appearance enhancement.

There's also a cultural strand. In 2006, research among amateur athletes in Cameroon revealed that while awareness of banned substances was high, understanding of what constituted doping remained shallow and frequently distorted. Many athletes believed substance use was normal, necessary for success and simply part of competitive sport. Football, athletics, boxing and cycling emerged as the most affected disciplines, reflecting similar patterns seen globally in amateur and masters sport.

Substances used were often crude, locally available or misused pharmaceuticals. Cannabis-based stimulants, anabolic agents and cocaine featured prominently, with access driven by friends, coaches, dealers and even medical staff. In a further study, 8 per cent of amateur footballers admitted taking cocaine before and after matches.

A significant number of athletes reported involuntary doping, highlighting how blurred the lines were between lawful supplements, traditional remedies and prohibited substances. The use of occultism with performance-enhancing intentions reported by key informants in the study added another dimension to the problem, the authors said, with bloodletting popular, albeit presumably this ancient practice to cleanse the body is performance-diminishing rather than enhancing, involving blood removal without the infusion part.

It's clear that performance-enhancing drugs are not the preserve of the professionals. In fact, that 2017 BBC State of Sport investigation found that more than a third (35 per cent) of the 1,025 women and men polled from amateur sports clubs and teams said they knew someone who'd doped.

By sport, around 57 per cent of tennis players admitted to knowing someone who'd 'enhanced' followed by contact sport (52 per cent), football (48 per cent), running (47 per cent), cycling (45 per cent), gym/weight-lifting (43 per cent) and swimming (42 per cent).

Then UKAD chief executive Nicole Sapstead described the figures as 'incredibly alarming'. Which they were. But the results must be put in context as they grouped legal substances like pain-relief gels and over-the-counter anti-inflammatory medicines as PEDs. A category oversight? Further studies suggest not.

*

In 2023, research in the open-access journal *Sports Medicine – Open* found that more than one in ten recreational athletes admitted using over-the-counter (OTC) medication to enhance performance.

'We surveyed around 7,000 recreational athletes,' says lead author Ask Vest Christiansen, associate professor of public health and sport science at Aarhus University, Denmark. 'About 45 per cent had used OTC medication for reasons unrelated to performance. Things like pain relief. But around 10 per cent openly admitted using OTC medication to improve performance.'

That equates to roughly 700 recreational athletes using substances such as salbutamol not to calm inflamed airways, but to expand them in search of marginal gains.

Christiansen is quick to point out that the study wasn't designed to draw legal lines. The researchers didn't differentiate between substances permitted or prohibited by WADA. What interested Christiansen and his team was an athlete's attitude: how non-elite athletes think about drugs, fairness and performance.

The respondents spanned more than 200 sports that Christiansen divided into four broad categories. First came CGS sports – those measured in centimetres, grammes and seconds, including cycling, running and swimming. Then artistic sports such as gymnastics and dance; combat sports like judo and karate; and, finally, games, including football, rugby and tennis.

The researchers hypothesised that OTC use for performance would be highest in CGS sports, where gains are easily measured and transparent: VO_2max, watts, times . . . It would align with the logic that marginal improvements matter most where outcomes are numerical. Yet the data told a different story. OTC performance use was more prevalent in games than in CGS sports.

Does that mean cyclists and runners are ethically purer?

Christiansen doubts it. 'The obvious explanation is participation structure,' he says. 'There are huge numbers of people who run or cycle recreationally without ever competing. They might fall into CGS sports, but they're exercising for health, not results. They never pin on a race number, so they never even consider performance-enhancing medication.'

Games are different. You can't play football without keeping score. Even five-a-side has winners and losers. 'Most people playing games are in some kind of league or club structure,' Christiansen adds. 'That gives outcomes more meaning. Competition is built in.'

Painkillers are where this argument complicates things. A 2009 study found that 30–50 per cent of Ironman and marathon participants reported using NSAIDs (non-steroidal anti-inflammatory drugs), most commonly ibuprofen. But, as the participants fed back, this wasn't about going faster. It was about survival, of ensuring months of dedication and sacrifice, balancing work, family and life, didn't come to nothing.

'I suffer from sciatica and often take ibuprofen before a ride,' says Jacek Kapela, a Warsaw-based cyclist in his 50s to whom we chatted in chapter three. 'Sometimes I'll take something stronger if it's bad. It's not about performance, it's about getting through the ride.' Many of his peers do the same. This is where ethics blur. Ibuprofen doesn't boost power, but it dulls pain. Is that enabling participation or enhancing performance? Does it matter? Maybe.

Some have argued these drugs should be banned from sport, not because they improve results but because of their health risks. Chronic NSAID use is linked to gastrointestinal bleeding, kidney disease and increased cardiovascular risk.

Those concerns prompted organisers of the Ultra-Trail du

Mont-Blanc (UTMB) World Series running event to ban painkillers within 24 hours of racing and during events. 'The most common self-medication we see is for joint pain and digestive issues,' announced UTMB medical director Patrick Basset on the ruling. 'That means NSAIDs and anti-diarrhoeal drugs.'

Laura Lewis, director of science at USADA, found the decision noteworthy, though not without reservations. 'They're not part of the WADA system,' she says, 'so it's unclear how much testing or enforcement there really is.'

Lewis doesn't believe ibuprofen belongs on the Prohibited List. To recap, a substance must meet two of three criteria: enhance performance, pose a health risk or violate the spirit of sport. 'Ibuprofen might be harmful at very high doses, but it's not performance enhancing. And I don't think it violates the spirit of sport.'

For amateur athletes who are unsure where they stand, Lewis recommends Global DRO, the online database that clarifies what's permitted and when.

Paracetamol muddies the waters further. Long considered benign, studies suggest they can deliver small performance gains. In 2013, Dr Lex Mauger of the University of Kent found recreational athletes rode further in time trials after taking paracetamol, not just because it dampened pain but because it reduced core temperature. A 2009 study showed amateur cyclists rode a ten-mile time trial around 30 seconds faster with paracetamol than without.

The potential cost? A 2011 study from the Royal Infirmary of Edinburgh warned of 'a very real concern of severe liver damage'.

From the professionals to recreational athletes, the anti-doping framework stresses the importance of education. Read, learn, sidestep PEDs. But education doesn't always deter. We're in an age of information. It's at your fingertips. It's inescapable. With a little research, your 'hobby' can mimic a professional's.

'At the moment, my friends and I are discussing ways to improve performance by way of better oxygen flow,' says Jacek Kapela. 'We follow a nutritionist called Asker Jeukendrup. He's shown that supplementation of L-citrulline with L-arginine improves your blood flow and your oxygen intake. It's like beetroot [a proven blood-flow booster]. I don't use the shots but I do eat a lot of beetroot. I also use DHEA. That last one has helped enormously.'

DHEA, or dehydroepiandrosterone, is a hormone that gives your body a nudge in producing testosterone. It's often used by men who, like Kapela, are over 50. 'My testosterone levels dropped quite markedly,' he says. 'It's illegal in cycling [you would need a TUE] but it's helped my recovery, my riding and my general health. I take a 100-milligramme capsule once a day.'

Kapela stresses it's for general health as much as cycling, though he is aware of ex-professionals and good amateurs he rides with that dope. 'You realise that in amateur cycling, there are a lot of ambitious people who want to show up and simply ride strong to look good,' he says.

Christiansen says that seen through an academic lens, doping, be it amateurs or elites, comes down to 'moral disengagement'. It's a concept derived from developmental psychology and refers to the process by which individuals persuade themselves that ethical standards don't apply to them in a specific context, in this case recreational sport. This occurs by 'deactivating the mechanism of self-condemnation'. As such, moral disengagement entails a process of cognitive reinterpreting or reframing of potentially harmful behaviour as morally acceptable, without altering either the behaviour itself or the underlying moral standards.

A powerful driver behind this moral disengagement is immersing yourself in your hobby. The more you engage with an activity, the more you know . . . the more you become aware of novel ways to boost your performance.

'We undertook a study years ago into what's been called "student doping" or "cognitive enhancement",' says Christiansen. This covered smart drugs that are most often stimulants or cognitive-enhancing drugs like prescription medication. Ritalin and Modafinil are two examples.

'We found they were much more prevalent in the health faculties than the art department. The more people know about a drug, the more they're immersed in that world, the more they might use it. That differed to the philosophy department, who'd go, "No, this is absolutely wrong. I'm not taking that." There's an element of this as a recreational athlete. The more you invest time and energy into something, the more immersed you are in that world.'

But how far are you willing to morally disengage for the winning try in front of one woman and her dog or the fastest time at your village fun run? In the case of former actor Giovambattista Iera, pretty far. During a multi-stage amateur cycling race in France back in 2024, the officials targeted Iera.

'We suspected potential cheating,' said race director Frédéric Lenormand. 'On Saturday, in the stage between Beauvais and Maignelay-Montigny, he caught up with a breakaway in an abnormally fast period of time. On Sunday, several people mentioned an abnormal noise when he was riding.' A sign of motor doping where you secretly power your bike by a battery and motor.

Iera raised suspicion when, as Lenormand approached, he escaped in his car. 'I wanted to hold him back, but he ran away. He ran into me with his car and I drove a hundred meters on his hood. It couldn't have been more dramatic.' Iera's AC Bellaingeoise team was excluded from the race and didn't participate in the last stage.

'It's inconceivable to me why he would cheat,' Lenormand said. 'There is no money. The winner wins a jersey, a trophy, a bouquet of flowers and . . . a steak.' Team manager Daphnée Boss said that it was a betrayal to the squad and 'intolerable behaviour for an amateur race'.

Or any race.

Iera furiously denied all allegations of wrongdoing through a statement distributed via his lawyer, claiming an investigation found him innocent of the charges levelled against him.

'I did not "run-away" or strike an organiser,' Iera said. 'On the contrary, I was quick to contact the Gendarmes to immediately resolve the false accusations. Since then, the police investigation has demonstrated my innocence and has cleared me of any involvement in any act of violence against the organizers. With regards to the alleged "mechanical doping," all the bicycles have been inspected and scanned via x-ray by the investigators and technicians.'

That was February 2025. This author contacted the race organisers for an update but, at time of writing, had not received a reply.

Ultimately, technological doping simplifies the complex area of anti-doping because, as Christiansen says, when you dig a little deeper, there's an incoherence and inconsistency that pervades when an athlete 'enhances' his or her body.

'When I do talks to students, I ask what's the definition of doping? They reply that it's performance enhancing and unnatural. I say, so Coca-Cola then. It contains caffeine, which is a proven performance enhancer, and not natural. "Okay, but what about if something's natural? That is fine," they reply. "Of course," I say, "so you can extract your blood and reinfuse it. That's pretty natural as it's all your own blood. Is that okay?" "Not at all," they reply.

'You find with "doping", whether at recreational or elite level, the less you know, the clearer your views. The more you look into this area, the less clear you are.'

INSIDE THE MIND OF A DOPER

The 10th of February, 2023, was a day like any other for American professional triathlete Collin Chartier. Train, eat, sleep, repeat. It's the mantra for multisporters, for whom 30-hour-plus training weeks are the norm, even more so for the likes of Chartier, who competed on the Ironman circuit. For the unfamiliar, that's 3.8km swimming and 180km cycling, all finished off with a marathon run. In 2022, the journeyman had enjoyed the season of his career, winning August's Ironman Mont-Tremblant in Canada and the PTO US Open in Texas the following month. Chartier approached the biggest event in the sport, October's Ironman Hawaii, in peak condition. But a disappointing debut left him down in 35th. Still, he finished the year ranked 16th in the end-of-year PTO rankings, adding another £14,000 to the $100,000 he'd won in Texas. Not Premier League riches, but comfortable.

Chartier lived the nomadic lifestyle of an endurance athlete into the off-season, seeking the oxygen-boosting benefits of altitude training in California, Ecuador and then, on this crisp February Saturday, in Girona, Spain.

'That's when I received a call,' says Chartier. 'It was the doping control officer. I'd given the wrong address on purpose, but said I'd meet him at the pool. Looking back on it, I didn't have to show up because it was out of my one-hour window. I could have just taken the hit of a missed test. My mistake for answering the phone!'

Soon after, Chartier received a letter informing him that his samples had flagged up an adverse analytical finding for EPO. And exogenous EPO delivered via a vial not the endogenous EPO generated by Chartier from training high. On Monday 24th April, 2023, the news broke. And the torrent of disappointment rained down on him.

Australian Josh Amberger, who finished second to Chartier in Canada, turned to Instagram: 'I feel physically ill. I'm not celebrating, rather I'm completely and utterly in mourning. It wasn't just me and my competitors that were robbed that day. The whole sport was robbed.'

Chartier's coach Mikal Iden: 'I never thought I would have to make a statement like this. I'm in shock and crying just now, learning that an athlete I've been coaching for the last year has been doping. I can't distance myself enough from this action. It's such a complete crash in my values it's unthinkable. The only positive I see from this is the anti-doping organisation catching the athlete.'

And Ben Hoffman, winner of Ironman Texas in 2022, 'F@%K DOPERS.'

Chartier's response to his EPO positive was rare: he immediately admitted his wrongdoing on Instagram. 'I am not going to give myself or anyone else the bullshit excuse like a tainted burrito or tainted Covid vaccine. I made a terrible choice, and now I face the consequences. Own it and move on.' His ban was reduced from four to three years for the frank omission, though Chartier announced his immediate retirement.

'On the day the news became public, I remember curling up in my house alone. I had sweats and chills and couldn't eat. I had an immense feeling of shame and guilt, to the point I felt physically under attack. The stuff online was horrific.'

That shame and guilt, Chartier says, stalked him from the moment he started taking EPO in November of 2022, following the Hawaii result where he felt as if he'd 'failed' and let down the people that supported him. (Those who question Chartier's story suggest this is a convenient doping start date to avoid returning the 100-grand he won in Canada three months before.)

'That period of my life I suffered palpable anxiety. I kept looking over my shoulder. How do I deal with this? How do I keep training hard and moving forwards? It wasn't a good place to be in. It's the exact opposite state of high performance you're seeking. Wrestling with constant anxiety, worrying about the future, that really prevents anyone from being present and extracting the most from their sessions.'

Chartier's anxieties were reflected in his erratic EPO administration. The American's adamant he doped alone, pointing to his undergraduate background that involved blood work. Many cast doubt over Chartier's lone-wolf account, with 2014 Ironman Hawaii champion Sebastian Kienle commenting, 'That's the problem with a liar. He lied once, so is he now telling the truth? Is he telling part of the truth or is it a whole lie again?'

'I micro-dosed intravenously,' Chartier recalls. 'But though I've worked with blood, I'm not a trained professional, so things were a little all over the place. I used insulin needles, which are really small, and I think I must have kept missing the vein. If you do that, the half-life of EPO is ten times longer than if you hit the vein. It's a massive difference. So, I assume that's what happened. I tried on my forearms, hands and feet. I was a complete mess.'

Crossing the legal line had resulted in bleeding limbs, paranoia and sub-par training. It begs the question: why? Why, if we're to believe his EPO regime began in November, 2022, did Chartier dope off the back of a career-defining season? Why, when he could have been celebrating his success, did he trap himself in a world of mistrust and suspicion?

'I believe on a subconscious level I wanted to be caught as it was my only way out of the sport. I was stubborn enough to never quit. Quitting is not me. "I will do this for the rest of my life, even if I'm lonely and tired and injured all the time." My identity was wrapped around the sport and it was killing me.

'I'd just enjoyed the biggest season of my career. But I looked at the other guys, the top guys in our sport, and was like, "I need to make more. I need to make a million a year." As soon as I achieve a goal, the next one must come along straight away. So that constant chasing, it's never satisfying. You're never content. You never celebrate anything. It was just a constant cycle of never enough. You could have said, "This time in three years you'll finish top three in Hawaii and be financially sorted." I wouldn't accept that. I had to expedite things. "It has to happen now." It's probably to do with ego and self-worth.'

That resonates with Alex Smith, senior researcher at the University of Bern in Germany. Smith, originally from the Wirral in England, has extensively studied mental health in athletes – both those who are clean and those who have doped. 'I compare doping in sport to addiction in that it's viewed as some sort of moral failure,' he says. 'But there are shades of grey. Academia has started to reflect that. Public perceptions haven't. There's a tendency to call someone a cheat without considering the broader determinants, of which there are many. They might be social pressures, socioeconomic pressures and even the pressures of one's personality.'

You've likely heard of the type-A personality, which you could perceive as a doping warning sign. That the traits of competitiveness, time urgency and even hostility deliver an aggressive push towards the ethical line. Current thinking, says Smith, has shifted towards more nuanced and behaviour-specific models including the 'dark triad', a psychological concept coined in 2002 that describes a cluster of three distinct but overlapping personality traits: psychopathy, narcissism and Machiavellianism.

'We all have them but to varying degrees,' he says. 'Psychopathy is typified by manipulativeness, deceitfulness, superficial charm, impulsivity and grandiosity. The narcissism and Machiavellianism are similar. These traits are considered "dark" because they're characterised by socially malevolent qualities, such as emotional coldness, duplicity and a manipulative interpersonal style. We used to think of psychopathy as categorical, whereas now we know it's on a spectrum.

'There's evidence linking accentuated psychopathic and dark triad traits with positive attributes in sport. Take the will to win. If you're willing to give everything you have, arguably that's admirable. But that can extend to doing absolutely anything to win, which can obviously bring doping into the equation. Interestingly, a lot of these traits take on an anti-social dimension, but in a more accentuated form. That's advantageous in specific contexts. Sports is one, politics is another, big business is another. There's a lot of material about psychopathic chief executives who bring the money in. These traits wouldn't generally be accepted in normal social situations. But many who reach the top of these domains do exhibit dark triad traits.'

Nike's marketing team clearly did their homework in 2024 with an advert entitled, 'Winning isn't for everyone. Am I a bad person?' You can find it on YouTube. Featuring a string of sporting legends, including LeBron James, Jakob Ingebrigtsen, Kylian Mbappé and Serena Williams, actor Willem Dafoe narrates what it takes to be the best. 'I'm single-minded. I'm deceptive. I'm obsessive. I'm selfish. Does that make me a bad person? Am I? Am I?' After two minutes of sporting theatre, the ad concludes with the sign-off, 'Winning isn't for everyone.'

'They must have had psychological consultation because they nail nearly every indicator of psychopathy,' says Smith. 'It's a neat ad and shows the complexity of personality structure.'

Made even more complicated when exhibiting 'dark tetrad' traits. That's when sadism is sprinkled into the mix and entails a complete disregard for others' well-being. Those who have sadistic tendencies experience joy and pleasure inflicting pain on others. For Chartier, it was all about inflicting pain on himself.

'I started working with renowned sports psychologist Dr Jim Taylor,' he says, emphasising that Dr Taylor had no knowledge of his doping. 'We spoke extensively about the topic of pain. He said to me that to achieve my goals, I had to push through pain. I replied, "I am chasing pain."

'I once visited Costa Rica and spent time with an expert on mindset and beliefs. He told me, "Go to a memory, a place, where you felt happiest. Like joyous. Utopia." He said to think of times with friends and family. There's a pause, he's looking at me and says, "Where's your energy? There's nothing going on. What are you thinking about?"

'I reply, "Well, I'm trying to think about good times with people and I'm coming up blank." I guess it was a bit sad. But he told me to persist. I then got to thinking about three to five experiences I'd had in training where I'd pushed beyond the barrier of pain. When you go beyond that barrier, you keep on pushing because you're flooded with endorphins. You're euphoric. It's incredible. You're pushing the limits and you've transcended the body because pain is no longer a limiter.

'I realised that was one of the few things that made me happy and I was constantly searching for it. That guy in Costa Rica said I lit up. The problem is when you train really hard, it beats up your body. A lot. So, that's when tramadol first came in, followed by prednisone. They helped me to keep pushing that pain threshold higher. Working with Dr Taylor, we realised this pain-seeking had become an addiction and something I'd developed from an early age. I thought improving was about pushing through the pain. But that wasn't the healthiest of mindsets.'

Elite athletes walk the fine line between peak performance and injury. It's no headline-maker's dream but consistency of training is the cornerstone of progress. Sport is littered with athletes who failed to match the hype due to injury. Juan Martín del Potro burst onto the tennis scene at 21, beating Roger Federer en route to winning the US Open. A series of wrist and knee injuries robbed him of further majors. Basketballer Grant Hill's early career trajectory suggested greatness before ankle injuries derailed him in his prime. And England footballer Darren Anderton endured such an extraordinary run of injuries that he was nicknamed 'Sicknote'.

Consistency equating to success is supported by science. Australian researchers followed 33 international track-and-field athletes over five seasons, tracking their weekly training status, episodes of illness and injury, and whether they achieved key performance targets. Those who completed more than 80 per cent of planned training were about seven times more likely to triumph, and training availability accounted for 86 per cent of successful seasons.

'Injury shines a light on the grey area of anti-doping,' says Chartier. 'I used the corticosteroid prednisone out of competition, which is allowed – it's not allowed in competition – because it reduces pain and inflammation. Now, both of those are a daily occurrence for elite athletes. It's powerful, and you see athletes trying to get off it. But I was trying to get on it because, in training, it also helps you to recover faster and enjoy stronger workouts. That is not a healthy thing. You start to think, how much can I use to maximise training?'

Chartier reflects that he's never been mentally healthy, and that up until his doping revelation, he's lived a mentally unhealthy life.

'I guess it started from an early age. I was homeschooled and felt huge insecurities when I moved to public school. I didn't have a comparison with my peers. When it came to sport I also had coaches that really didn't think much of me at the time. One of them called me "Charmin Ultra", which is a toilet paper brand here in the US. It was his way of calling me soft in front of the whole group.

'Instances like that fired something in me. I thought, *I'm not going to be soft. I'll prove them all wrong.* I've had a persistent desire – or should I say, persistent pressure – for most of my life to win.

To be the best. And it's always worked on a timeline of "now". I've been operating a system of a horse with blinkers on.'

Chartier's doping epiphany is that an athlete's belief system is a major driver on whether they chose to take performance-enhancing drugs or not. His stemmed from his childhood and believing he wasn't talented enough, leaving him flattened by low self-worth and low self-esteem. Once that seed's sown from an early age, he says, it becomes engrained and you'll do anything to pick yourself up off the floor. Anything to gain an edge.

'What I've learned is that what separates the real winners from the rest of us isn't drugs but the mind. In triathlon, within about 5 per cent, we all do the same training and workloads. But what is your mental construct? Dr Taylor taught me several obstacles to success, including overinvestment. You've overidentified with the sport. That was a big one for me. Then there's negativity, like negative self-talk, fear of failure and perfectionism. The best athletes can remove all of these hurdles. They handle adversity. Is it all or nothing? For the best of the best it isn't because all or nothing is a very weak mindset.'

Chartier, self-inflicted it may have been, spiralled out of control, but he is here to tell the tale. Many athletes aren't.

'There are clearly massive negative associations between doping and suffering mental-health issues afterwards,' says Alex Smith. 'Just look at Terry Newton.'

Newton was a former England and Great Britain rugby league international who, in 2010, tested positive for human growth hormone (HGH) while playing for Wakefield Trinity. It was a landmark case: the first positive for HGH in British sport. Newton received a two-year ban, lost his contract and sponsorship, and became the public face of a new era of anti-doping detection.

Within months, Newton was found dead at his home in Cheshire. An inquest later ruled his death a suicide. The coroner heard that Newton had been struggling with depression, financial stress, loss of identity and shame following the ban. Friends and family described a man who felt he had let everyone down and couldn't see a way back. The sanction, public scrutiny and sudden collapse of his career were significant stressors layered onto existing mental-health difficulties. The mental-health charity State of Mind Sport was set up in the wake of Newton's death.

'Media scrutiny, people turning up at your home, loss of earnings . . . your entire identity is connected to sport and has been since childhood. When that suddenly disappears, many athletes are in trouble,' says Smith. 'You're living in this massively structured environment. Your training's scheduled, your food is cooked for you by the team chef and you know you must perform, in the case of a sport like football, every Saturday and possibly Tuesday or Wednesday, too. Then you make a mistake and it's all gone. There's such a lack of sympathy for these individuals. Yes, we must uphold fair play, but there are nuanced shades of greatness.' (Chartier, it seems, is an outlier, happily jettisoning his identity and triathlon.)

The suicide of Antonio Pettigrew in 2010 is a case in point. The former 400m world champion, who admitted taking EPO between 1997 and 2003, was found dead in his car. The coroner ruled death by overdosing on sleeping pills. 'Drugs cheat Olympic sprinter found dead,' reported Sky News; 'Drugs cheat Antonio Pettigrew found dead in car,' said *The Telegraph*; 'Disgraced sprinter found dead in his car,' *The Times* . . . Little compassion in life and death. Life is a spectrum of complexity. That is until an athlete dopes. It's then black and white.

Byron Juma is assistant professor and programme co-ordinator at Emporia State University in Kansas. Juma was born and raised in Kenya before moving to Swansea, Wales, and then the US in pursuit of a Masters in sports ethics and integrity. In Kenya he'd worked in sports and developed an interest in the doping athlete, specifically, what happens next? He formalised his curiosity, resulting in the 2025 research paper, 'The Hidden Cost of Doping Sanctions: Examining the Experiences of Kenyan Athletes Sanctioned for Violating Anti-Doping Rules.'[32]

'It was challenging research,' Juma says. 'Doping is such a sensitive topic and I knew recruiting athletes who'd been banned would prove tricky. Eventually, the Anti-Doping Agency of Kenya (ADAK) pointed me in the direction of one athlete who was four months into her sanction. The interview was so raw that she'd tear up when we reflected on her experience. But she agreed to reach out to fellow athletes who were sanctioned.'

Juma eventually recruited ten Kenyan track-and-field athletes – six men, four women – who'd tested positive for prohibited substances and were sanctioned for between two and four years. 'I drove halfway around the country for some of those in-person interviews,' he says. 'I did not do one Zoom interview because of the emotional subject matter. There's no human touch. Whereas with these interviews, I'd be there for around three hours. We'd have a meal; I'd meet their family.

'They admitted negligence and lack of knowledge and agreed with the verdicts, but it became clear that much more needs to be done to empower athletes, especially younger ones, into making the right decisions. They have a lot of pressure from support teams

---

32 https://www.sciencedirect.com/science/article/pii/S2211266925000763#:~:text=Social%20
stigma%20led%20to%20shame,concerns%20about%20their%20well%2Dbeing.

and are in a vulnerable position. In the end, they were pleased to speak to me. They told me that no one had ever spent time listening to their side of the story without judging them. That hit me hard.'

Juma categorised their reaction into two themes: 'seeking meaning', where the athletes tried to rationalise why they had tested positive; and the 'psychological and physical distress that followed'.

Each athlete received a pseudonym. This from his paper:

Chira, Dua and Gathoni, still visibly affected, recalled their struggles. Fighting back tears, Gathoni shared, 'This is the most disturbing time I have ever had in my life.' Chira, sanctioned while representing Kenya abroad, felt as if 'the world had come to an end'. Many athletes coped through avoidance and self-isolation. Dua recalled, 'All I wanted was to sleep and not think about anything. As long as I had slept, I was okay.' For some, this withdrawal lasted months. Gathoni turned to alcohol, saying, 'I stayed alone. I did not want anybody in the house. I was just staying alone, drinking, and then trying to figure out things'.

Insomnia accompanied uncertainty over the future, as did oversleeping and physical symptoms like peptic ulcers. This distress escalated into darker thoughts.

Anti-doping officials reported no known doping-related suicides in Kenya, though Angaya [pseudonym of anti-doping officer interviewed] attributed this to limited suicide statistics. He acknowledged speaking with athletes whose distress sounded severe enough to raise concerns about suicidality. These fears were not misplaced, as seven athletes in this study described experiencing suicidal thoughts.

Some avoided the term 'suicide', instead using euphemisms, such as stating they might 'commit something bad'. Others were more forthright. For instance, Wanjala admitted having suicidal thoughts but worried how this would impact his family.

Musyoka said media sensationalism surrounding his case led him to contemplate suicide.

Chira's account was particularly stark: 'I remember thinking, *Why don't I just die?* I even contemplated throwing myself from the top of the building and letting everything come to an end.' He continued: 'Luckily enough, something just came to my mind. I thought about my friends, even compared myself to them, and saw that I was better [off]. I have my own house . . . I also have children. Why would I want to take my life?'

One athlete, Wangui, attempted suicide after months of isolation. She recalled, 'In the third month, I felt like things were at a climax, so I tried committing suicide.' Her neighbours and friends intervened. With her coach's help, she spoke with her military commander, entered a mental-health clinic for several weeks and took extended leave from work. Her case underscores the critical importance of timely intervention and support in mitigating suicide risk among sanctioned athletes.

Juma says that these suicidal ideations weren't a surprise, but he didn't expect them to be communicated. 'That was particularly true for the male athletes. The Kenyan culture is one of stoicism. It's doubtful that the men would have been that open with their wives. It makes them look weak. In Kenya, you must be strong.

Amid all trials and tribulations, we must show that we have everything under control.'

Which was far from the case as, says Juma, there is no support network for athletes who are sanctioned. He says that's regrettable but understandable with the budgetary pressures endured by every national anti-doping organisation and WADA itself. 'Who do you look after, the sanctioned athlete or the up-and-coming star who has the potential to represent their country and break a world record? I get it. They don't have infinite resources.

'Then again, they didn't kill anyone. When someone commits a heinous crime, they're sent to prison with the hope of rehabilitation. You'd hope there'd be some form of rehabilitation programme for athletes.'

Juma sees research like his as a starting point, and that by illustrating the very human cost of sanctions athletes will read his work, educate themselves and refrain from doping. 'In Kenya, especially when it comes to running, the media and social media will kill you if you're banned. "Oh, you're a cheat. You should be ashamed of yourself." From all fronts you're under attack. That's especially true of high-ranking athletes as the media amplifies the story in search of clickbait and selling newspapers. Well, papers like this one can hopefully act as a deterrent. We're educating people by giving the sanctioned athletes a platform to recall the pain they've gone through.

'Hopefully this helps to educate anti-doping authorities, too. When you look at the WADA Code, one of the cornerstone anti-doping principles is respecting the health of athletes. But that doesn't seem to apply if they're sanctioned. How can you penalise the athletes without helping them to avoid permanently damaging their mental health?'

Casting his eye on the future, Juma plans to dig deep into injury rehabilitation programmes and, while recognising the two are very different, see if lessons can be learned for sanctioned athletes. 'I'm not sure what that would look like but it's about forging pathways for humans who are suffering. Humans who have shown vulnerability. Structured programmes that promote constructive activities, alongside mental health and family support, could turn the sanction period into an opportunity for positive transformation and long-term resilience. Whether that will ever happen . . .'

Collin Chartier's road to Damascus began when his EPO positive became public. 'On the day the news came out, I got a call from one of my friends in Boulder who runs a Bible study group. He said, "You're coming tomorrow." I said to him that I couldn't. That I was a liar. That I was not worthy. But he insisted.

'I drive the hour to Boulder and knock on his door. I'm crying. He opens the door. He's crying. He then gives me the biggest hug and assures me that those who love me know that there's more to my life than this moment. I discovered the power of community. Friends would call me and share their stories of difficult times they went through, including going to jail. I felt that this was not the end.'

Chartier packed up his life and embarked on a six-month bike-packing trip from California to Colombia. He had time to think. And breathe. 'That's when I found breathwork. That was key as it calmed down my nervous system and brought me into the moment. The cycle of shame and guilt disappears when you can only think about the present. Those emotions keep you stuck in the past.'

Whether you lean on the conservative or compassionate side of the debate, there's no doubt a sanctioned athlete's mental health is impacted by doping. And not solely down to the psychological – there are pathological repercussions, too.

A 2025 study, 'Psychological Correlates of Performance-enhancing Drug Use', examined how PED use, particularly anabolic steroids, relates to emotional, cognitive and social functioning among gym-goers.[33] Comparing long-term users, short-term users and non-users, the research revealed that chronic PED users reported significantly higher levels of depression, anxiety and muscle dysmorphia than their PED contemporaries. Users also demonstrated reduced executive functioning in cognitive testing, suggesting that sustained PED exposure may impair attention and mental processing.

An earlier paper examined the association between long-term oral corticosteroid use – which are legal for out-of-competition use – and subsequent mental disorders in a large clinical population.[34] Researchers at King Abdulaziz Medical City in Saudi Arabia reviewed records of 3,138 patients who'd taken oral steroids for more than 28 days and found that around 5.5 per cent developed a new mental disorder during or following treatment.

The most common psychiatric effects included anxiety, depressive episodes, mixed mood disorders and psychological sexual dysfunction, and these effects appeared across age groups and both genders, though anxiety was particularly prominent among females. There's also evidence that human growth hormone can lead to depression, stimulants to anxiety and insulin to mood swings.

The likes of WADA and national anti-doping agencies look to educate athletes on the significant detriments of doping. But what

---

33 https://www.frontiersin.org/journals/psychiatry/articles/10.3389/fpsyt.2025.1710046/full

34 https://pmc.ncbi.nlm.nih.gov/articles/PMC10185922/

about the mental-health repercussions of proving you're clean? In chapter five, we chronicled the importance of the whereabouts system to the anti-doping framework. We also came across professional cyclist Rory Townsend in chapter one.

'I'm a great believer in clean sport,' he says, 'but the system can be stressful. I recently grabbed a later train back from Belgium, so wasn't in the location I'd said I would be on ADAMS. I flew to Thailand for our honeymoon, so I was in the air for 18 hours and couldn't change it. Thankfully, it was all fine.'

Alex Smith and his colleagues examined the impact on an athlete's mental health when adhering to the anti-doping system in the paper, 'Coercive Compliance? Anti-doping Systems in Tennis and Athlete Mental Health'.[35]

It was off the back of a civil antitrust lawsuit filed by elite tennis players against multiple authorities, including the Association of Tennis Professionals and the International Tennis Integrity Agency, arguing that current anti-doping and integrity systems create psychologically harmful conditions. The plaintiffs contend that invasive testing procedures, compulsory disclosures and rigid enforcement processes compromise personal rights, exploit players and exacerbate mental-health stressors.

From a sports psychiatry perspective, Smith and his fellow authors argued that elite athletes are already vulnerable to stress, burnout and psychiatric disorders due to competitive pressures, travel demands and performance scrutiny. They suggest anti-doping procedures, when overly rigid or lacking transparency, can intensify these vulnerabilities, contributing to anxiety, depression and fear of inadvertent violations. The paper highlights cases of

---

35 https://www.frontiersin.org/journals/sports-and-active-living/articles/10.3389/fspor.2025.1636161/full

prominent players reporting insomnia, anxiety and distress linked to anti-doping proceedings.

Smith and his team call for a balanced approach that maintains sporting integrity while safeguarding athlete well-being, recommending greater procedural fairness, mental health support and clearer communication, and stress that anti-doping systems should incorporate sports psychiatry expertise to reduce unintended psychological harm.

As for the lawsuit, at time of writing it had yet to be resolved.

'I've done a fair bit of work in that area, including viewing the anti-doping system through the lens of athletes with ADHD [attention deficit hyperactivity disorder],' says Smith. 'The stimulants used to treat ADHD, like methamphetamines and amphetamines, are banned in competition by WADA. That means these athletes must apply for a TUE. This is important and the athlete is liable to a suspension if it doesn't happen.

'Applying for a TUE is a relatively involved process for any athlete, let alone an athlete who has a disorder that's associated with forgetfulness, disorganisation and impulsivity. If you have ADHD, there's a very good chance that you simply won't fill in the form, opening yourself up to an unexplained positive test. Or the athlete, so anxious, will simply stop taking their medication. Clearly, neither scenario is desirable.'

Smith says it's potentially a massive issue, of which British Cycling for one has started to address by running ADHD-specific TUE courses. 'ADHD also impacts an athlete completing their whereabouts information. I wonder how many athletes with ADHD have racked up missed tests because of their condition?'

★

Pressure, they say, is a privilege. The life of an elite athlete can be rewarding, both intrinsically and financially, but at what cost? Every performance is scrutinised, every night out plastered over social media. For many in elite sport, whether clean or doping, the stress of perpetually being on trial can weigh heavy.

Michael Liebrenz-Rosenstock works with Alex Smith at the University of Bern. He heads up the forensic psychiatry department. Liebrenz-Rosenstock has undertaken numerous studies into elite sport and mental health, especially cycling. The results are stark.

'In one of our papers, we found that 22 per cent of cyclists reported substance use or addiction-related behaviours,' he says. What Liebrenz-Rosenstock observes most often, particularly among riders struggling with insomnia, anxiety or depression, is a growing dependence on prescription sleep and anxiety medications, such as benzodiazepines or so-called Z-drugs, especially during multi-stage races like the Tour de France.

'Anecdotally, prescribing medication during long tours appears relatively casual, with limited discussion around duration, tapering or exit strategies. Riders may sleep well for a week or two, but then return home and stop suddenly, only to experience rebound insomnia or even mild withdrawal.

'In a small number of cases, this escalates into longer-term dependence or the use of multiple substances. One case we reviewed involved both benzodiazepines and cocaine. But most situations aren't about reckless misuse. They're about incremental coping mechanisms in a high-pressure environment where asking for psychological support is still viewed as weakness.'

Whatever shape the struggle assumes – be it disordered eating, chronic overtraining or substance misuse – riders often exhibit the same underlying neurobiological susceptibility, says Liebrenz-Rosenstock. The risk intensifies when performance be-comes the athlete's primary way of managing emotion. In that setting, the slide is rarely sudden, but it can be quietly perilous. Liebrenz-Rosenstock holds particular concerns for younger athletes.

'The teenage brain is still developing, particularly in areas related to emotional regulation, impulse control and long-term planning. Dropping a 16- or 17-year-old into the high-stakes world of professional sport with contracts, performance tracking and media exposure leaves little room for error and essentially asks them to function like fully formed adults in a system that rarely tolerates vulnerability. That's not just unrealistic, it's dangerous.'

Liebrenz-Rosenstock argues that managing the mental health of young athletes isn't a problem that can be fixed by a team psychologist or a motivational speaker working in isolation. What's required is a clinically robust, preventative mental-health framework, one that brings in specialists experienced in neurodevelopmental conditions and complex psychiatric illness. That support needs to extend beyond athletes to the wider staff. Elite sport is a pressurised ecosystem. If those inside it don't understand how, for example, ADHD presents under strain, or how depression first surfaces, warning signs will go unnoticed until they become acute.

'In the case of young athletes, the goal shouldn't be to slow down talent development, but to balance it with appropriate psychological scaffolding. Young athletes need space to be human, not just high-performance machines. Teams and organisations that recognise this, and act on it, will not only protect their athletes but also improve longevity and performance outcomes.'

Liebrenz-Rosenstock is a proponent of the REACT framework

that involves: Routine mental-health check-ups, not just when in crisis; External help from confidential independent options outside the structure or team; Assess early, refer early (if there's even a suspicion of trouble, act); Collaborate with specialists, especially for complex cases like ADHD; Treat early, manage long-term.

'Mental health doesn't end when an athlete stabilises,' he says. 'It requires ongoing care, monitoring and support across seasons.' With these structures in place, not only will athletes perform to their peak but it'll reduce the likelihood of doping.

Collin Chartier's emotional empowerment sadly came after he'd crossed the line and become headline news, though he now recognises that the informal support system he enjoyed during his Ironman career delivered a much safer and more significant boost to performance than any PED could.

'In my mind, I was always seeking massive jumps in performance. Where could I find the next bump in speed and stamina? But the reality is that the biggest improvements came from training partners, coaches, training environments and gaining confidence through being in a community. There was a benchmark. "I'm training with him. That must mean I'm okay." When I trained alone, that benchmark disappeared. So I reverted to type, "Oh, I'm not good enough." And when you go into a race believing you're not good enough, you won't perform. Your belief systems, your environment – they're massive. PEDs? They made a difference but not much. Maybe 2 per cent.'

Chartier version 2026 works in real estate and teaches his breathwork. Now he's desynced his identity from an activity that was all about pain and self-flagellation, he's discovered joy. It means he's also returned to the sport that caused him so much distress – triathlon – but from a coaching perspective.

He's happier. More content. And, as he scrolls through his phone, thicker-skinned. 'Wow, here's an Instagram comment today from my number-one troller. It reads, "Collin, I'm not trolling you, but you're just a sad loser who can't accept that you're not good enough." Ooh, here's another one: "You shouldn't be allowed anywhere near professional sport and anyone who chooses you as a coach is delusional. You're a convicted doper with a Masters in doping".'

Does that not affect you, I ask? 'I've become immune to it, though I do engage with them. The first one I'll say, "You were my favourite troll," but then the second one, I'll add, "Now you are my new favourite troll," with some heart emojis. Because, at the end of the day, it doesn't affect me. It just looks sad for them.

'There's enough people who follow my story and defend me. They're like [to the trolls], "Really, you haven't moved on. You're still letting this fester." They're still engaged emotionally in a story that's no longer relevant. The idea of forgiveness is for ourselves. It's letting go of the past, letting go of the shame, and it's allowing us to be present.'

Goodbye guilt, goodbye drugs. It's a fairy-tale ending. Maybe not . . . 'I like the mission of the Enhanced Games,' says Chartier, 'and will be working with them in some capacity, maybe as a chaperone to ensure the athletes have an experience similar to the Olympic Games. But, ideally, I want to be a presenter. I don't know if it'll happen. I'll put it out there.'

ENHANCED SPORT — ENHANCED RISK?

'The goal has changed, James. When we started this project, we were about building a competition to challenge the Olympics. Now our goal is to bring in the next age of mankind. It is to build superhumanity. This is about changing the whole of society.'

Dr Aron D'Souza is not a man short of confidence. The Australian led Peter Thiel's litigation against Gawker Media involving the wrestler Hulk Hogan, which saw the digital news organisation file for bankruptcy with debts of $140 million. In 2014, *Men's Style* magazine recognised him as one of Australia's most influential men. He's Oxford-educated, ambitious and inhabits a world of tech billionaires. He's also the brains behind, as its website proclaims, the Enhanced Games, 'a global annual competition that celebrates human potential through safe, transparent enhancement, offering fair play, record pay and unmatched athlete care.' Or, as CNN called it, 'A doping free-for-all.'

DOPE

Competitors of the first Enhanced Games, taking place at Resort World Las Vegas on 24th May, 2026, are allowed to take performance-enhancing drugs – banned by WADA – under medical supervision. Male and female athletes will compete in swimming (50m and 100m freestyle; 50m and 100m butterfly); athletics (100m sprint; 100m/110m hurdles); and weight-lifting (snatch, clean and jerk).

While many of the entrants cite the desire to 'test the limits of human potential with the tools and possibilities of our time' (swimmer Ben Proud on sign-up in September 2025), the biggest attraction is the 'life-changing' sums of money on offer, with prizes of $250,000 per event and $1 million for breaking a world record. Appearance money is thrown into the mix for the top draws.

As of the end of January, 2026, the headliners included American sprinter Fred Kerley, two-time Olympic medallist and three-time world champion; swimmer Megan Romano, the American 200m short-course record holder; and the world's strongest man, Iceland's Hafþór 'Thor' Björnsson, who's looking to break his non-assisted deadlift world record of 510kg.

The Enhanced Games flies in the face of traditional 'clean' sport and its notions of 'fairness' with a host of Olympic legends lashing out. 'It lacks purpose and honour,' said Carl Lewis, one of only four Olympic athletes to have won nine golds; 'A ludicrous PR stunt,' slammed four-time gold medallist Michael Johnson; and 'It's bullshit . . . if anybody is moronic enough to feel they want to take part in that – and they are from the traditional, philosophical end of our sport – they will get banned. They will get banned for a long time,' Lord Sebastian Coe, the president of World Athletics.

Like Coe, international and national federations were quick to voice their disapproval, threatening career-ending sanctions. The

Enhanced organisers immediately retaliated, filing an $800-million lawsuit against World Aquatics, WADA and USA Swimming, stating their efforts to dissuade athletes from competing in its new series were illegal. A federal judge threw out the claim in December, 2025.

Controversy has focused minds.

'Firstly, it's not the ultra-libertarian vision that you can just show up to the Games after taking whatever drug you like,' says D'Souza. 'That doesn't sit with our thesis. Doesn't sit with our vision that technology will enhance the human condition.'

It's not the Wild West, where you can inject novel chemicals spawned from underground laboratories. Instead, athletes are permitted to use substances approved by the US Food and Drug Administration (FDA). These include steroids, testosterone, EPO and growth hormone, although, as we'll come onto, those are approved for therapeutic reasons and not performance-enhancing ones. Sport is entering the unknown. A risk?

'Let's calibrate risk appropriately,' says D'Souza. 'If you head into space, currently there's around a one in 16 chance of you dying. In the early days of climbing Mount Everest, you were looking at one in ten. Now I think it's about one in a hundred. Then we have free-diving and skydiving, both sports that are deemed dangerous. But just because something is perceived as "unsafe", should we not challenge that notion? Should we not climb mountains? Should we not fly to the moon? We would be much less of a human civilisation if we said we'll only do things that are absolutely safe. I believe that individuals with free and informed consent should be able to take risks.

'That said, the PEDs that might be used by the Enhanced athletes are all time tested. The 1939 Nobel Prize was awarded for work on sex hormones, including testosterone, of which around 2.5 per cent of American men use today. Around 6 per cent of British men have taken anabolic steroids at some point in their life.'

But, the counterargument goes, these numbers are based on a population health level. That taking testosterone for many users is about normalisation, not elevation to supraphysiological quantities.

'Okay, let's take that population health level,' says D'Souza. 'We know that steroids are used by millions beyond the therapeutic reasoning, but do we see an epidemic of bodybuilders and powerlifters showing up to emergency rooms? No. In contrast, something like the painkiller fentanyl – which you can easily access from a chemist – has caused havoc in the US.'

And destruction. According to the Drug Enforcement Administration (DEA), fentanyl is responsible for nearly 70 per cent of the 107,000-plus drug overdose deaths in the past year. It's 50 times stronger than heroin and 100 times stronger than morphine.

D'Souza cranks up the defence of the disruptor, suggesting that the medical screening systems in place for the Enhanced athletes will make his competition safer than the Olympics.

It's a point picked up by academics including Dr Luke Turnock, criminology lecturer at the University of Lincoln, in his commentary on the Enhanced Games,[36] 'A reality which has long been understood – if comparatively underacknowledged – is that drug testing inherently encourages use of drugs that are harder to detect, which are often more harmful to health. Robert Voy, former chief medical officer for the US Olympic Committee, acknowledged in 1991 that: "A sad paradox is that after drug testers and sport federations worldwide have worked so hard to eliminate

---

36 https://www.sciencedirect.com/science/article/pii/S221126692400032X

the steroid problem, we have in a sense steered athletes towards more dangerous drugs".'

The medical safety protocols are overseen by the Enhanced's medical commission, including the provocative recruitment of Dr Michael Ashenden. The Australian is one of the most influential figures in modern anti-doping. He was a driver of the athlete biological passport and worked on landmark cases, including Lance Armstrong's.

In his Substack post 'Not So Fast', Ashenden 'advocates for the concept of an Enhanced Games to co-exist with the Olympic Movement, provided their athletes do nothing illegal'.

One of his major arguments for the legal medicalisation of sport is that: 'Elite sport is now a competition between engineers, strength and conditioning specialists, recovery scientists, movement analysis technicians and nutrition experts. And the enhancements they bestow. Consequently, the Olympic Movement cannot escape the contradiction that it promotes itself as a test of natural human limits, yet it simultaneously endorses scientific and technical enhancements to surpass those limits. When viewed through this lens, the issue becomes: "Which *additional* enhancements should society tolerate participants using in the Enhanced Games?"'

Ashenden suggests societal attitudes towards the risks associated with enhancements have shifted. Injectable dermal fillers are a cosmetic norm, he argues, but even with medical supervision, injectables can lead to stroke, blindness or death. 'Hence it is not entirely clear why, provided there was medical monitoring, contemporary society would condone the health risks associated with *cosmetic*, but not *performance*, enhancements.

'It is relevant that all substances on *banned* lists that have regulatory approval can, by definition, be taken safely with medical monitoring,' he continues. 'Even [some] steroids, ruthlessly stigmatised by the media and therefore misunderstood by the general public, have some clinical applications and are considered reasonably safe if taken under medical supervision, with the physician evaluating the benefit and risk ratio.

'Harmful effects from virtually all *banned* substances may occur after prolonged or excessive use, but it is possible to address both via medically monitoring participants in the Enhanced Games. Of course, how that monitoring process is implemented and executed will determine its efficacy.'

Ashenden questions the evidence linking EPO to historic cycling deaths and says it's distasteful to weaponise the forced administration of steroids on East German female athletes against the safe protocols that'll be used by Enhanced athletes.

With echoes of D'Souza, Ashenden proceeds to point out that elite sport carries inherent risks whether enhancements are used or not. That in ski-jumping, risk is seen as a valuable element of the activity. 'Spectators call it bravery when taking higher risks leads to success; tragedy when it leads to injury . . . In the United States, over a 27-year period from 1980 to 2006 [which spans the height of *drug* use in sport], from a total of 1,866 athletes who died while participating in organised team or individual sports, autopsy results concluded that only 2 per cent of deaths were attributed to drugs.'

In a compelling post, Ashenden concludes, 'Unfortunately the Olympic Movement no longer epitomises the athlete's quest for excellence. It has morphed into a marketable commodity sold to the highest bidder. Its stewards must take their share of responsibility for transforming sport into a multi-billion dollar, multi-national entertainment business.'

And, says D'Souza, one that is massively hypocritical. 'Who are two of the longest-serving sponsors of Olympic sport in the United States? Coca-Cola and McDonald's. The IOC are supposed to be the guardians of health, but are those sponsors, who've ploughed millions into the IOC, the foundations of a healthy lifestyle? I know that in the UK, gambling companies are popular sponsors of sport. Again, is that conducive to a healthy lifestyle?

'Honestly, there's a certain moral righteousness to the Olympic Movement. But if they are so "right", why won't the likes of Kirsty Coventry [president of the International Olympic Committee] and Witold Bańka [president of WADA] sit down on live television and debate me? I've offered them many times but they don't take up the invites. Why? Because they know they will lose as they have no moral standing.'

D'Souza argues that the IOC are corrupt and greedy, meaning the majority of Olympic athletes survive on slim pickings. The Enhanced Games, on the other hand, rewards its competitors handsomely, especially if they break world records. Where does the Enhanced funding come from? We're not party to the finances but there's a clear biotech-billionaire theme emerging.

You have co-founder Christian Angermayer, the brains behind Ribopharma, who later founded investment firm Apeiron, which now manages more than $2.5 billion worth of assets. Notably for enhancing the human race, that includes longevity companies. On his website, Angermayer writes that ageing can be 'prevented, cured and reversed'. Peter Thiel, who D'Souza helped bankrupt Gawker, is a financial backer. As is Balaji Srinivasan, former chief executive of cryptocurrency Coinbase.

'And then there's funding from 1789 Capital. You know who's behind that, James? Donald Trump Jr. Can you believe that?

Honestly, if the Enhanced Games goes ahead – and I still think it might not – I wouldn't put it past that lunatic father of his to turn up at the Opening Ceremony. The whole thing is absurd.'

John Hoberman is the author of several books about the history of steroids and a University of Texas professor. To say he's sceptical about D'Souza and the Enhanced Games is an understatement. He's been a staunch critic of both since the idea went public in 2024.

'Honestly, people like D'Souza are so well-connected to the American billionaire class, they feel they can do what they want,' he says. 'When I met him, I told him to quit while he was ahead.'

He didn't. That was in August, 2024. Both Hoberman and D'Souza travelled to Aarhus, Denmark, to attend an anti-doping conference. The event was co-founded by Verner Møller, a sports scientist and long-time critic of the current anti-doping framework, who professed that the idea of an Olympic-style competition openly allowing performance-enhancing drugs had long circulated in the field as a bit of a joke.

D'Souza delivered one of the two keynote addresses. The other was given by Ines Geipel, who survived East Germany's state-sponsored doping programme of the 1970s and 1980s – a system that left many athletes with lifelong health damage. While D'Souza attempted to win over the audience from the stage, the mood shifted during questioning, with Hoberman launching a blistering critique. 'I told him he was naïve to think that drugs equates to better performance. He haphazardly mixed transhumanist nonsense with his interpretation of science.'

D'Souza pushed back, accusing Hoberman of 'ideological bias'. 'Some people aspire to remain Homo sapiens,' he said. 'To live, suffer, age and die. I believe technology and science allow us to move beyond that. Others disagree – that's their right. It's Professor Hoberman's right to age and die.'

Hoberman argues that 'D'Souza's most daring rhetorical ploy has been to turn the condemned status of doped athletes inside out by extolling these rule-breakers as pioneers of enhancement'. He directs me to a statement from D'Souza early into the Enhanced journey, where he announced, 'The IOC has committed itself to vilifying Enhanced athletes . . . It is time to end this oppressive cycle. The Enhanced Games hereby reinstates the world records set by the following athletes and commends them for their bravery.'

D'Souza's modus operandi, says Hoberman, is 'predicated on the assumed authority of elites' and their alleged 'world-class' expertise is invoked to certify the validity of his ideas. He points to The First Conference on Human Enhancement that was held at the House of Lords in London in February, 2024.

The conference convened 45 leading scientists, clinicians, thought-leaders, academics, entrepreneurs, government officials and investors, including individuals from or previously associated with the Olympics, the Human Engineering Research Laboratories, the Rejuvenation Olympics and Bryan Johnson's Blueprint (a marketing scheme for longevity supplements). 'D'Souza was there, too, and they discussed the present realities and near-future enhancement and longevity,' says Hoberman. 'Honestly, his science just doesn't add up. He dresses things up as a libertarian dream, but at the heart of things, he's a moneymaker. These guys are trying to create the biggest drug market in history.'

At the beginning of this chapter, D'Souza talked about the goal of the Enhanced Games changing. That was between the first time I interviewed him in 2024 and the second in September,

2025. The original pitch focused on liberating athletes from the manacles of the antiquated anti-doping system, to maximise scientific innovation in pursuit of smashing through the limits of humanity. Come our follow-up, the tone had changed. He talked about the Enhanced team being the figureheads of the Age of Enhancement. That their intention was to become the Amazon of Enhancement. It's why a 'Products' tab popped up on the Enhanced Games website.

'We're still working on exactly what the consumer can tap into, but it'll definitely include testosterone therapies and certain peptides,' says D'Souza. As of late January, 2026, only three products were featured – oral and injectable testosterone, and Enclomiphene, to block oestrogen receptors and increase natural testosterone production (all on the WADA Prohibited List) – but no products were yet available for purchase. If it does go live, the course of action would involve a biomarker test, online clinical consultation and personalised plan.

'Initially, it'll be available in the USA only because the US has the most accepting prescribing guidelines and drug marketing ability,' says D'Souza. 'It's the simplest business model. There are hundreds of anti-ageing clinics that'll charge you up to $1,000 to access a cocktail of hormone therapies and peptides. We're going to make that available to absolutely everyone at a much lower cost.

'And the best business models in history are to take what's available only to the wealthy and make them accessible to everyone. That's what Uber did. They made a private chauffeur available to everyone.'

In late November, 2025, the Enhanced Group announced their intention to float on the Nasdaq stock exchange, valuing the company at $1.2 billion – a staggering amount for an organisation that has yet to host its debut competition and sell its first vial.

'Beyond live events,' the press release read, 'Enhanced is developing a comprehensive telehealth and direct-to-consumer business focused on performance medicine products. This division aims to democratise access to performance-enhancement tools and protocols, allowing consumers to "Live Enhanced" through scientifically backed products and services. The Company expect to launch this product offering in Q1 2026 . . . Enhanced aims to establish market leadership in this emerging sector while building sustainable competitive advantages through its unique combination of elite sporting events and health products.'

Will Enhanced become the PED-fuelled equivalent of the indoor-fitness-competition phenomenon that is Hyrox? I ask D'Souza if the humanitarian headlines from Enhanced's early days were a mask for the commercial intent?

'No, not at all. I've spent two years working on this project and realised through it that the business model of start-up sports leagues is terrible. Just look at the recent Michael Johnson debacle.' D'Souza's referring to the Grand Slam Track, an athletics league fronted by Johnson that offered six-figure prize money for top runners. The league filed for bankruptcy in December, 2025, after cancelling its final event and failing to pay athletes and vendors. 'Honestly, UFC is probably the only sporting competition in recent memory that has flourished.'

'What's the best business in the history of sport?' D'Souza continues. 'In my eyes it's Red Bull. It's the world's largest energy-drink company and one of the largest beverage companies. They use stunt sports marketing to sell their drinks at an incredible margin and were originally banned in many countries because of regulatory concern over taurine. In the public eye, they invented the category of energy drinks. Well, we're inventing the category of performance medicine. It's taken the Olympics 120-plus years and huge capital expenditure to bring in annual revenue of around a billion dollars a year. I believe we can do that in a significantly shorter period.'

Sceptics would suggest that this commercialisation of PEDs was always the intention, tempting investment from those interested in longevity.

Josh Torrance, a drug researcher at the University of Bristol, England, who we've heard from several times throughout this book, is concerned.

'You'll have a really big problem if you have corporate interest driving IPEDs. Inevitably, there isn't proper regulatory oversight when these things first become established. It's a bit of a freak war. And who loses out? People who actually shouldn't be pumping all these IPEDs into their bodies, who are led to believe they should be by persuasive social-media feeds.

'I see it all the time. Inject yourself with testosterone and have the body beautiful. Honestly, young men really don't need testosterone. They're full of the stuff. Corporates know their target audience. Many youngsters watching the Enhanced Games will watch it and want to buy those products. This could be trouble.'

Does D'Souza have concerns that these products will be used and abused by impressionable young people? That they'll be tempted by the Enhanced product offerings but won't have the resources, so go underground?

'It's a silly argument,' he replies. 'Does anyone look at Kim Kardashian and start ordering Botox online and injecting themselves at home? No. Well, maybe there are but it's not my job to manage idiocy in this world.'

For once, WADA and USADA were united in condemning the event, but did the very public disagreements between the two create a vacuum for the Enhanced Games advocates to make their case? Perhaps. Even in reproachment, their divisions are clear.

'This circus, this dangerous event is irresponsible,' says WADA president Witold Bańka. 'It's a ridiculous idea. Taking all of these prohibited substances, it's completely against the values of sport. I hope that this event will not happen. But we really want our colleagues from the USA to do more to ensure that this event will not happen, or at least to hold a strong position on this. Despite our discrepancies, despite our different views, we must be united, together with the IOC, together with the entire anti-doping community.

'I haven't heard anything from USADA's side. Maybe it's time for the US perspective to convince them, these people who decided to finance it, that this is a dangerous event. It's their responsibility because this event is going to be in the US.

'From the IOC and governments' perspective, I didn't meet a single minister, prime minister or president who supported this idea. We have consultations in all our bilateral meetings which I had in the past month. The position from European Union, Council of Europe, African Union, ministers responsible for sporting in Asia was very clear.

'Being a private event, I know we don't have the power to stop it. But we all have the power to be vocal. We are vocal.'

'They [Enhanced] have been attacking anybody and every-body, including us [USADA], the IOC and WADA,' says Travis Tygart. 'We've been very clear. It's a bad idea. It's a clown show. But we don't have any authority to do anything about it. But in democracies and free markets, our power comes through contracts. And we don't have a contract with them or any other sporting events that have been open about their doping, like bodybuilding or powerlifting.

'Why would WADA attack us? They're either blissfully ignorant of that fact or they're intentionally trying to use this for political gain. Are they trying to divert attention away from their own failures and their refusal to hold China accountable in the system that actually does impact our athletes that we have clear jurisdiction over?

'Away from anti-doping, I'm also honest and real enough to listen to comments from the likes of Olympic 2024 silver medallist Ben Proud, who's saying the money he could receive is the equivalent of winning 17 world titles. Arguably, that has to be looked at and good on sport leaders like Seb Coe who are trying to get more money into the system and into the hands of athletes, as opposed to flying leaders of WADA around the world in business class, staying in five-star hotels and eating at Michelin restaurants. Let's do right by the athletes, though that's not necessarily my lane.

'The Enhanced Games isn't the answer to the failures of our system. But we should look at competition, if that's how it's being characterised, as reasons to make ourselves better and deliver on the promise that we give clean athletes, and use this as a moment, if we're going to use it as anything, to hammer home the point.'

Enough from the politicians. What about the views of the non-enhanced? 'It's morally reprehensible and it shouldn't happen. It's actually gross,' says professional cyclist Rory Townsend. 'I hope for the athletes involved that they're being looked after in terms of what they're taking. But then you're conflicted, as in a way you need something relatively bad to happen. You don't want this to set a precedent; that people think you can just get geared up and become a world-class athlete.'

Townsend sees the Games as the end-point to the medicalisation of sport. That sport science has spiralled out of control, blinding many to the fundamentals of consistent and committed training.

'At my last team, it was a sport scientist's heaven. We'd do heat-acclimation training in Hazmat suits, sodium bicarbonate testing [studies show this can improve sustained power output] . . . every time I saw a sports scientist, I'd be doing some test or other. But is it for us or them?

'A nutritionist can sit there and say, "Well, I've given this rider 400 beetroot shots this year [that reportedly boost endurance]." I'm sure that goes down well with management but is it actually making a rider reach the finish line faster? I'm sure there are merits in some of these interventions, but for me, it's more important to put in the training, at the right intensity, at the right time of year, to build your aerobic engine. That is vital. All the rest is peripheral.'

Nick O'Hare is a former international swimmer who competed for Ireland for eight years, including the men's 50m freestyle at the 1996 Olympics in in Atlanta, USA. He later covered six Olympics as a commentator. At the time of writing, two Irish swimmers had signed up to the Enhanced Games: three-time Olympian Shane Ryan, and Ryan's teammate in the Paris 2024 Olympic 4x100m medley relay, Max McCusker. Both said they were lured by money, Ryan telling the *Irish Sun*, 'Financially, I'm making over six figures for nine months and then potentially making over $600,000 when it comes down the line.

'I'm going to be doing two events, the 100m freestyle and the

50m backstroke, and if I win one of those events, I get $250,000. If I win both of those, that's half a million dollars on top of what I'm earning right now. For me, as an athlete that's 31 years old, this is kind of a jump-start financially. I've talked to a lot of people that are super-excited.'

O'Hare isn't one of them. 'It flies in the face of what sport is and what sport is supposed to be about,' he says. 'Shane Ryan is sanctimonious. His decision isn't brave. Just a few weeks before, he was talking to youngsters about clean sport. In fact, I remember him telling me a few years ago that, once his swimming career was over, he wanted to inspire the kids. Well, you can't tell a youngster that discipline and hard work matter, then embrace a competition that normalises pharmaceutical products.

'Honestly, he's so naïve. He said that after the Enhanced Games, he's now not looking to stay in swimming. Instead, he wants to go into medical sales. Well, no one will go near him because of his lack of ethics. He'd be a reputational risk to pharmaceutical companies, to biotech companies, to medtech companies . . . Whatever role he goes for, people will question his moral compass and integrity. They won't touch him with a bargepole.'

And work, he must, adds O'Hare, as Ryan will be subject to the American tax system rather than the Irish system that's generous to sports people and artists. 'If he can't find a job, half a million over 30 years isn't a lot.'

O'Hare's damnation of Ryan is in stark contrast to his admiration for 2016 Olympic 100m freestyle champion and former world-record holder Kyle Chalmers of Australia. Chalmers turned down a lucrative offer worth millions of dollars to compete at the Enhanced Games. He admitted it was one of the hardest decisions of his life, especially with the recent arrival of his baby, but he declined because his legacy was more important.

O'Hare says the Enhanced Games and the likes of Ryan and McCusker do a disservice to clean athletes. That their signing up raises suspicion of clean athletes. It's something he had to contend with himself when competing for Ireland through the Michelle Smith period. 'Until Smith came along, I don't think anyone would have thought Irish swimmers would take drugs. She changed that view.'

Smith stunned the world at the 1996 Atlanta Olympics with three golds and a bronze, but her rapid improvement sparked suspicion of performance-enhancing drug use. She passed all drug tests at the Games, yet critics questioned her dramatic rise and her coach-husband's own doping history. In 1998 she was banned for four years after a ruling determined she'd tampered with an out-of-competition urine test. Smith always denied using banned substances, and held on to her Olympic medals, but the scandal left a lasting mark on her legacy.

'You're a sports person, you've got to have integrity. What's the point else?' O'Hare says, before detailing his own Chalmers moment. 'You'd look at swimmers, those with acne on their back, and you knew they were on something. Well, in 1998, I was offered drugs myself. I'd been training in Hamburg, Germany. Before I'd headed over, I'd really struggled with a bad respiratory infection and was still suffering the after-effects, so wasn't swimming as well as normal.

'Later on, I'm driving down the motorway with one of the assistant coaches from the club and he goes, "Nick, you know, you did not swim fast today." I reply, "Yeah, I'm still wrestling with this sickness." He then opens the glove compartment and gives me a box. "I fix you," he says. "With this you grow big and strong. Just infuse every second day." Out of curiosity – one of my degrees is in analytical science – I opened the box. Inside were 30 bottles with "nandrolone" written on them, plus a couple of syringes. I declined, packed my bags the next morning and flew home. I was shocked at the brazenness of it. It transpired that coach got busted down the line.'

Once O'Hare drew the curtain on his swimming career in 2000, his scientific background saw him forge a career in the pharmaceuticals industry, where he's now worked for 25 years. He suggests that Ryan, McCusker and all the other Enhanced competitors are little more than guinea pigs, lab rats for the 'products' arm.

'You can't deny that they've done a good job of selling the Games, especially off the back of that libertarian idea. But Thiel, Angermayer, they all have interests in biotech. I know how this stuff works. They'll be using the athletes' data for case studies. It's what you call "patient-level data". So essentially a clinical trial.

'They'll pump these guys full of drugs and look at what their baseline is. Then they'll assess the level of improvement, which they can publish. They can make a real thing of saying "this is Shane Ryan, who recorded the sixth-fastest 50m backstroke ever and he's improved by 'X' per cent".

'You'll then get local, recreational rugby players, footballers, athletes, whoever, who'll be like, "Well, if they're already peak performers and they've enjoyed this improvement, how much could I benefit?" It'll be a persuasive sell. Because at the end of the day, this is all about selling drugs. Those athletes will soon be cast aside, while the likes of Thiel will make millions.'

The disposable Enhanced athletes, O'Hare adds, may be set adrift. But in good health. The medical screening will see to that. 'The worst that'll happen will be maybe muscle ripped from the bone because the ligaments and tendons won't be strong enough to cope. Painful but not life-threatening. But what about the unmonitored, the athletes who'll buy these performance packs?

'We know how it works. Say you have a paracetamol. If it doesn't clear your headache, you have another one. It'll be the same with the PEDs. If athletes don't enjoy the claimed benefits at the prescribed dosage, they'll take more. And more. Believe me, people will die from taking this shit.'

For those new to the Enhanced Games, this isn't their debut in testing the limits with PEDs. In February, 2025, Greece's Kristian Gkolomeev swam 20.89 seconds in a 50m time trial in the US, 0.02 seconds faster than the official world record set by Brazil's César Cielo in 2009. Gkolomeev, who finished fifth at the 2024 Olympics in 21.59 seconds, began taking banned substances in January. He received $1 million for beating a world-record time, though how much of a boost he enjoyed from his programme was impossible to unpick as he wore a full-length polyurethane 'supersuit', which was banned from competition just a few weeks after Cielo had set a record in one.

Although Gkolomeev and the Enhanced team didn't reveal what substances he'd taken, citing personal confidentiality and concern that others would follow Gkolomeev's regime unsupervised, the Greek did add that come the April of that year when he swam 21.03 seconds in textile 'jammer' shorts, which do comply with current World Aquatic regulations, his body shape had changed considerably.

'On the second attempt I was on a full two-month cycle,' he

said. 'I had an extra 10lbs of lean muscle. My coach and I did a pretty good job in that short amount of time to get used to my new strength and weight in the water. It was a good result.'

Australian James Magnussen lined up alongside Gkolomeev as part of the Enhanced experiment. The three-time Olympic medallist retired from competitive swimming after the 2018 Commonwealth Games but was the first athlete to signal his intention when news broke in early 2024 that the Enhanced organisers would offer that $1-million world-record-beating prize. 'I'd juice to the gills for that money,' he said.

In 2025's trial run, Magnussen failed to break the world record after piling on too much weight. 'Within ten days, I put on ten pounds [4.5 kilogrammes] of muscle,' he said. 'I was getting bigger and stronger and my strength just went through the roof. I was just getting so big and so strong, and we didn't know that would happen. In terms of health metrics, my resting heart rate lowered, my blood pressure lowered, my cholesterol lowered – my fitness was really good.'

Magnussen said he reached 115kg (253 pounds), compared to the 95kg (209 pounds) he raced at during his Olympic career.

Speaking to *The Sydney Morning Herald*, he went into more detail on what specifically he'd taken. 'I'm definitely allowed to say that I was taking peptides and testosterone, which is pretty much it, to be honest. We tried a few different things on top of that. We used BPC-157, CJC-1295, Ipamorelin and Thymosin. The BPC-157 and Thymosin is for recovery and to prevent injuries. It promotes healing in the body. The CJC and Ipamorelin enhances your body's natural production of growth hormone. You're not injecting growth hormone into you – you're maximising your body's own potential. The testosterone is the superpower –

that's what gets you bounding out of bed in the morning, lifting massive weights and feeling your best.

'It all felt safe because I did it all with doctors and under medical supervision,' he added. 'I'd go for weekly check-ups at the doctor's, where they were checking a full suite of health markers. It's quite confrontational and intense.'

Both Magnussen and Gkolomeev worked with Australian Olympian Brett Hawke, who's the head swim coach of the Enhanced Games. I catch up with Hawke over Zoom to dig deep into the training and PED protocols. He's in Las Vegas and, on greeting me in what looks like a car park, he points over his shoulder into the distance.

'The swim event will take place just over those tennis courts,' he says. 'It's a Myrtha Pool, like they installed at the [2024] Olympics. It's portable. It'll take them two weeks to build it at Resorts World.'

Or it might. Hawke adds that swim bodies have threatened to cancel any contracts with Myrtha if they go ahead with constructing the Enhanced pool. Politics around every corner. But that's no concern of Hawke's. He's charged with optimising his supercharged athletes and, at time of writing, there were 16 swimmers signed up, of whom he'll coach them all. For an experienced athlete and then coach, he says it's been a steep learning curve.

'I learned a tonne from James [Magnussen, who he began coaching first]. I went into it blind. Within a month, he'd started on his enhancement protocol with a team of doctors in Australia. That was separate from the Enhanced Games at that time and I didn't have a lot of information around what he was doing. But what I noticed is that pretty quickly he grew big, lifting very heavy weights and growing very strong. He kind of had that all-in mentality of, "I'm just going to go for it".'

And he did. Too much. Hawke compares Magnussen's debut Enhanced effort to a thoroughbred sprinting from the gates at the Melbourne Cup. 'The jockey needs to reel in that energy at times to ensure they can really push at the end of the race. In the pool, that's where coaching comes in. You can't just see a doctor and go faster. A coach needs to keep an eye on the signals and feedback from the athlete. They need to be cautious if needed, as elite athletes just want to go harder. You have to be patient and we didn't nail that with James.'

Hawke credits the performance enhancers with accelerating recovery, resulting in Magnussen's significant muscle gain. 'What I hadn't accounted for was the impact on the neurological system. Some people think you take PEDs and don't have to do the work. If anything you can do more work because you're recovering faster. The problem is your nervous system can't keep up. So, it's really important that you optimise everything – sleep, nutrition – and keep a close eye on the biomarkers and see what your blood's telling you. If you don't, you can very quickly push yourself over the limit.'

Hawke applied these load-managing learnings to Gkolomeev, with whom he started working two months later, and ensured the programmes – both training and PED – didn't result in the noticeable bulk Magnussen carried.

'We adjusted how much time was spent in the gym and I worked more closely with the doctor. We ensured we micro-dosed whatever PEDs Kristian chose. It worked.'

Although Hawke's not involved in the PED selection process, he says that ahead of the Las Vegas event, athletes will continue to micro-dose for safety reasons. He's also mindful that similar to all training interventions – be they amount of sprint work, heading to altitude or modes of recovery – every athlete will respond differently.

'Many think it's a magic pill and it'll transform your performance. That's just not the case. For me, it's like your vitamin regime where you might notice a small difference but nothing major unless it's something you're deficient in. I'm not looking for these athletes to drop a second off their times. We're looking for hundredths of seconds, maybe tenths if it goes really well. That's a much healthier way to look at this.'

Though, he continues, elite sport is far from healthy. It's one reason why the Enhanced project piqued his interest. 'When I was an athlete, I constantly pushed my body to the absolute maximum. You're always trying to find what your limits are. And I did the same with my athletes.

'But that's a very dangerous space to inhabit. When you're pushing your body to the extreme every day, when you're beating yourself up, that can have a seriously negative impact on your physical and mental health. There's nothing healthy about high-performance sport. Now, I have a chance to look at the science and see how these interventions can help athletes recover better, overcome injuries and illness faster, and hopefully extend their careers in the sport.' Hawke says that losing faith in the 'clean' system was another driver of his decision. That these PEDs, customisation and the medical screening will level the playing field.

As for the build-up to the Las Vegas late-May event, when we speak around Christmas time 2025, he stresses that none of the 16 confirmed swimmers had yet to begin a programme of PEDs. Nor had the athletes or weight-lifters.

'In February [2026], all of the athletes – the swimmers, weight-lifters and track athletes – are heading to Abu Dhabi to live and train together. Until then they won't be on anything stronger than coffee. In UAE, the athletes will be part of a study.'

O'Hare, the former Olympic swimmer whose career flowed into the pharmaceutical industry, knows his stuff. Presumably the end-point of the trial is the Games themselves followed by analysis of the results. And then, if successful, the Enhanced products will fly off the online shelves. That's the Enhanced dream, albeit there will be a grey area in the pool at least in that the swimmers are having bespoke super-suits designed and made for them. How the researchers will unpick the impact of the PEDs and their high-tech clothing remains to be seen.

Hawke represented Australia at the 2000 and 2004 Olympics. He's coached at the top level for 20 years. What to this high-performer will success look like? 'I want to see personal records broken. I want each one of these athletes to walk away from this saying, "That's the best I've ever swum." You know, I have one girl who hasn't been competitive in nine years. Imagine if I could return her to her best – maybe even better – after just six months of training. That would speak to the average human. That you can improve your life and physical fitness in a safe way. To recreational athletes, that's far more relatable than looking to smash every record. That's not just realistic.'

At the end of 2025, D'Souza stepped down from the Enhanced's day-to-day operations, with co-founder Maximilian Martin appointed as CEO. D'Souza, brash and bold, revelled in the limelight and is still involved in the background. But does this signal a more pragmatic move? That for their competition and products to be taken seriously, the PR needs to be cranked down a notch. That they are in it for the long haul.

'Long term, I fundamentally think that other sports leagues will follow our approach, changing from a punitive testing system to one that is focused on the athletes' health and safety to compete,' Martin told BBC Sport soon after taking up the post.

He hopes to stage a winter edition of the Enhanced Games, making it a biannual event, as well as hosting one-off time-trial attempts to better existing world records. He also plans to expand into triathlon. The business model, of promoting supervised PEDs, relies on the exposure.

Will it work? Is Enhanced the future? From weight loss to Botox, modifying bodies and minds with technology has become more normalised. Why not sport?

Or is it simply a freak show with billionaires preying on vulnerable athletes in the twilight of their careers who seek to secure their financial future? How can it grow if Olympic athletes aren't permitted to compete? How much appeal will these one-off events hold for elites at the peak of their career, who thrive on regular competition?

Will it transpire that the superhumans are the enhanced or non-enhanced?

THE FUTURE IS . . . ?

It's the year 2040. Saudi Arabia hosts the Summer Olympic Games for the second time in a row. 'There is no corruption here,' officials proclaim. 'It's just that Saudi Arabia is the only country in the world that has the air-conditioned facilities to cope with global warming. We are proud to once again host the greatest show on earth. We know that more eyes will be watching than ever before because, with regulated enhancement allowed for the first time, records are guaranteed to be broken in every discipline.'

Dystopian? Unlikely? Inevitable? Time will tell. But the regulated enhancement angle, at least, seems less far-fetched in 2026 than 20 years ago. In the last chapter, former anti-doping scientist Michael Ashenden opined that the legal medicalisation of sport has created a conundrum; that the International Olympic Committee sees itself as the promoter of pushing human boundaries, encouraging scientific and technical breakthroughs but then limits them. This, he says, goes against society's changing attitudes to lifestyle enhancements, like Botox injections and semaglutide weight-loss drugs like Ozempic.

'It is not entirely clear why, provided there was medical monitoring, contemporary society would condone the health risks associated with cosmetic, but not performance, enhancements,' the Australian said.

What might a regulated system look like? See the last chapter's Enhanced Games focus for an idea, but it might include approved substances (rather than a banned list), strict medical supervision, dosage ceilings, transparent disclosure, mandatory health monitoring and, arguably the hope of the Enhanced organisers, centralised distribution to avoid illegal markets. In many ways, it would resemble how some combat sports regulate cutting weight – controlled, monitored and standardised.

Grey areas, like TUEs, altitude tents, ketones and advanced recovery methods, would disappear, with proponents praising honesty over hypocrisy. Open medical oversight could generate research rather than secrecy. 'If enhancement is allowed under equal conditions, everyone will compete under the same pharmacological framework,' the medicalised defendants will argue.

Contamination cases would be a thing of the past; there'll be no worries about muscle memory and the performance boost delivered once doping stops; and the anti-doping organisations' jobs will be cleaner, thanks to the vastly trimmed Prohibited List. *Citius, Altius, Fortius* . . . *Pharmacius*. Faster, Higher, Stronger . . . Chemically.

But is that what the world wants out of sport? Would fans feel the same rush of joy if Athlete A drops the 100m men's world record to under 9.50 seconds when he insists his doctor joins him on the podium? The same awe-inspiring look when

Athlete A praises his family, friends and pharma for his epoch-making moment? Will parents happily buy the Athlete A duvet set, curtains and posters for their children knowing Athlete A is fuelled by enhancers?

As WADA's director of education, Amanda Hudson, says in chapter two, 'No athlete ever awakes and says that they want to participate in sport because they want to inject themselves with steroids. This is a very powerful, straightforward fact.'

In that same chapter, we delved into the doping prevalence figures that ranged from 0 to 50 per cent. Many see a figure of around 20–25 per cent as a pragmatic assessment of those who cross the ethical and legal line. That leaves up to 80 per cent of athletes competing 'clean'. If enhancements are permitted that, as Joe Papp told us earlier in *Dope*, 'can make you fly', those clean athletes will undoubtedly feel compelled to use drugs just to remain competitive, even if their values see it as cheating. They will be compromised for their belief system. Is that fair?

Then there's the health aspect. While medical supervision reduces risk, it doesn't eliminate it. Cardiovascular complications, hormonal disruption and long-term organ damage could all be on the cards for elite athletes who'd have begun their enhanced programme from childhood.

Fairness and integrity aren't always happy bedfellows in professional sport, but it only functions if competitors and fans believe the contest is genuine. 'I can't line up against any of the peloton knowing they have taken drugs,' professional cyclist Rory Townsend tells me. 'If I did, I've lost before I've started.' That's not Townsend being naïve. He knows that sports people will cheat. Why? Because sport reflects society. But where is the inspiration and drive to train, to be your best, if results reflect chemistry rather than preparation, talent and tactics?

Without trust in fairness, medals lose value and records lose meaning. Would sponsors and broadcasters invest in sport if performance is believed to be inauthentic? At its core, sport is about exploring the limits of training, the psychology of competition and the physiology of adaptation. If pharmacology defines performance, the philosophical basis of sport shifts from human excellence to biomedical optimisation. That might satisfy some, whose lives become defined by scientific advancement, but would that appeal to the majority who see the wider picture of the social value of sport?

There's also a clear psychological component that's often lost in the talk about boosting the physical. Current illegal enhancers like steroids can impact your mind as well as your muscle. Your author knows this first-hand. I undertook a blood test with UK company Forth. I'm approaching the half-century and, like many of the middle-aged athletes I talked about in chapter 10, my testosterone readings were at a level that ticked the boxes for exogenous testosterone.

I'd felt tired for a while, so was happy to go on a three-month course of gel. But two months in, despite upping the quantity, the major difference I noticed was mentally not feeling myself. Now, it'd be reductive to say the testosterone was playing with my mind (I was writing a book at the time, which was a little mentally challenging!) but something didn't feel right. I didn't feel any more energised, and physically I didn't morph into chiselled marble, either. (That said, training was also somewhat impacted by said book.) My anti-testosterone thesis wouldn't stack up because I was a very poor guinea pig, but it did hammer home that there's a clear psychological hurdle to leap over when taking any drug designed to boost health and performance if, like me, you've relied on a relatively natural and healthy diet.

All of this doping debating could be redundant, of course, if gene therapy becomes as normalised as taking an inhaler for asthma or an antihistamine for hay fever. The spectre of gene doping has haunted sport for 20 years, with WADA banning it back in 2003. Since then, those concerns have seemingly remained theoretical rather than real. But is it only a matter of time before that changes?

In Bryan Johnson's surprisingly heart-warming 2025 Netflix documentary *Don't Die: The Man Who Wants to Live Forever*, the face of longevity underwent experimental $25,000 gene therapy in Honduras to increase levels of follistatin, a protein that may enhance muscle growth and reduce inflammation. Johnson flew to Honduras because follistatin is not approved by the US Food and Drug Administration.

The rationale for using follistatin as a potential longevity therapy stems from animal research. Studies in mice have shown that introducing the follistatin gene can extend lifespan by nearly one-third, notably without increasing cancer risk – a common concern with many 'rejuvenation strategies'. Administering follistatin to both mice and non-human primates has also been associated with increases in muscle mass and strength.

In humans, research has been limited to small, open-label studies involving individuals with different forms of muscular dystrophy, where early findings appeared encouraging. However, these results have not yet been confirmed in larger, randomised controlled trials.

In 2025, Johnson gave LinkedIn a six-month update. 'My speed of aging has dropped to 0.64 (a personal best). I now celebrate my birthday every 19 months. My muscle mass is up by 7% (already in the 99th percentile). My follistatin levels increased by 160% (two weeks post-injection).'

That's not to say follistatin was solely responsible for that 7% muscle-mass increase, but Johnson's experiment is currently proving a literal and philosophical shot in the arm for gene therapy, not necessarily for sport but life as a whole. As I write this (February, 2026), the UK government has just announced that GPs will be paid to prescribe weight-loss jabs, like Mounjaro, to speed up the NHS rollout of the medication.

'This is just part of a wider public health package to help ease the £11-billion burden obesity places on the health service and economy,' said health secretary Wes Streeting. 'These new incentives for GPs will bring the principle of fairness – which has always underpinned the NHS – to obesity jabs, with the phased rollout to those with highest clinical need first.'

This is no altruistic investment. A healthier nation is a more productive nation. Lose weight and not only do you reduce your chances of becoming reliant on a creaking health system, you'll also be more industrious with your working day.

If gene therapy becomes normalised like weight-loss drugs, it's not outlandish to imagine a sporting world where gene doping becomes normalised. Though Professor Yannis Pitsiladis extols the virtues of his genetic doping test in chapter nine, as a society we're not yet at a stage where a test like Pitsiladis' would detect genetic changes, especially for an athlete who's been genetically doped from an early age. If gene therapy becomes omnipresent, it could well be goodbye to WADA and hello to the sub-nine-second 100m.

Like much of this book, predictions marry science and

(educated) speculation. But what of the near future? What simple steps can be taken to bolster the anti-doping framework? Here, we approach the *Dope* finish line hand-in-hand with Dr Robin Parisotto, stem scientist at the Canberra Hospital, Australia, and a key figure in modern anti-doping. Parisotto's (Anti-) Doping Doctrine is realistic and, he says, would strengthen global efforts to beat the cheats . . .

- A well-funded anti-doping programme that has 'buy-in' from athletes, sports teams, sponsors and broadcasters.
- Mandatory in- and out-of-competition testing programmes for all sports.
- WADA, the International Testing Agency and international federations could work with and accredit local pathology laboratories in more countries to extend the reach of the ABP [athlete biological passport] programme in particular.
- The banned list requires re-consideration. Which drugs are truly performance-enhancing and which ones are theorised to work, i.e. where is the evidence base for banning certain drugs?
- Contemporary research strategies must be developed. A centre or centres of excellence should be encouraged that concentrate on specific research areas. For example, research centres for steroids, growth enhancers, blood boosters, stimulants and gene doping. Current arrangements are ad hoc and usually dependent on researchers' previous track record. It's a very small scientific community and in need of innovation.
- Testing and results management should be performed by external independent agencies.

- Trust in the system has been compromised of late and mandates that sporting federations must be more transparent with results management.
- Make it a mandatory condition of athletes being allowed to participate in the sport that test results are publicly available.
- The current Therapeutic Use Exemption [TUE] system is being abused. A transparent TUE database would be a good means by which to rebuild trust in this system.
- Alternative penalties and sanctions strategies should be developed that could increase compliance. These include withholding of prize monies for statutory periods; creation of 'superannuation funds' that would quarantine a proportion of athlete earnings and not released until retired with no doping infractions; and heavy fines levied on individual athletes and team and sponsors in addition to suspensions.
- Finally, formation of a voluntary Clean Athlete database created by and managed by athletes with transparent oversight by an independent authority.

Parisotto's manifesto is fit for purpose, pragmatic and relatively easily actioned. But will these changes happen? As we've seen throughout *Dope*, the conflict that is stakeholders policing and promoting their own sport is one that not only limits funding but also limits the collective push for a stronger and more transparent system. All in all, while sport retains its capacity to enthral and inspire, always have your pen ready to add the footnote: *Record scrubbed, as enhanced.*

ACKNOWLEDGEMENTS

The list of those who deserve thanks for making *Dope* happen is far too long for this space, but you'll find many of them in this book. These are the scientists, academics, experts and athletes who were kind enough to share their thoughts, experiences and research.

Special mention must go to the whistleblowers, whose bravery in exposing doping cases and anti-doping inadequacies cuts through the politics and bureaucracy that protects the cheats. Within *Dope*, I've spoken directly or indirectly to those who went public – the likes of Renee Ann Shirley and the Stepanovs – but there are many more deserving of praise who remain off the radar.

Doping in sport is a somewhat sensitive subject, especially when a journalist comes knocking on your door, so many thanks to Christiaan Bartlett, who showed great faith and trust in guiding me around London's WADA-accredited laboratory. For some reason, elite athletic endeavour is far sexier than vials, data and spectrometers … but experts like Bartlett deserve their moment in the spotlight for working tirelessly in the background to protect the integrity of sport.

Many perceive WADA as a tired, cumbersome organisation that's lost respect, but that was far from the case when it came to its media head, James Fitzgerald, who helped to facilitate several interviews. His speed of reply was particularly impressive – and appreciated with deadline looming.

The topic of performance-enhancers in sport naturally stirs up a lot of misinformation, hearsay and gossip. So, chapeau to investigative journalist Trond Huso, who founded and runs antidopingdatabase.com. His trustworthy platform proved a valuable resource in painting a picture of doping in sports. As did Edmund Willison's excellent 'Honest Sport' Substack.

Thank you to Joe Hallsworth and the team at Blink Publishing for believing that I could make my idea and pitch come true (without ending up in court!). The same hat doffed to my agent, the mighty Kevin Pocklington of North Literary Agency.

Huge love to our two children, Mia and Harry. Not only are you becoming fine adults, but by fleeing the homestead, I could focus on book writing. Further love for my mum, who instilled my work ethic, and my dad, who instilled my love of sport. And to my sister, for whom I recommend a course of PEDs to break her Parkrun PB.

Finally, huge gratitude and love to my wife, Tara, who made me believe many years ago that book writing was not an impossible dream. Your support helped me over the finish line – and, yes, I promise that if I ever write another book, I will disappear in the final few weeks before deadline to remove a grumpy human from our home!